THE SEA
WAS ALWAYS THERE

THE SEA
WAS ALWAYS THERE

"IN SEA AFFAIRS, NOTHING IS IMPOSSIBLE,
AND NOTHING IMPROBABLE."

BY

JOSEPH F. CALLO

Fireship Press
www.FireshipPress.com

The Sea Was Always There

Copyright © 2012 by **Joseph F. Callo**

ISBN - 978-1-61179-207-2

BISAC Subject Headings:

BIO026000	BIOGRAPHY & AUTOBIOGRAPHY / Personal Memoirs
BIO008000	BIOGRAPHY & AUTOBIOGRAPHY / Military
HIS027150	HISTORY / Military / Naval

Cover photos by Sally McElwreath Callo

Cover design by Megan Eichenlaub

Address all correspondence to:
Fireship Press, LLC
P.O. Box 68412
Tucson, AZ 85737
Or visit our website at:
www.FireshipPress.com

To SALLY,

THE BEST OF SHIPMATES.

CONTENTS

PART III — SAILING
What I Learned in Boats

PHOTOS AND ILLUSTRATIONS

PART IV — SEA CONNECTIONS
What I Learned from Places by the Sea

PART V — LEADERSHIP IN STRESS
WHAT I LEARNED FROM HORATIO NELSON AND JOHN PAUL JONES

FOREWORD

For both the ancient Greeks and the authors of the Old Testament the sea is chaotic. Pontus, the pre-anthropomorphic god of the sea, comes into being from a single parent. Eventually Poseidon becomes ruler of the sea and he is as capricious as his unfathomable beginnings. From his depths come ship-destroying whirlpools like Charybdis and the sea-monster Scylla. His storms wreck ships. A blow of Poseidon's trident reverberates beyond the sea and trembles the earth. Odysseus's wanderings are prophesied to end when the hero of Troy carries an oar so far inland that men do not recognize it and ask Odysseus if it is a tool for separating wheat from chaff. There Odysseus is to sacrifice to Poseidon, his divine adversary: the sea's chaos is so powerful that it must be propitiated even among men who do not know it. In the Old Testament Genesis states that while the earth was merely "formless" a more sinister "darkness" covered the surface of the deep. Later, waters destroy the disobedient world from which Noah escaped safely, and—emphasizing again the waters' fearsome power—the sea churns violently when Jonah tries to avoid God by taking refuge on a ship.

In this book whose pleasures the reader is about to enjoy Admiral Joseph Callo, U.S. Navy, (ret.) finds a similar chaos. And, like the ancients, he respects the chaos including the calmness which is part of the sea. With a lifetime of experience he asks what can be learned from the sea. The answer is everything. *The Sea Was Always There* is one of those books whose heart lies not on the surface but in the vital currents that move underneath.

Certainly the anecdotes hold readers' interest and propel the book forward. The author was raised nearly within hailing distance of Long Island Sound and learned to sail on City Island. He spent childhood summers playing in the surf from Cape Cod to Jones Beach. From relatives, a live-in maid, and books came the stories that molded his soul. Admiral Callo doesn't use the word soul, but it reaches out from his writing and leaves as clear an impression as a sharply cut seal pressed into liquid wax. The live-in maid had grown up in Ireland and told stories from her childhood. Others might have clung to the particulars of the stories. Not young Joseph Callo. They turned his mind to what lay beyond the horizons he could see from the Atlantic's beaches. The author's grandmother was an accomplished storyteller. The author recalls the mythic Irish spirits plainly but the strongest impression came from the hero of her tales, a traveler and adventurer whose exploits meant travel. The grandmother's brother may have been an officer in the IRA, and grandmother was no friend of the English. Callo was immune to his grandmother's understandable antipathy. He jumps instead to his family's Christmas tradition of listening to Dickens' *A Christmas Carol* and his thoughts alight on London and the character of England. The ideas in the books he read strengthened the same adventurous synapses. What made the profoundest impression on him? A tale of Samuel Champlain's voyage and exploration in the New World.

Other children's imaginations might have been stimulated by the fantastic world of the Emerald Isle's fairies or turned against those who had oppressed the Irish or captured by Champlain's accounts of his encounters with the Indians. Or they might have continued to play stick ball in the Bronx and seen no further than their neighborhood's boundaries. Callo has another kind of soul. It is curious, adventurous, courageous, questioning, and open to unfamiliar ideas. These are exactly the qualities that have traditionally described a seafaring people who depend on the same characteristics to explore, benefit from learning in their voyages, apply lessons to seafaring, expand their commercial horizons, and possess the courage to defend what they have earned through their risk and labors.

Callo's book is thus comprehensive. He finds in the sea and seamanship an education in virtues as fine as those that apply to family life and as broad as those that shape the fortunes of empires. In between is his experience as a naval officer and his consistent effort to understand from experience. Again the book demonstrates its usefulness as guide to life. As a junior officer in *USS Sarasota*—an amphibious ship of nearly 3,000 tons laid down in April 1944 and launched two months later—Callo and much of the rest of the wardroom found the commanding officer personally disagreeable and ill-tempered. Then the ship ran into a hurricane. Callo and the other officers and men who manned the bridge that night saw a c.o. who acted calmly, confidently, and quietly. He brought his command unscathed through a tempest that threw the vessel over nearly on her side. Callo changed his mind about the captain. It's not a simple lesson. Mankind often judges things by their appearance. Callo learned otherwise from his experience.

He was an officer long enough to rise to the rank of rear admiral, long enough to apply the education in leadership he acquired as an officer to his family which vacationed in tents at the eastern tip of Long Island. Again, it's the qualities of soul that rise up off the pages. Freezing showers? They're an exercise in character building. Rainy days? A challenge to be mastered to ward off children's boredom. And, as letters from his sons and daughters show, Callo succeeded in passing along his love for the sea to his children.

The author also knows the virtues shaped by the sea on a much larger stage. His chapters on Horatio Nelson and John Paul Jones link remarkable character with achievements whose strategic consequences determined their nations' future in ways that only seapower can.

Before it became a navigator for consumers, multi-tasked parents, and mini-encyclopedia on health and nutrition Readers Digest was a guide that praised middle-class values such as integrity, frugality, loyalty, and courage in civilian and military life. It was a powerful affirmation of the values that everyday Americans cherished and an encouragement to its vast readership that these values were good and worth clinging to whatever may come. *The Sea Was Always There* does the same thing and it does it very well.

John Lehman

John Lehman was Secretary of the Navy in the Reagan Administration and a member of the 9/11 Commission

ACKNOWLEDGEMENTS

The first acknowledgement for *The Sea Was Always There* must go to the two people who set the course that took me to places around the world that they could never see: my parents. They dreamed the life I've led.

My sister Toni, who was a partner in my earliest contacts with the ocean and sailing, clarified recollections of my very early years and also filled in gaps of family history.

Many authors have contributed to my understating of the sea, and one in particular, former Director of the Royal Naval Museum the late Colin White, was a constant inspiration to get beyond the obvious when analyzing historical characters and events. Colin also reflected an enthusiasm for his subjects that was infectious. The counsel of friends and fellow writers on maritime subjects, Arthur Herman, George Daughan, and Jim Nelson was invaluable, as was that of Phil Siekman, friend and exceptional business writer. Author Bill Hammond was a huge help in my efforts to develop the book proposal for *The Sea Was Always There*.

Senior naval officers, such as Admiral John S. ("Profane") McCain, Jr., Admiral Joseph Metcalf, III, Vice Admiral Robert Dunn, Vice Admiral Robert Stroh, Rear

Admiral Bruce Newell, Rear Admiral Sig Bajak, and my first commanding officer, Captain (later Rear Admiral) Allan Roby, were better role models than I deserved. And along the way I have also learned much about seamanship and the definition of a shipmate from those I have led in the U.S. Navy.

President Emeritus of the National Maritime Historical Society and friend of many years, Peter Stanford, demonstrates daily how much there is to be learned about the sea and the importance of spreading the understanding of how the sea influences virtually every aspect of our daily lives.

To former Chief Executive at the U.S. Naval Institute and retired U.S. Marine Corps Major General, Tom Wilkerson and former editor-in-chief of *Proceedings* and former senior executive at the U.S. Naval Institute, Fred Rainbow, as well as others who urged me on when I allowed myself to be discouraged, I owe more than they will ever realize.

I am indebted to the Editor of *Military History,* Mike Robbins, Literary Editor of *The Weekly Standard,* Philip Terzian, Managing Editor of *Proceedings* Fred Schultz, and Editorial Page Editor of the *New York Post* Bob McManus for significantly improving my craft.

Chief Operating Officer at the National Museum of the Royal Navy, Portsmouth, Graham Dobbin has been a constant reminder of the importance of relevant history. Former shipmate and exceptionally skilled radarman, Charlie Amato, brought back memories of underway watches in the combat information center of USS *Sarasota*.

My wife Sally was an essential part of my discovery of some of the world's most beautiful sailing grounds, particularly those in the British Virgin Islands, and together we also discovered wonderful places connected with the sea, such as Sagres in Portugal, the Royal Dockyards of Portsmouth, and Museo Naval in Madrid. Sally also called upon her experience as a corporate communications executive and retired U.S. Navy captain to provide uncounted and much-needed "sanity checks" as the manuscript for this book developed.

Finally and enthusiastically, I thank Michael James and Chris Paige and the rest of the team at Fireship Press for their patience and professionalism as we brought *The Sea Was Always There* to life.

INTRODUCTION

The sea teaches, and as I've come to understand that plain truth, I've wondered why so many people seem to miss such an important aspect of the saltwater-world that comprises seventy-one percent of the world's surface.

Yes, the sea is fascinating for its beauty and challenging for its power and unpredictability. Yes, the sea is equated with adventure and exploration. And the sea is also an arena in which we observe the marvels of nature. But the ability of the sea to teach is an overarching quality. The nineteenth century writer, T.S. Eliot, put it in a poetic way: "The sea has many voices."

Being involved with the sea as more than a shore-side spectator forces you to get beyond your comfort zone. It lifts you into a special learning mode, and it delivers challenges that are never totally overcome. Off shore there is always a next level of skill and understanding to achieve, and no one ever conquers the sea. That too keeps one in a learning mode.

In addition, there is always the sense of dealing with an environment that, no matter how friendly at the moment, is constantly poised to expose the shortcomings in your skills. The more you learn about the sea, the more you understand how much more there is to know. The offshore domain can be wonderful. It can also be brutal, but above all it teaches, and it teaches its lessons with extraordinary effectiveness.

Sometimes my experiences related to the sea were intensely pleasant; sometimes they were harsh, even dangerous. Sometimes the lessons were subtle, but just as often they were blunt. Often there was considerable humor involved. But without doubt, what I learned from the sea stuck.

It was during two years at sea in a U.S. Navy ship that I really grew up. I was challenged and there was no escape route from that steel, navy-gray capsule. At that point the sea was my life. During another period, when I was under heavy pressure with family and the day-to-day stress of managing my career, a simple activity involving a very small sailboat sustained me. During another phase of my life, I learned the twin joys of discovery and appreciation in larger sailboats among the exotic islands of the Caribbean's West Indies.

Often what I learned had to do with practical, every-day matters. Sometimes what I learned was profound. But when all was said and done, the most important thing was that the sea taught me truly significant things about myself. And beginning with my earliest recollections of childhood, the sea was always there.

All of the above elements are woven into the stories that follow. The venues vary from evocative beaches to a ship of war and a wide variety of sailboats, each with a distinct personality. The venues also include a unique variety of places that are inexorably joined to the sea and that stretch from the eastern shores of the Indian Ocean, through the Pacific and Atlantic Oceans and into the Mediterranean. Also woven into the narrative is a cast that includes friends, family members, shipmates, and even characters from times past.

One special member of the cast from the past is Great Britain's Admiral Lord Nelson, who is perhaps the world's best known naval officer. During his implausible career, about which I have written three books and which included battles during the Age of Sail that shaped the course of history, Nelson learned a lot about the sea and seamen. He was also a prolific writer of letters and military dispatches.

That latter quality was important, since Nelson's words provided much more than a narrative of his astonishing career. They were often startlingly perceptive and thought-provoking in unexpected ways, and they frequently instruct us in the ways of the sea that extend beyond combat under sail. He had a sailor's way with words that grew directly from the way shipboard life through the ages tends to compress language: few words but rich content.

In *Nelson—The New Letters,* Colin White, arguably the most insightful of his recent biographers, focused on the spontaneous quality of Nelson's written words: "The words tumble out of him...almost as if he is speaking."

Often Nelson's words have implications that soar beyond the specific situation at hand. They were plain but forceful, and when he wrote to the Russian Plenipotentiary at Corfu in the Ionian Sea in 1804 they described an over-arching truth that has a lot to do with this book:

"In Sea Affairs, nothing is impossible and nothing improbable."

PART I
BEGINNINGS
SETTING A COURSE

CHAPTER ONE

EARLIEST YEARS

The sea! the sea! the open sea!
The blue, the fresh, the ever free
Without a mark, without a bound
It runneth the earth's wide
Regions round.

Barry Cornwall 1787-1874

My mother's parents emigrated from Ireland, and I am not aware of any specific seafaring history in her Irish ancestry. My father's parents came to the United States from Sicily, and as is the case with my mother, I am not aware of any immediate seafaring connections in his Sicilian background.

Since both Ireland and Sicily are islands, however, and since in far history the Celts, as well as the Greeks, Phoenicians, and Carthaginians who colonized early Sicily were never far from the sea, I'm sure there was a strong sea connection embedded in my genes. It was only a matter of time for the influence of those genes to become evident.

Where and When I Met the Sea

My mother was a painter, and the artist colony in Provincetown, Massachusetts was a familiar family vacation site during my earliest years. The Provincetown Inn was built on the farthest tip of Cape Cod at the site reputed to be where the Pilgrims first set foot in the "new world." There was an aura about the place, a feeling that filled my childhood memories of being there.

The Provincetown Inn was built in 1925, and my first recollections of the Inn were formed when I was probably about three or four years old. In fact I have no mental images that predate those of playing on the strip of beach between the Inn and the Atlantic Ocean. The building was low, possibly a single story, but not more than two stories, and it had a weathered-white tone.

In my mind's eye, the Inn and the ocean are softly focused. Both are distant. One looms upward behind our beach blanket base on the sand. The other stretches away in the opposite direction, towards places and things that were simultaneously formless, fearsome, and beckoning.

The figures of my mother, father, and older sister move silently in and out of my vision. They are outside the imaginary world into which I immigrated on the beach. It was not a lonely place however, since I filled it with characters that I invented to fit the day's play.

In sharp contrast, my recollections of the immediate space that I occupied on the beach are quite vivid. It was limited to only a few feet beyond the blanket that was the center of family activity for a few hours. A carved wooden sea captain in a blue peacoat and white cap and about five inches in length was one of the two key elements in that imagined world. I can still picture the details of that roughly carved and evocative figure. The sand was the other key element of my pretend world at the edge of the ocean.

The space we occupied on the beach could be tape-measured in a few feet, but in my mind it had no boundaries. With little effort and the beginnings of my imagination, my small place in the sand became miniature roads, caves, hills, forts—a world without limits, a world that I controlled.

Building and rearranging that limitless place was all-engrossing, and those days on the beach at Provincetown were the beginning of my conscious relationship with the sea, something that would expand, and at times during my life, come to the fore in surprising ways.

Narragansett Avenue

My earliest years were spent growing up in a two-story, semi-attached house at 1947 Narragansett Avenue, where I was born in my parent's bedroom. The house was part of a newly created residential neighborhood in a northern section of The Bronx, one of New York City's outer boroughs.

There was nothing nautical about the Narragansett Avenue neighborhood, but Long Island Sound was only a few miles away and the Atlantic Ocean was not far beyond the Sound. And that first home was also only a few miles from the unique and little-known New York City nautical community called City Island, where, a few years later, I eventually learned to sail.

The Narragansett Avenue neighborhood was a 1920s precursor of the housing tracts that sprang up in America in the 1950s. To be sure, there were much rougher parts of The Bronx, but they weren't evident in that neighborhood. It was quiet, tidy, and infused with upward mobility. And it was also a family affair with two of my uncles—one on my father's side and one on my mother's side—living with their families within a block of our house.

The house on Narragansett Avenue was the next-to-last at one at end of a row of semi-attached, red brick structures that extended for an entire block. It wasn't large, but it was comfortable, with a small backyard, a smaller front yard, a brick front stoop with four steps leading up to the front door, a separate one-car garage set to the side and back from the house, and a gravel driveway. The crunch of the gravel in the driveway announced my father's arrival home from work each evening. That house, its yards, and driveway were pretty much the limits of the day-to-day world of my early childhood.

I played alone most of the time. In those days, learning to "play nice together" was not an essential part of early childhood development. And I remember what an important place radio had in my daily life, even in those very early years. We had several small table-top radios and a large floor model with a wood cabinet that stood about three feet high. The floor-model radio was a

3

handsome piece of furniture and one of the centerpieces of the household. It provided news, family entertainment, and a distinct physical presence. It was almost as if it were a member of the family.

The Lone Ranger was at the top of my listening list, but characters such as Jack Armstrong ("the All-American Boy"), Little Orphan Annie, and The Shadow held secure positions as well. The characters were all defenders of "the American way of life," and they were sponsored by household staples, such as Wheaties and Ovaltine.

I generally listened to my shows while draped over a stool right in front of the radio. In that position and at that location, it was virtually impossible for anyone to get between me and the make-believe world created by the words and sounds that flowed from the radio.

A Lass Named Bridie

Growing up during the 1930s in The Bronx was on balance a positive experience. In some ways, the most important feature of my pre-school childhood was Bridie Breen. Bridie, who was born in Ireland, was a live-in housekeeper. She had a sturdy look about her and she spoke with what was for me an intriguing brogue. In my child's eyes, she was both an ever-present companion and a part of the family. It usually was Bridie who was charged with "watching" me. In her quiet way she was also a purveyor of an intriguing combination of grown-up wisdom and visions of a mysterious and far-away place. When she spoke about Ireland, she was beginning to expand and introduce reality to my visions of what was beyond the shoreline of the Provincetown beach.

Bridie had grown up on a farm in Ireland, and I'm sure it had been a hard life. One of my clearest recollections of her was that she was missing part of a finger. When I asked what had happened to her finger she said that if had been cut off by a piece of farm machinery, in her words, "because I didn't do what my dad told me to do."

In the course of things, Bridie talked about other aspects of her home in Ireland. She described it as a beautiful place, and the

4

word "lovely," always delivered with an Irish lilt, seemed to stand out. But there was also a perceptible sadness in her recollections. For me one of the most important things about Bridie was that she built a mental image of a mysterious green island, populated by hard working and friendly people, someplace very far away and across the ocean. She added some specificity to the vague idea of an undefined something over the sea, to which I had been introduce on a beach at Provincetown.

It was a happy day for Bridie when she married a New York City policeman and moved on to a new life raising her own family, but her departure left a gap in the house at Narragansett Avenue and our family that was never really filled.

Stories

My grandmother Brennan was also a regular part of my earliest years; and during my bouts with measles, mumps, and chicken pox, she was virtually a full-time nurse. She was the best storyteller I've ever known. It's almost impossible for me to hear the word "story" without thinking of my grandmother Brennan.

The hero of most of Nana Brennan's stories was a boy name "Johnny Magory." He had epic adventures, usually involving a journey of some sort, sometimes in Ireland and sometimes on or across the sea to some exotic place, but always ending in his triumphant emergence from nearly insurmountable difficulties. The Johnny Magory stories were even more evocative than the adventures I heard on radio.

Nana Brennan's repertoire also included stories about Ireland's Leprechauns, frequently referred to as "the wee people," and Banshees. The latter were spirit women who could be heard wailing—and on very, very rare occasions seen—in the forests. The Leprechauns were adventurous and could be mischievous, but the Banshees were bad news, literally. If you heard a Banshee wailing, it meant only one thing: someone you knew was going to die. It was clear at the time that Johnny Magory was an imaginary figure, but the stories about the Leprechauns and Banshees fell into a different category, one where it was not clear where Nana Brennan's fictional story-telling talents and her belief separated.

It was probable that my grandmother Brennan believed her stories about Leprechauns and Banshees, and they were always delivered in a serious manner. But there was a twinkle in her eye, the faintest glimmer of a smile, and a tilt of the head that added up to a license to wonder about the reality of the characters she described. And I am now convinced it was that child's wondering that was her real objective all along.

As was the case with Bridie, my Grandmother Brennan's telling of a beautiful and far away island across an ocean was tinged with sadness. In my Grandmother Brennan's case, it's doubtless that sadness had something to do with the circumstances of her departure from her birthplace.

An older sister had immigrated to America before her, and as was common, her older sister then arranged for my grandmother, then about eighteen years old, to join her in America. She had been brought to America to escape the terrible suffering in Ireland caused by a potato famine and the bloody conflict between England and Ireland, which by that time was centuries old. In one of the great Irish understatements of all time, the bitter fighting was referred to as "The Troubles."

At one point, I was told, her family was suspected — we now know that her brother Johnny was an officer in the IRA — of involvement with an IRA plot. And one day the British soldiers arrived at the family's front door and accused them of hiding documents related to the IRA's activities. The household was given ten minutes to vacate the building. The soldiers searched the house; then it was dynamited.

My grandmother Brennan was a gentle woman, but she hated the English. To her credit she never volunteered those feelings to me, but at times it was clearly there in her eyes.

In the household of my early youth, one of the essential events in the preparations for Christmas was listening to a radio performance of Dickens' *A Christmas Carol*, which was always broadcast a few days before Christmas. The day and time that the program would be on were carefully noted, and when the time came for the broadcast, we all gathered around the radio listening intently and spinning up Charles Dickens' scenes and characters such as Scrooge, Bob Cratchit, Tiny Tim, and "old Fezziwig" in our imaginations.

Dickens' England became another faraway place that existed in my mind. It wasn't beautiful, at least not in the way Ireland was, but it was peopled with a fascinating array of characters, and it had a curious quality of its own. In later years the mental images created by *A Christmas Carol* would eventually translate into an ongoing interest in Great Britain and particularly London.

Around the House

The concept of nursery schools was not yet popular when I was a kid, so my early childhood was pretty much a matter of self-entertainment. For that reason, books were, in an unusual way, very much a part of even my pre-reading years. On rainy days, books, shoe boxes, empty Log Cabin Syrup cans, and other household items became makeshift building materials for playing with my toy soldiers.

The toy soldiers came in two variations. Most were bought at an F.W. Woolworth "Five and Ten" store, where almost all items were priced under a dollar, and many actually did cost only five or ten cents. My soldiers, for example, cost ten cents each. They came in a variety of U.S. Army uniforms and poses. There were three basic positions for the soldiers from the "Five and Ten": firing a rifle while standing, firing while on one knee, and firing while prone on the ground.

A second variety of toy soldiers was more expensive, was more detailed, and they were bought in sets of perhaps fifteen or twenty pieces. Each set represented a distinct British regiment, and they were kept carefully in their original boxes. One set that I remember was Scottish, with kilts and pith helmets. Most of the sets of toy British soldiers were bought on periodic car trips we took to Montreal or Quebec.

The books and improvised household ingredients made wonderful ramparts, buildings, plateaus, tunnels, and other features for the impromptu military dioramas generated by my imagination and spread out on the rug on our living room floor.

The process could occupy an entire afternoon, or when it rained, even the better part of the day.

At the end of the play sessions, the books were returned carefully to their shelves and my toys were put away in a very large copper water pitcher, which was kept in a prominent part of the living room and which was about the size of a farmer's large milk can. I'm not sure where the copper water pitcher came from, but I knew that it came from some place across the ocean. In a corner of my mind, there is the dimmest of recollections that the water pitcher came from Portugal.

A Crucial Discovery

At some point, I realized that there was something worthwhile *inside* the books, and I remember the excitement of having the first book of my own, *For the Glory of France,* by Everett McNeil. I was probably six years old. I still have that book, and when I look at its heavily scarred cover, I marvel at the genius of its selection as a gift for me. The book was an adventure story that began with a trans-Atlantic voyage by two stowaway boys. The book was characterized in its Preamble:

> Being the Tale Told by Noel Bidoux of How He and Robert De Boville, Two French Boys Fleeting for Their Lives from the Swords of Their Enemies, Hid Themselves in the Hold of the Ship of Samuel De Champlain Just Before He Sailed for the New World; and Narrating their Thrilling Adventures on Board the Ship and with the Savages and Wild Beasts of That Strange and Marvelous Land; Together with a Full Account of the First Settlement at Quebec and the Discovery of That Long Lake, which was Named Lake Champlain...Giving the Remarkable and Thrilling Happenings That Caused Them to Hurry Back to France and Led up to the Kinless and Homeless Noel Finding both Home and Kin.

The book's inside front cover and first page were occupied by an illustration depicting the west coast of France, a foreshortened

Atlantic Ocean (with stylized illustrations of a whale, a sea monster, the god of the east wind, a square-rigged bark, and a compass rose), along with the St. Lawrence Seaway and the east coast of Canada. On the left edge of the scene there were two insets, one showed two young men with muskets and dressed in frontier garb, including coon-skin hats. The two young men are looking intently to something being pointed out by an American Indian. The other inset was a sketched portrait of Samuel de Champlain.

In the lower right corner of the illustration there was an artfully lettered and elaborately framed statement:

A map of the
Adventurous journey to the New World of
Robert de Boville and Noel Bidoux who
stowed away of the ship of Saml de Champlain
which sailed from HONFLEUR Ao Do 1608
FOR THE GLORY OF FRANCE

For days as I read the book, I was wrapped in the world represented in that illustration. I had answered another call of the sea. It was another step in the life-long process that would stretch across the Atlantic, Pacific, and Indian Oceans, as well as the Caribbean and Mediterranean Seas.

CHAPTER TWO

ON THE EDGE OF DISCOVERY

[I]t is your friends who make your world.

William James

By the time I outgrew my toy soldiers, we had moved to a somewhat larger house on Gunther Avenue, roughly two miles from the house in which I was born, and still in The Bronx. It was a move of a short distance, but it was in the direction of Long Island Sound and the Atlantic Ocean, apparently meaningless at the time but at least symbolical of my getting closer to the sea.

I was about nine years old and at that point my focus had shifted. It had moved beyond my immediate family and the confines of my house and its front and back yards. At that age, my primary interest had become my neighborhood friends. The main object on a given day was to be with your friends, whether it was playing touch football on an empty field, playing stickball in the streets, playing street hockey on roller skates with an improvised puck made of wood, or just standing around on a favorite corner and "hanging out."

Yes, we really did hang out on a particular street corner. In fact the corner was a meeting place, an informal clubhouse, and at times even a schoolroom of sorts, where there was a lot of informal but useful learning going on.

A Kid's Life

In the fall and winter there was attending Holy Rosary Grammar School, precisely a one mile walk from my house, where many of my classmates and the Irish Presentation Nuns were part of a tougher side of life. I was smart enough, however, to avoid the more extreme character-shaping tactics of the Nuns, at least most of the time.

During the winter there was also sleigh-riding on our Flexible Flyer sleighs down one of the lesser traveled streets of the neighborhood, building snow forts, and snowball fights. The latter activity was enhanced by an inexplicably enjoyable variation of the normal snowball exchanges: throwing snowballs at girls who came within range.

By late spring, there were games like football, plus baseball and a street game called "ringoleavio." The latter game involved two sides of four or five kids. The object was for one side to physically capture the members of the other side. In some ways, it was a little like rugby—but without a ball.

None of the games required uniforms, referees, coaches, or formal playing fields. The equipment was basic: a football, a bat, ball, and baseball glove, or in the case of stickball, a tennis ball and a broomstick handle for a bat. "Ringoleavio" required no sports equipment at all.

In order to play our games, we simply went to an empty field or a convenient place in the street to "choose up sides," and play. We were our own referees, and somehow it worked just fine. If you became known as a person who constantly argued the close plays or refused to "give in" at some point in the disputes, you were simply excluded from the games as "a real pain in the ass."

The summer was much like spring and fall, except you added swimming (usually with the family on weekend excursions to Jones Beach on the north shore of Long Island) and the daily visit of the Good Humor ice cream truck, which occurred at the same time every day. Some of us actually ran a credit tab with the Good Humor man. And most important about the summer, there was no school.

On occasions during the summer, my mother would drive my sister and me to Wilson's Woods, a public swimming pool in Mount Vernon, in lower Westchester County. It wasn't the beach, but the diving board almost made up for that. Diving for a coin that you threw into the pool was an introduction to the secret and fascinating world below the surface of the water and was a preamble to the snorkeling I would enjoy in the years to come.

The biggest drawback at Wilson's Woods was the iron-clad, pool-side rule: NO RUNNING! At nine or ten years of age, you have to concentrate very hard to *not* run, but that diving board made the effort worthwhile.

Up the Hill to Grandmother's House

At this stage of my life, there was one common denominator during all seasons: the best thing was being with your friends, even when you were just "hanging out." The worst thing was being pried away from those friends by such things as going to a restaurant for dinner with your mother, father, and sister.

One exception to the never-wanting-to-go-out-for-dinner problem was the periodic Sunday visits to my Grandmother and Grandfather Callo. They lived on the other side of The Bronx, at the top of Gun Hill Road. Nana Callo's meals simply were the best Italian cooking I have ever experienced, and that covers a lot of Italian food, including some very good meals in Italy.

One of the special features of the Sunday visits to my Callo grandparents was that before and after dinner I was allowed to go the basement, where there was a workbench next to a pile of scrap lumber. The scrap lumber consisted of odds and ends from two-by-fours, molding strips, one-by-ones, dowels, remnants of plywood sheets, shelving, and more. There were strips, triangles, and an almost infinite variety of shapes. I was turned loose with a hammer and nails and permission to "build something." It wasn't like being with my friends but it was interesting in its own way.

For reasons that were not understood at the time, just about every session at the workbench involved building a boat. My finished products would have been excellent examples of abstract art. The important thing, however, was that I enjoyed the process, and each time I was turned loose in my Callo grandparents basement the scrap-wood pile was different.

Sports

When you were with your friends, the best thing you could be involved with was sports, and to a significant degree, my interest in sports had a lot to do with my father. He had played semi-pro baseball as a young man and was an avid sports fan. I also recall being told by my father that my mother had been a good athlete in her youth. He described how she had excelled in the competitive games that were part of the scene at Edgewater Beach, a local resort area on the Long Island shore, where they had met.

Seeing a Yankees' baseball game at Yankee Stadium, the Football Giants at the old Polo Grounds, the Rangers hockey team at the old Madison Square Garden, and even local sandlot football teams at a neighborhood field were highlights of any weekend. And my father was a serious fan. When the team he was rooting for lost, he really suffered. By that time I was also allowed to go to the movies on Saturday afternoon with my friends, and movies about football and baseball stories were special events.

Social Structure

As life in the Gunther Avenue neighborhood progressed, it involved two distinct subsets within the young male society: The Big Kids (roughly from 17 to 19 years old), and The Little Kids (roughly 9 to 13). For some reason, there didn't seem to be any kids in the gap between 13 and 17. I was one of The Little Kids.

The relations between the two groups were not friendly, and communication was mostly limited to exchanges of verbal insults. For example, we nicknamed one of our nemeses "Crisco" (fat in the can).

One of the periodic rituals carried out by The Big Kids, when they were particularly annoyed by The Little Kids, was to give one of The Little Kids a "ride on the green trolley." That meant that several of The Big Kids picked up one of The Little Kids by his arms and legs and heaved him into a nearby hedge.

Entering the hedge on the fly and then disengaging oneself from its branches was somewhat painful. But the humiliation was the worst part of it. Retribution was required, and on some occasions, things got out of hand. On those occasions rocks were the weapons of choice. One well aimed missile from a Big Kid during a rock fight left me with a facial scar that reminds me of those good old days.

Nonviolent Alternatives

At any time during the year, particularly on rainy weekends, there was scale model building. Most of the models were aircraft. The Flying Tigers' shark-toothed Curtis P-40 "Tomahawk" fighter was one of the most popular model kits. Some of the aircraft models were simply carved from solid balsa wood and glued together. Others were so-called flying models that required a higher level of skill and patience. The flying models were constructed like actual planes, with exteriors covered with special paper and painted with "model dope." They were propeller driven and powered by a wound-up rubber band. Flying models were more fun than solid models, even though their flying range was usually about twelve to fifteen feet.

Many of the completed aircraft models were displayed by hanging them on strings that were thumb-tacked to the ceiling of my bedroom, suspended in never ending dives, banks, and climbs. Lying in bed in the dark and watching the barely visible planes as they twisted ever so slowly in "the sky" was the most efficient sleep inducer I have ever come across.

Although aircraft seemed much more interesting at the time, there also were boat models in my one-person production line. One that I particularly remember was a PT boat, similar to the torpedo boats involved in the escape of General Macarthur and his family from the Philippines at the grim, early stages of World War II. At one point, I can remember reading W. L. White's *They Were Expendable*. The exploits of the four young officers who related the story about the naval war in the Pacific made a profound impression on me.

The man at the center of the story, then-U.S. Navy Lieutenant John Bulkely, became a national hero at the beginning of World War II. Yes, I still have that book too, and I believe it had a lot to do with my decision to choose the navy for my military service.

There was also a model of the classic, two-masted New England fishing schooner *Bluenose*. Shaping the beautiful and yet functional hull of that ship from a sold block of balsa-wood was probably the beginning of my appreciation of how form follows function in boat design.

Another nautical, built-to-scale model project was a recreational sloop built much like a real boat, including a hull with a lead-weighted keel, ribs, planking and a hollow mast. The sloop model was the beginning of my curiosity about small boats, something that would grow to significant proportions as I matured. And the rudimentary knowledge of boat construction that I learned would help me get started with a real boat within a few years.

Jones Beach

As the beach at Provincetown was my introduction to the beach as a playground, Jones beach on the north shore of Long Island was my introduction to the more active joys to be experienced in the surf. Those joys included diving into waves at the precise moment they broke for their final run onto the beach and alternatively body surfing the waves to the edge of the beach. In both cases timing was the key and a timing miscalculation was often punished with a chaotic "ass over tea kettle" ride that ended in being deposited in sputtering disarray in the shallow water at the edge of the beach.

The trip to and from Jones Beach was accomplished in a four-door Buick, with a clutch and floor gear shift, usually on a Saturday. The journey began with the packing of a picnic lunch— deviled eggs were a must—several beach blankets, and a large, folding beach umbrella, the pole of which separated into two parts, and heading for the ocean.

It was a fairly long drive—probably more than two hours under the best conditions—and the drive included a ferry across the lower end of Long Island Sound, between Schuylerville in The Bronx and Whitestone in Queens. The actual ferry ride probably wasn't more than fifteen or twenty minutes, but the waiting line to board the ferry, especially on weekends, could take an hour. In 1939, the ferry was replaced by the Whitestone Bridge. The Bridge was certainly a lot faster, but it took something of the adventure and challenge out of the trip.

Because of the traffic, which generally was a major frustration, it was important to get an early start. The early start also was important at the beach itself, where our favored parking area, Lot Six at the east end of the beach, filled up fast. And of course it was important to get there early in order to claim a spot on the beach as close to the water as possible but just above the high tide line.

One of the special features of Jones Beach was its extensive boardwalk. And the boardwalk involved another immutable childhood rule: never, never, *never* walk on the boardwalk with bare feet. I recall that there was a special first aid station on the boardwalk dedicated to removing nasty splinters from the feet of those who violated the never, never, *never* rule.

Once across the boardwalk, it usually took only a matter of minutes to find a choice location for the day, which had to be not only close to the water but also somehow not too close to other beach-goers. Sometimes, less experienced beach-goers would pick a spot that looked like it would be safe but actually wasn't above the high-tide line. Eventually they provided a few moments of special entertainment as high tide inevitably arrived. As the waves swept higher and higher up the beach, one would eventually reach the rookies' blanket. That would precipitate a frantic effort on their part to pick up clothes, beach blankets, food and whatever else was on the beach all at once to prevent soaking. Knowing looks and smirks always passed among my father, mother, sister, and me as one of those scenes erupted.

The basic idea at Jones Beach was to stay in the water as long as possible. In addition to the primary attraction of diving into waves and body surfing, climbing onto my father's shoulders and then diving off would go on for as long as allowed. The diving off my father's shoulders was an extension of the diving for coins at the Wilson's woods pool. Only at the beach, one could, at times, actually grab a shell off the bottom. Those shells, no matter how mundane in design, were trophies to be carried up to the blanket and kept *forever*, or at least until it was time to go home.

Periodically, my mother or father—usually my mother—would come down to the edge of the water and call us out for brief periods, presumably to keep us from suffering hypothermia. Despite the appeals for "just another few minutes," we were condemned to brief periods of sitting on the blanket, while anxiously awaiting the release to reenter the water.

Yet another immutable childhood rule, "The Forty-five Minute Rule" was strictly enforced after eating lunch at the beach. If you returned to the water, even after *forty-four* minutes, you could get a cramp and drown. During those out-of-water periods there was burying one another in the sand. My favorite was to dig a long, shallow hole in which I could sit and then be buried up to the waist, with a car shaped and traced around me in the sand by my father and sister. It wasn't nearly as much fun as swimming, but it could occupy the better part of forty-five minutes.

The drive home from Jones Beach was tedious; especially since you had exhausted yourself in the water, but the pleasant glow from being in the sun for the better part of the day and the smell of the salt air that clung to everything were reminders of a day of perfect play. Jones Beach remains one of the most beautiful in the world, and its place in my mind is unique.

Miami

At some point, perhaps when I was about three years old, my Grandmother Brennan established herself in the real estate business in Miami. It was a modest business, but it had a tremendous fringe benefit for my parents, my sister, and me: an annual winter trip to Miami. The trip was made by car, with me and my sister assigned to the back seat of the family's Buick sedan.

At some point, an Irish terrier named Rusty was added to the lineup.

I have no idea how long the trip took, but I do remember that there were no motels for car travelers. There were tourist "cabins," but they somehow had a shady connotation that I never really understood, and they were never considered, even for a moment. Other than hotels, which were a rare option, overnights were spent at "tourist houses."

As we reduced speed (small towns were notorious speed traps) and entered a given town, there was always a series of private homes with small signs on the lawn or front porch advertising accommodations for tourists. A likely selection would be identified by my parents. We would park in front of the house, and my parents would go in to inspect the premises. They would invariably return with the simple endorsement, "This is fine," and that was it. My only recollections of the people who took in tourists are that they were an easy-going, friendly, and obviously a both trusting and trustworthy lot. They were a part of Americana that was displaced by motels.

Miami was exotic, even magical. Ubiquitous palm trees, lemons and oranges growing in backyards, under-sized Austin cars flitting along the streets, alligator wrestling exhibitions, Seminole Indian reservations, and the Tamiami Trail with roadside tourist shops stocked with intriguing gift items such as painted coconuts and beaded Indian moccasins for kids were all part of the fascination. It was a kid's tropical paradise. Even the prospect of confronting a scorpion or a snake was seen as an intriguing part of Miami's exotic character.

There was a favorite restaurant in downtown Miami, called the Seven Seas, where the waitresses wore sailors' uniforms. How good could it get? With waitresses in sailors' uniforms, it was automatically and emphatically a great place to eat. Who really cared what kind of food they served?

But it was the palm-lined stretches of beach along Biscayne Boulevard, with their unusually—for us—warm and transparent waters and fine sand, that were the main attraction for me. Just being *in* the warm, crystal-clear water seemed like an adventure.

And just being *on* the beach in Miami was somehow even more inviting than the beach at Provincetown that occupied my memories of earliest childhood and Long Island's Jones Beach that occupied my interest as a young boy.

Miami was an unbelievably fascinating sea-dominated environment, an exotic place that set my imagination about tropical lands in motion. It was the preamble to even more magnetic tropical and semi-tropical places, such as Key West, Puerto Rico, Cuba, Jamaica, the Dominican Republic, the British Virgin Islands, St. Lucia, Bermuda, Gaeta, Rapallo, The Canary Islands, Hawaii, and Fremantle that I was to discover as an adult.

Wayward Ways

My friends and I weren't bad kids, but we weren't angels either. I smoked my first cigarette by the time I was eleven and I drank by first beer at about the same age. At that age, a significant degree of ingenuity was involved in getting cigarettes and beer, and although my neighborhood honor code prevents me from revealing our methods, we had them. For example there was a particular candy store where a kid could buy "penny loose" cigarettes at a penny-a-piece—with no questions asked. But there were no real benefits to beer and butts at that age, and with a few exceptions we were able to figure that out fairly quickly.

Those years were good years. In hindsight they might seem to have been awkward and even a bit aimless, but actually there was a lot of learning going on. Much of the learning involved the games we played and particularly how we played them.

Just hanging out with my friends was an important dimension of my own learning process, and the street corner was the principle classroom. The natural conversations were a form of constant information sharing, with bits of useful knowledge being spread casually among inquiring minds. Those pre-teen years were the time when I learned how to get along with my peers, and that was a process that involved exclusively unwritten rules. I certainly didn't see it those terms, but that's the way it was.

It was a time for learning about such things as "how to take care of yourself" in a wide variety of situations, situations that were part of everyday life in The Bronx. You learned, for example, that bullies could not be avoided and that showing fear or reasoning with them only prolonged the unpleasantness.

I didn't realize it at the time, but those years when being with my friends was everything were also a phase of my growth when connections with the sea were edging into my life.

CHAPTER THREE
WAR AT SEA

World War II, which changed history forever, was the largest war that man has brought upon himself. Since the sea inevitably decides world wars, World War II was also the largest naval war.

Rear Admiral E.M. Eller, USN (Ret)

On December 7, 1941 my life changed radically. The change was triggered by the Japanese attack on Pearl Harbor. My memory of the moment when I learned of the attack is still clear. I was standing on the sidewalk about a hundred yards from my house, when one of my friends ran out of his front door and yelled, "The Japanese bombed Pearl Harbor!"

My childhood ended then and there; fun wasn't much fun anymore, and constant anxiety permeated everything we did. Hawaii was no longer an exotic Pacific Island; it had become a deadly epicenter for a hideous war. The gently swaying palm trees that could always be counted on previously in the newsreels about the island were transformed into stripped and shattered trunks, signaling how war converts beauty to ugliness.

It was an abrupt transition, and I'm sure it had a lasting impact on my personality. The early, almost exclusively negative trajectory of the war's initial events was particularly formative. In any event, the result of the attack was all too clear: the country that I had known up to the Japanese attack on Pearl Harbor would no longer be the same.

The War at Sea

World War II was one of the greatest sea sagas in recorded history. The sweep was global, with major actions in the Atlantic, Pacific, and Indian Oceans. There were also significant actions in the North, Mediterranean, Caribbean, Baltic, Philippine, and Coral Seas, and many previously lesser-known waters.

Broad concepts of maritime power became abundantly clear as Great Britain's crucial food imports were reduced to a trickle by German submarine tactics and the War in the Pacific cut U.S. imports of crucial raw materials from that area of the world. America had suddenly joined the other previously prosperous people of the world who were learning "to do without."

Pursuing German surface raiders and submarines in the Atlantic, maintaining seaborne supplies to beleaguered islands like Malta, complicated amphibious assaults over the beaches on Pacific islands, amphibious assaults in North Africa and Sicily, aircraft carrier actions against the Japanese in places like Midway Island, the Coral Sea and Leyte Gulf, the miraculous evacuation of a major portion of the British Expeditionary Force from Dunkirk, and ultimately the landings at Normandy in the European Theater and Okinawa in the Pacific filled the newspapers, radio broadcasts, newsreels—and our minds.

The events of the War were all connected by the sea, and chapter after chapter of dramatic sea stories—mostly negative in the beginning but positive as the tide turned—were described in the news constantly. Day by day the life-and-death relevance of what went on at sea was etched into my consciousness, along with the other daily realties of "the war to make the world safe for democracy."

No Debates

Twenty-four hours after the attack, America declared war. There were no significant debates or hesitation, just an evocative statement by President Roosevelt and an overwhelming vote for a declaration of war by Congress.

There were no public opinion polls at the time that I can remember, but initially there was absolutely no doubt in my household and neighborhood about how long the war would last. The overwhelming initial consensus was that it would be over in a matter of months. The basic reaction, especially from those who had scoffed at the possibility of an attack from Japan in the first place, was that the Japanese had to be crazy to attack the United States.

We were going to have to teach "those Japs" a lesson, and that wouldn't take too long, no more than a few months—a year at the most. What didn't take too long was for that opinion to unravel. Accompanying that new consensus was the sobering two-part realization of just how inadequately prepared the United States was militarily and just how high the cost in blood and national resources would rise.

It was a different time, however, and there were virtually no verbal attacks on President Roosevelt when the war stretched on, initially with one defeat after another and without a predictable end in sight. Frighteningly large areas on the map of the world were coming under the control of the Axis Powers, and U.S. military personnel were dying by the thousands. There were, however, no body counts of U.S. military dead in the media. There were only the small gold star flags in the windows of many homes, indicating that a member of the military from the family had been killed in the war.

There were an awful lot of the gold star flags in windows of homes everywhere, and everyone could see how they were multiplying steadily. They were a quiet, painful, ubiquitous report on the status of the War. What they lacked in context, they more than made up in their simple, terrifying eloquence.

The initial overconfidence after December 7, 1941 was replaced quickly by an understanding and acceptance that the war was going to be hard and costly in terms of treasure and human life. The new attitude was captured, not in flowery exhortations but in a three-word admonition that spoke volumes and that became the companion to the Gold Star windows: "Remember Pearl Harbor."

There was a universal understanding that the Allies could lose the war, and during that time, fear was a perpetual companion. But there was also determination and a willingness to pay the price in blood and effort to win a war that absolutely had to be won.

When the War started, my father was a principal in the small advertising agency he had founded in 1929. Before starting the business, he had joined the U.S. Marine Corps at age 17 and gone to France with the American Expeditionary Force during World War I. Immediately after the Japanese attack on Pearl Harbor, he tried to reenlist in the U.S. Marine Corps. He was turned down, however, because of his age and his two children.

My mother went to work as the chief clerk in a local Draft Board. She didn't talk about it much, but it was pretty clear that she didn't like it. I believe the fact that she was sending draftees to war and in many cases to their death was almost too much for her to handle.

There were four houses and several empty lots on our side of the block on which we lived, and two Big Kids from two of the three other houses joined the military as soon as the war began. They both joined the U.S. Navy. One, Joe McMahon, was an officer who fought in the South Pacific and the other, Al Staiger, was a Navy diver who fought in the Aleutian Islands. Both had younger brothers I hung around with, and both came home at the end of the war and went right to work building civilian lives. They were among the lucky ones, contrasting with those who did not return and those who returned with wounded bodies and minds.

The Home Front

Shortly after the attack on Pearl Harbor, we were introduced to food and gasoline shortages and the rationing books that measured out one's life during the war. I clearly remember the lettered sticker on the windshields of our family cars that identified the level of gasoline ration to which each was entitled. There were a lot of cars that were put up on blocks in their garages.

I also remember the food rationing books that were a part of every grocery store and butcher shop visit. Sugar, coffee, and meat were among the very scarce items. We knew that everyday things in Great Britain were worse, but I don't think there was a realization that the people in the British Isles were close to a state of starvation.

Every grammar school had a War Stamp savings program for its students, and the newspapers, radio reports and movie newsreels were dominated by war news. During the first year of the war, the news was very, very bad. Much of it showed London and Londoners being bombed to bits and Japanese troops marching inexorably through newly conquered territory in the Pacific. There also were daily scenes of German troops marching through and occupying countries, and daily reports of merchant ship sinkings in the Atlantic, some right off the U.S. east coast, and most accompanied by footage showing half-drowned merchant seamen being dragged from the icy cold waters of the Atlantic. Newsreel maps constantly showed the growing shaded areas of the globe coming under the control of the Axis Powers. Those shaded maps of huge global swaths were my first lessons in the geopolitical relevance of the world's seas in war. They illuminated indelible lessons about what A.T. Mahan explored in his book: *The Influence of Sea Power on History,* and they provided a foundation for all of the variations on that theme I came across later in researching for my own books. [1]

The War pervaded everything and changed how we lived and how we thought, and along with the accounts of the ongoing War, there was palpable fear in America and in my own home at that point. Attitudes had radically changed, and everyone realized that it was possible for the Allies to lose the War, in fact, we *were* losing it. The major barriers that stood between us and our worst fears were the Atlantic and Pacific Oceans.

There actually was fear that America would be occupied by a conquering army, and the images that provoked were terrifying. But no matter how bad things looked, there was virtually no dissention among politicians or the media. A demonstration against the war would have been unthinkable, and there was no parsing of patriotism. Virtually everyone was part of The War Effort, and those who were perceived to be "war slackers" were despised.

In my neighborhood, those men who were physically and otherwise eligible served in the military, either as a volunteer or a draftee. Either was OK, but a volunteer was clearly better. And a draft dodger ranked with out-and-out traitors, a disgrace to himself, his family, and his friends. There were five men within a block of our house who went into the military: two in the navy, two brothers in the army, and one who joined the then Army Air Corps.

Men who were not physically qualified for the draft were classified by the draft system as "4F," and among my peers, all of whom were something less than mature observers, that was something to be pitied. "He's just a four-F" was a pejorative that reached beyond military draft classification. It was used to describe any male you *really* didn't like. The idea that there were men who were legitimately unqualified for military service never broke through the powerful aura of patriotism that engulfed me and my friends.

Women went to work outside the home. Many filled factory jobs on production lines that produced aircraft, tanks, guns, and other war materiel, the kinds of jobs that had been performed only by men before the War. Others took office jobs with companies that were classified as essential industries, such as shipyards and refineries.

Families grew vegetables in "victory gardens" to supplement supplies of food. Spam became a food staple and women's silk or nylon stockings disappeared. Women were known to paint stocking seams on the backs of their bare legs. Kids collected scrap metal, rubber, and newspapers. Nothing was more patriotic than buying War Bonds, and kids bought War Stamps, usually in programs set up in their schools. In movie theaters, collection cans were passed around after the double features to collect for "war relief" for refugees and other "displaced persons."

There also was "civil defense" training, mostly dealing with anticipated German air raids. After all, the Germans were bombing the British, so we expected the same. It was only a matter of time. Neighborhoods had "Air Wardens," who wore steel helmets and had special armbands. The only weapon they carried was a whistle.

The wardens' main job was to assure that everyone was off the street and there were no lights showing during air raid drills. They were armed with whistles that they blew in front of a house that might be leaking light. And they "wielded" their weapons aggressively in the pursuit of their duty. I also remember the training everyone got about dealing with incendiary bombs. Rule one was never throw water on an incendiary bomb. Rule two was to try to get it on a long-handle shovel and move it away from flammables. Rule three was to suffocate it with sand or dirt. Everyone involved was very serious about the air raid drills, and there were zero complaints about any inconveniences they caused.

I had a specialty during the war: building up two very impressive scrapbooks of pictures of military aircraft clipped from newspapers and magazines. One book was of Allied aircraft; the other was for Axis planes. To this day I still can identify many of the aircraft that were flown by both sides during the War. Several years ago, I was able to actually touch the wing of a Spitfire at the Imperial Air Museum at Duxford, England. The result was a flood of images and emotions associated with the life-and-death battles fought in the skies over Britain during the early 1940s. I was stunned at how emotional the experience was after so many years.

Today those two scrapbooks would be worth a considerable amount of money to a collector of World War II memorabilia, but like the aircraft and ship models and almost all of the other tangibles of my childhood, they eventually went out with the trash.

Silver Linings

There were two aspects of World War II that were not negative for me personally. The first involved what were called "blackout parties." The parties were scheduled periodically at the home of one or another of my school classmates—interestingly, always one of the girls—to coincide with the blackout drills that were intended to prepare us for the German air attacks that we knew were inevitable.

The second aspect of the war that wasn't negative involved one girl in particular. At the edge of our neighborhood there was a small campus of two- and three-story buildings called the Gould Foundation. It was an orphanage, and during the war, there was a group of approximately 20-25 kids from Great Britain who were in the United States to avoid the German air raids decimating London and other targets in England. Not surprisingly, the kids from Britain became known in my circle as "The English Kids." They pretty much kept to themselves, but there was some limited fraternizing, especially towards the end of the War.

The first one-on-one date of my life was with one of The English Kids. Her name was Babette MacKenzie. My guess is that she was 15 years old at the time, and she was pretty. I was thirteen years old, and I have to admit that I misrepresented my age to her by telling her that I was a freshman in high school.

I don't think I fooled her for a minute, but that didn't matter. I had attained the unattainable and was thrilled when Babette agreed to go to the movies with me on a Saturday night. Sadly there was no second date, although I did ask. I'll never forget that courteous but unequivocal "no thank you"; and I never again dated a girl who was taller than I was. That was also the last time I lied about my age.

I have often wondered what life was like for Babette and The English Kids when they got back home after the war. They deserved to have some good things come their way, but they were returning to cities and a nation that were beginning a difficult rebuilding process, literally. They were kids whose childhoods were never free of anxieties that they didn't deserve, and they had been shipped across an ocean to an unfamiliar place where they had no friends or family. Remembering my own insecurities during the war, I can only imagine how difficult it must have been for The English Kids.

An End and a Beginning

The end of World War II was a strange combination of emotions. Good had triumphed over evil. The United States was safe. Most of those who fought the war and won were coming home. But not all of them were coming home, and that was a terrible reality. Everything seemed a lot better overnight, but the gold star flags in the windows weren't coming down.

More than 400,000 members of the U.S. military had died, roughly three-quarters were combat deaths. Approximately 20 million military personnel worldwide had died in the War. Approximately 40 million civilians worldwide had died as a result of the War. These were mind-boggling statistics. Peace had been achieved, but at a dreadful price.

As a country we had come through a desperately testing time. As people we had seen the essence of humanity, its best and its worst. We were changed forever, in ways that no future generation could possibly grasp.

CHAPTER FOUR
A BOY AND A BOAT

Our life is closed—our life begins,
The long, long anchorage we leave,
The ship is clear at last—she leaps!
She swiftly courses from the shore,
Joy! Shipmate—joy.

Walt Whitman

As World War II was winding down, there was a special happening in my life, something that involved a sport that was not well known in my neighborhood. It began with my mother falling in love with the idea of having a family sailboat, and the follow-on result was that she convinced my father that it was a good idea. I was probably thirteen years old when this momentous family decision was made.

My sister Toni, who is three years older and was at the time dedicated to saving me from my ruffian ways, was no doubt complicit in the proceedings. In any event I wasn't involved in the discussions, being the junior member of the household and much too busy with my friends in the neighborhood to get involved in discussions about a *sailboat*. Further, there was another distraction for me: the emerging concept of girls as something other than just soft boys.

The Alden O Knockabout

As a result of my mother's instigation, a somewhat aged sailboat was purchased at City Island on nearby Long Island Sound. She was one of a class of day-sailers called Alden O Knockabouts and was designed by famous boat designer of the time John Alden. But the Callo family's "new" boat had seen better days and was probably at least ten years old when my father bought her.

The new addition to the family was 18 feet long and had a wood-planked hull, an open cockpit, and a small deck area forward. She had originally been designed as a centerboard boat with a gaff-rigged mainsail and small jib, but her previous owner had eliminated the centerboard and added a permanent keel. He had also replaced the gaff-rigged mainsail with a taller and what was for its time a more modern triangular mainsail. His changes also included the addition of a one-cylinder, in-board engine that had a will of its own. Adding an in-board engine, particularly one that usually refused to start and was inordinately noisy when running, was a nasty thing to do to any sailboat.

In theory, the previous owner had "modernized" the boat. But in terms of the delicate design balances that make a sailboat both fast and seaworthy, he hadn't done the boat any favors. A well designed sailboat is a harmonious compromise among a series of physical and mathematical realities. When a near-perfect balance among all of the design factors is achieved the result is peak performance and functional beauty. But when some of the elements that have been brought together to achieve that near-perfect balance are changed, the resulting functional disharmony shows in performance and appearance.

As I've looked back after sailing a lot of boats over the years, it seems to me that the previous owner of the newly acquired Callo family boat had challenged that truism—and lost. But the Callo family boat was sturdy, and she provided the means for me to begin the never-ending learning journey involved in sailing. For those attributes, I remember her fondly. And although I didn't realize it at the time, the boat was going to not only be the means of my learning new things about a hitherto unknown sport, it would become the means of discovering important things about myself.

A Clash of Cultures

To my dismay, I was elected by my father, mother, and sister —I probably was hanging out with my friends when the election took place—to learn how to sail. The idea of sailing rather than playing street games was, to say the least, radical. But despite my preoccupation with more important things, including that new area of interest involving girls, I was talked into accepting my new responsibility.

As I was adjusting to the idea of sailing, things got worse, much worse. My mother and sister got their heads together and came up with a name for the boat. The name they settled on was *Ree-Raa,* which in Gaelic means "A place or state where exuberance and revelry prevail." Try explaining *that* to my friends in The Bronx.

Suddenly it was not only a matter of telling the guys that I wouldn't be around on a given day because I was *sailing;* what if they found out the boat's name was *Ree-Raa*? In my crowd that was living on a razor's edge.

But there was no escape, and I accepted my fate. My initial sail training lasted perhaps three or four days and consisted of relatively short training sails in *Ree-Raa* on Long Island Sound with the former owner of the boat. His skill as a teacher was on a par with his skill as a naval architect, but he did his best to cram the basics into me on those brief occasions. Since I was starting from a pinnacle of ignorance, the process did have some limited success.

Given the circumstances, I was fortunate in also having several opportunities to sail with one of my uncles, Norton Brennan. Uncle Norton was a physics professor at Penn State University, and he was at least able to explain the basic principles of energy transference involved in propelling modern sailboats. Those principles had escaped me completely during my initial training sessions with *Ree-Raa's* former owner, a seriously inarticulate person who would never have won an award for interpersonal communication. Lesson one with Uncle Norton began with an explanation of why the boat wouldn't move ahead if you stood on the deck and pushed forward on the mast. Yes, I really did ask him that question.

The result of the process was that in truth I had to become a self-taught sailor, and my first excursions with my mother and sister were trying for me and no doubt more than a little nerve-wracking for them. I even managed at one point to ground the boat on Cuban Ledge, a sand bar in Long Island Sound. I'll never forget the sickening feeling of *Ree-Raa* surging to a stop with her sails filled. The experience left a mental wound that never healed, some dark thing that lurks in the back of my mind every time I take the helm in a sailboat.

The days that I spent learning to sail in *Ree-Raa* were by no means marked by "exuberance and revelry," and I have to admit that I really felt put upon and at the same time intimidated by the whole situation. But gradually the sense of constant anxiety diminished, and I began to realize that there was a kind of magic in using the wind to power a boat. I didn't recognize it at the time, but I had actually crossed over a threshold into a special process of learning that would continue for a lifetime. In fact what was involved was just as much a state of mind as a process. And it was a state without borders.

A Healthy Byproduct

Learning to care for a wooden boat—an old one at that—turned out to be a blessing in disguise. It was hard labor that again involved on-the-job training. The challenge of getting the boat ready after winter storage in the boatyard was mitigated by a high school pal Bob Simms. Bob traveled from his home on the opposite side of The Bronx on innumerable Saturdays and Sundays to share the scraping, caulking, sanding, painting, and varnishing that went with getting the boat out of the yard and into the water in the spring.

By the standards of experienced sailors, our work was nothing special. And I should add that I was able to avoid ever painting *Ree-Raa* on the boat's transom. But my deep satisfaction at seeing a freshly painted and varnished boat I had worked on riding with grace and confidence at her mooring was a surprisingly profound pleasure, my first clear epiphany of the sea.

There were two additional things I learned with *Ree-Raa*. First, when I became a junior member of the venerable City Island Yacht Club, I began at least faintly to understand how the fascination with sailing could infect one. The City Island Yacht Club was also where I learned important lessons about caring for a boat from the Club's yard master, a no-nonsense Scandinavian named Eddy Quest. Mr. Quest introduced me in blunt terms to the philosophy of taking care of your tools and doing your work on a boat only one way, the right way. Eddy Quest was not a tolerant man. In fact I considered him to be a seriously unpleasant person. Over time and long after I had moved past my earliest sailing years, however, I realized it was my ignorance that angered him, not my person. That was a bit of learning that has helped me in surprising ways over the years.

Ree-Raa was also my introduction to City Island, a small and truly unique community that implausibly marries the quaintness of a small New England fishing town to the edginess of the city whose astonishing downtown skyline is visible from its southern tip. City Island is a true time warp. There's a sense of salt in the air and a sailor's attitude among the people who live and work there. Whenever I return there, it seems to be exactly the same as when I was first introduced to the technology of efficiently using wind to power a boat.

On City Island there were several boat yards and sail makers that clearly contributed to the nautical aura, and the aroma of tarred line in the local hardware store was an evocative hint of the Age of Sail. When you walk along City Island Avenue, which travels the full length of the long axis of the island, you are not in an urban world; you are in a world of boats and sailors.

Ree-Raa, the City Island Yacht Club, and City Island were the start of my learning about sailing. It was a somewhat awkward but clearly formative experience. Like some things that may be thrust upon the life of a teenager, sailing turned into one of the best things that could have happened to me. It became a crucial early stage in my relationship with the sea, something that would evolve in exotic places and evocative circumstances—sometimes joyfully, sometimes painfully and frequently edifyingly.

Sailing in *Ree-Raa* also was the beginning of understanding that no matter how long I have been learning about the sea, I remain forever at the beginning of the process. There is no point at which a true sailor can say, "I now know enough about the sea." With my reluctant introduction to *Ree-Raa,* however, my continuing learning journey on the subject had begun an important phase. I had embraced the sea and the sea had allowed me to do so. When that happens, there may be separations along the way—but never a divorce.

A former editor of *Yachting* magazine captured the spirit of the particular aspect of the sea that I had entered with *Ree-Raa:*

> Sailing is far more a state of mind and heart than it is a method of getting from Point A to Point B. For many sailors, the simple act of hoisting the sails puts them in a mellow mood, and a destination is far down the list of importance. [2]

As my formal education progressed through high school, there was a negative that related to what I was learning with *Ree-Raa:* there was a steadily diminishing amount of time that could be devoted to what I had begun to think of as "my boat." It became harder and harder to maintain *Ree-Raa* at the level she deserved, and it was increasingly difficult to even take the time to get out on the water. After a few years, the boat was sold, and that was the end of the beginning of my interest in sailing.

Dealing with Death

During my four years of high school, while my interests were moving beyond my home and neighborhood, there was a decline in my mother's health that turned out to be devastating. She was in fact dying, but I wasn't really aware of the terminal aspect of her illness until the very end in 1947. My mother was only 47 when she died.

If I had been more mature, I would have seen it coming. In addition, my father—I believe intentionally—never put it to me that her illness was terminal. I'm sure that he wanted to spare me the distress that he knew that knowledge would have brought. As well intentioned as that was, however, it would have been better to be fully aware of the situation all along than to deal with not only the shock of my mother's death but the element of guilt I felt at not having been aware of the real situation.

My memories of my mother are overwhelmingly positive. Her sensitivity to the feelings of others, the trips to Jones Beach and Wilson's Woods, an understated but make-you-laugh-out-loud humor, quiet but irresistible ambitions for me, and unflagging encouragement for whatever I tried to accomplish were for me her dominant traits. And there also were her paintings, which I always loved. Fortunately some of her paintings remained in the immediate family. One, a depiction of an organ grinder in a snowy courtyard, hangs in our living room.

Nothing is more important, however, than the realization that it was my mother's ideas about the joy of sailing that introduced me to something that would have a profoundly positive effect on my life, something that I would not in all probability have sought on my own initiative. And once that introduction really took hold, she was gone.

Besides my reluctant introduction to sailing, my mother played an uncanny role in another series of major events in my early life: my application to and acceptance by Yale University. For reasons that I never understood, my mother and father had decided when I was quite young that I was destined to attend Yale. Neither had attended college, and there was no family connection to that school, but for as long as I can remember, they spoke of my attendance there as if it was preordained. For my own part and as I approached the end of high school, my interests were in other directions.

Through a series of unlikely events, including a chance meeting with one of my former high school coaches at my mother's wake and a subsequent introduction to Bob Geigengack, the track coach at Yale, it was decided that I would do a fifth year of high school. It was hoped that the additional, fifth year of preparation for college would result in admission to Yale. The prep school of choice was Trinity-Pawling School in Putnam County, New York.

After the relative freedom of living at home, the restricted life of a boarding school was a major shock. But there was a major short-term compensation: sports. In the fall I played football. In the winter it was basketball, and in the spring there was track. What I couldn't understand about the sports program at Trinity-Pawling was that it was obligatory. How could anyone not want to play football and basketball and run on the track team?

Awakenings

There were two truly important intellectual factors involved with my year at Trinity-Pawling. The first was that it was during that year that I learned how to study. In that environment there really was no option. The second was that my intellectual horizons greatly expanded. It began to dawn on me just how much there was beyond my neighborhood.

The result of the combination of factors was that my motivation to attend Yale, which had been at best lukewarm, began to increase. And at Yale I found another major link with the sea.

CHAPTER FIVE
YOU'RE IN THE NAVY NOW

In after-years, should troubles rise
To cloud the blue of sunny skies,
How bright will seem, through mem'ry's haze,
Those happy, golden by-gone days!
So let us strive that ever we
May let these words our watch-cry be,
Where'er upon life's sea we sail:
"For God, for Country, and for Yale!"

From the song "Bright College Years"

My letter of acceptance from Yale arrived on the day I graduated from Trinity-Pawling School. I remember looking at the unopened letter and thinking, "Everything has come down to this piece of paper." I opened it and read:

Dear Sir:

It gives me pleasure to report that you have been voted tentative membership in the Freshman Class entering Yale University in September....We shall inform your school of the action of the Board of Admissions and send for your final record.

I had made it. The fact that I had received the letter so late meant that I was perilously close to the very bottom of the acceptance list. But that didn't really matter. I had tried to accomplish something that had involved a difficult challenge, and I had succeeded. It was a personal victory, but my view at that point shifted quickly beyond the immediate victory to the challenges I inferred from Yale's rather off-hand description of their verdict.

In the fall of '48, I showed up in New Haven, somewhat off balance. I was in yet another radically new environment, but my fascination with my rapidly expanding horizons was more than enough to overcome my anxieties. And the challenge of being part of a student body, all of whom were among the top students in their respective high schools, forced me to bear down academically, immediately. In addition, I was pleased and reassured to find that there were a number of very good runners from New York City high school track teams among my freshman classmates. I found that somewhat reassuring in my new and very different environment.

A Really Big Step

I was 18 years old when I entered Yale, and had already registered for the draft, as required, by the time I showed up in New Haven. In my household, military service was simply part of one's citizenship. Patriotism was not a situational value, and military service was something you did. There was no angst, no heroics, and no doubt; you just did it. The only significant question was how you would serve.

To assure finishing college before my military service, I sought out the Naval Reserve Officers Training Corps (NROTC) program at Yale. It seems the logical choice, since I was interested in sailing. I had received recruiting letters from the Army and the Air Force for their ROTC programs, and had learned by word-of-mouth about Yale's NROTC program. I sought out the NROTC office and an interview with the professor of naval science, a U.S. Navy captain, was scheduled.

The captain was a brilliant recruiter. During a courteous but brief interview, he thanked me for my interest and explained that there were 400 applicants for 110 openings in the part of the program (referred to as the "contract program") for which I was eligible.[3] There was no sales pitch; the session was strictly informational. He neither said nor needed to say anything more. I was determined to be one of the 110 soon-to-be Yale NROTC midshipmen.

Many years later, I learned that not every Yale NROTC student in history was a volunteer. One, the late Vice Admiral Jerome H. King, Jr. told how, just after he arrived at Yale in 1937, he went to the university post office to mail a postcard to his parents telling them of his safe arrival in New Haven. Somehow, he got on the wrong line and "before I knew it, I was signed up in the Naval ROTC." [4]

I passed the physical, which is undoubtedly the toughest I have ever taken. As I recall, the full test involved two days. I also remember that my entire body was so sore after the physical that I could barely get into my upper bunk for several days after it was over.

Although I didn't realize it at the time, my nascent association with the U.S. Navy was in many ways the continuation of a process that had begun as a small child playing in the sand on the beach in Provincetown. I didn't think much about it in these terms, but I was at that point back in touch with the sea, this time big time, and that renewed contact would play out in a very different way. The context was a lot more serious and a lot more expansive than my previous connections with the sea, and it was the beginning of a navy relationship that would continue for the rest of my life.

The NROTC program involved several classroom sessions and one naval science lab each week. All labs were in uniform. The freshman year was mostly indoctrination into U.S. Navy history and organization. There was also a considerable amount of close-order drilling, which, I believe is fair to say, had limited appeal for me and my fellow freshman midshipmen.

It didn't take long for me to figure out, however, that the U.S. Navy not only had a special history, it had a distinct culture as well. Now I had two new cultures to which I had to adapt simultaneously. Life was accelerating.

A Unique Academic Program

The NROTC program for sophomore and junior years involved the application of math, physics and geometry to such naval functions as navigation, ship handling, gunnery, and ship design. It also was my introduction to computers, in the form of a crude, solenoid-driven antecedent of the modern computer. That precursor of today's computers was about the size of a small refrigerator and it was used for heavy weapons fire control.

The sophomore and junior years of the program were especially challenging for me academically, since math, science, and engineering were not my strongest suits; in fact, as a liberal arts major, my subjects were concentrated in literature, history, and psychology. My senior NROTC year involved applied sociology, psychology, and history with the emphasis on effective management and leadership. There also was emphasis on naval strategy and tactics. For good measure, study of the Uniform Code of Military Justice (military law) was worked into the curriculum.

The four-year NROTC academic program was no pushover. There were a number of other courses in my four-year undergraduate experience at Yale that were less intellectually challenging than those in my NROTC program.

The Midshipmen's Cruise

Between the junior and senior years for "contract" students, there was something deceptively called a midshipmen's cruise. It involved six weeks of intense instruction that made me wonder about the use of the word "cruise." I was ordered to the then-heavy cruiser USS *Macon,* whose main armament was her eight-inch guns. I reported on board in Norfolk, VA with my seabag, my book knowledge of the U.S. Navy, and a little knowledge of sailing, and we departed for an Atlantic Fleet training exercise in the Caribbean.

That was yet another culture shock. A major warship such as *Macon* is a self-contained society. The overused comparison to a floating city is accurate but only up to a point. And what makes it different from a city isn't the salt air. A U.S. Navy ship is, when all is said and done, an oligarchy. The oligarch is the captain, and in that position, the captain has your life in his hands. But that's only the top of the chain of shipboard authority, and as a midshipman one answered (promptly) to department heads, division officers, and senior petty officers. The main objective of the cruise was not just learning how to do certain things, but how to do them the right way. At sea, and particularly in a military context, that was an important distinction.

A U.S. Navy ship is a military module designed to deliver, when called upon, extreme violence upon an enemy. There were specifics to be learned—up close, personal, and fast. Some of those specifics involved technical knowledge, the operation of an eight-inch gun, for example. There also was a lot to learn about how things got done safely, and I was surprised how many times the words "safe" and "safety" came up during each day.

There were also things to be learned about my own capacities. I found out, for example, that the basic four-hour, under way watch schedule for a ship means that one rarely gets more than three or four hours sleep during a 24-hour cycle. But to my astonishment, I also discovered that I could actually function despite such sleep deprivation. I also found out during engine room watches, which we stood in 135 degree heat, the meaning of *extended* physical stress. Arguably the most important discovery of all was that I could perform in circumstances that were difficult beyond anything previously experienced. The learning curve was steepening, and it was happening rapidly and in a challenging environment.

One of the more interesting aspects of the midshipman's cruise involved my general quarters assignment in one of *Macon's* three gun turrets, where I was instructed in the duties of gun captain. The experience in the eight-inch-gun turret during firing of the guns was an attention grabbing introduction into the day-to-day, minute-to-minute dangers of even basic military operations.

The process of handling and loading an eight-inch shell and powder bag and then firing the gun safely had to be highly disciplined. Small mistakes could be catastrophic. In the process of actual firing, the fact that my own safety depended on more than my own performance was inescapable. It also depended on the faultless performance of the others in the gun crew.

One of the most enduring memories of my experience in the *Macon's* eight-inch turret, the assault on the senses in that confined, steel-enclosed space at the moment even one of the three guns was fired, would be reprised in an eerie way many years later in a 34-foor sailboat, anchored in the British Virgin Islands' Road Town Harbor.

There also are softer memories of my midshipman cruise. For example, it was the first time I had been at sea and out of sight of land for an extended period of time. And despite the lack of sleep and intensity of the training, there were quiet moments when I had an opportunity to absorb the unique experience of being in a ship at sea surrounded with nothing by sky and ocean. I liked it.

Patrick O'Brian, author of the Aubry/Maturin series of novels described the sense of it: "This life, with its rigid pattern punctuated by the sharp imperative sound of bells, seemed to take on something of the nature of eternity." [5]

First Liberty

The only liberty port we visited in the Caribbean during the six weeks was Kingston, Jamaica. I had visited Havana with my sister—who was working for then-National Airlines and who was entitled to family passes—for a quick one-day visit a year before. So Jamaica was my second trip to the Caribbean, a region I have come to love over the years.

The fact that I approached the island in a ship rather than in a plane gave me a sea-focused perspective, something radically different from an arrival through an airline terminal. The difference is another one of those things one has to experience to fully understand. For some reason, arriving by sea gave me an immediate and strong sense of the history of the place, so much of which had to do with the sea. And because of Jamaica's turbulent and often harsh history, there was a palpable tension between the overwhelming physical beauty of the island and the mostly unseen residue of historic violence and hardship that had been woven into the fabric of the place and its people. The beauty mitigated the inescapable poverty, and the poverty compromised the incredible beauty. In a sense, each intensified the impression made by the other.

As midshipmen, our liberty in Kingston was tightly controlled. The Navy, it seems, was determined to divert us from the seamier side of downtown Kingston and the legendary ways of sailors on liberty in exotic ports. And those efforts at control were not without justification. There was clearly a much rougher side of my first liberty port that was evident, despite the restriction on our activities ashore.

The limitation notwithstanding, there was an opportunity to do some shopping, plus a hair-raising bus ride along a series of narrow mountain roads that ended at the Tower Isle Hotel. The exotic beauty of the mountainous tropical countryside was astonishing to a kid from The Bronx.

We swam in the Tower Isle pool, had a beer, and stared out over the lush countryside. It was the pivotal step in my personal discovery of the Caribbean, and I realized that I had fallen irrevocably in love with the place. That day at the Tower Isle also illuminated a paradox: while we were enjoying the incomparable tropical beauty and typical serenity of the Caribbean Sea, we were in the process of learning the efficient use of manufactured violence, the object of which was killing one's enemy. Contemplating that contrast on the ride back to *Macon* made for a quietly introspective trip.

That first liberty in the Navy was more than memorable; it was profound. And it would be repeated in different ways during my forthcoming two years of sea duty with the Navy. With each liberty over those years and subsequent civilian visits, I discovered more of the infinite variety of natural beauty of the Caribbean. I also continued to learn about the often overlooked and amazing cultural variety of the people of that region.

A Group within a Group

My recollection is that there were 300-plus midshipmen in the program at any one time during my four years at Yale. My class slowly became a cohesive group during our four years and we felt comfortable in the military dimension of our college experience. It was a very accommodating environment for the military aspect of our four years of "higher learning." There were, for example, campus memorials that spanned history from the American Revolution to World War II and that recognized in overt and positive terms the many Yale students who had served their country in its armed forces.

For me the most evocative of the memorials continues to be the statue of Nathan Hale, which stands alone in front of Connecticut Hall, Yale's oldest existing building. Hale, a Connecticut schoolteacher and Yale graduate, was a member of a Continental Army militia unit who became a spy in the Army of George Washington. He was captured behind enemy lines by the British near Flushing Bay on Long Island. He was 21 years old when he was taken prisoner.

Hale's reported last words—believed by some to in reality be a distillation of his final statement—before being summarily hung by his captors were "I only regret that I have but one life to lose for my country." That astonishing and thought-provoking statement of patriotism is carved at the base of the Hale statue on the Yale campus. The bronze image of the Continental militiaman just before his execution, with arms bound behind his back, is something I try to revisit each time I return to Yale.

There were other, less tangible elements of the positive links between Yale and our country's military. One of the most intriguing is the record of "The First Yale Unit," a group of undergraduates who underwrote the costs of their own aircraft and flight training during the run-up to World War I.

The leader of the group, F. Trubee Davison, spent several of his undergraduate years convincing the Navy that the unit could serve a useful military purpose. Then in 1917, on the eve of the

United States entry into the war, the group was given official Navy status and mobilized.

Members of the First Yale Unit earned a reputation as skilled and courageous pilots during the war, and many went on to distinguished careers in business and government after the Armistice was signed in 1918. The unit was the beginning of the Naval Air Reserve, which continues to serve our country.

As undergraduates and volunteers, Davison's group received very public support from the university as its members transitioned from student to military status. The university even promised to allow returning veterans academic credit for the time they had served in the military.

The First Yale Unit epitomized the tradition of service to the United States in its military by those not dedicated to lifetime careers in the Army, Navy, Marine Corps, or Air Force. In our modern era of the all-volunteer military, this tradition has continued to benefit our military and our nation in general.

Perhaps the most obvious evidence of Yale's tradition of support for America's military during my years there could be found in the seven words carved in granite over the main arch of the university's signature building, Harkness Tower: "For God For Country and For Yale." There was no campus debate during my time about whether or not those words included the U.S. military. It was a given.

To the best of my knowledge, all members of my NROTC unit went to duty assignments either at sea or in the Marine Corps. Most of the members of the Unit served their obligated service and returned to civilian life to pursue non-military careers.

A few remained on active duty and pursued full Navy or Marine Corps careers. In what has to be an unusual circumstance, three members of my Yale NROTC class went on to be submarine commanders during their U.S. Navy service. The submarine commanders included Earle DeWispelaere, George Graveson, who was a champion intercollegiate wrestler, and Doug Williams, who served as an enlisted man in the Navy before entering Yale. Horace MacVaugh III, another classmate, reached flag rank as a flight surgeon in the Navy's Medical Corps.

PART II
IN DEEP WATERS
WHAT I LEARNED IN THE U.S. NAVY

CHAPTER SIX
THE GATOR NAVY

You are Athenians, who know by experience the difficulty of embarking in the presence of the enemy.

Demosthenes

Going to sea in the U.S. Navy was an intense and important learning experience. There were sharp contrasts involved. For example there was grinding fatigue and constant stress, but there was also the incredible and infinitely varied beauty of the sea, plus the camaraderie among shipmates working hard towards common objectives.

"You are hereby ordered..."

For members of my NROTC Unit there were two initial options upon commissioning: The Navy or the Marine Corps. For those who chose the Navy, the next choices included heavy combatants (cruisers, battleships, aircraft carriers), small combatants (destroyers), and amphibious (a wide variety of specialized amphibious warfare ships).

Based in my interest in small boats, I requested assignment to the amphibious forces, and the ship to which I was ordered was part of the U.S. Navy Atlantic Amphibious Command. My orders were delivered to me on 9 June 1952, the day of my graduation from Yale and commissioning as an ensign. The orders were in strict Navy format:

Subj: Orders

Encl: (1) Appointment as ENS, USNR, (2) Form DD 93

Upon receipt of appointment as Ensign, U.S. Naval Reserve, you are hereby ordered to active naval service in time to proceed to Little Creek, Va., in order to report to the Commander, Amphibious Training Command, Atlantic Fleet at the Naval Amphibious Base, Little Creek, Norfolk, Va., on or before 11 July 1952, for temporary duty under instruction in amphibious indoctrination for a period of about two weeks. Upon completion of this temporary duty and when directed by the Commander, Amphibious Training Command, Atlantic Fleet, you will regard yourself detached; will proceed to the port in which the USS SARASOTA (APA 204) may be, and upon arrival report to the commanding officer of that vessel for duty.

With those two breathless sentences, written in lyrical navyese, I was officially ushered into the most laudable organization I have encountered during my adult life. It isn't perfect, and inevitably I came across individuals who were far from praiseworthy. But when measured in terms of overall quality of people, the United States Navy—from the most junior enlisted people to the most senior flag officers—is significantly above any large group with which I have had extended contact during my lifetime.

My opinion of the U.S. Navy is validated by a credible claim of objectivity. That claim is based on two facts: I was not a career naval officer; I have no close family ties to the Navy.

The day after I was commissioned and received my orders, I married my first wife Susan Jones. We had been planning on getting married when I graduated for the better part of my four years at Yale. Our decision to wait until after my graduation to get married was consistent with the U.S. Navy's determination that midshipmen didn't take on the distractions of married life before commissioning. In fact, the NROTC agreement stipulated that if a midshipman was married before commissioning, he was automatically discharged from the program. "If the U.S. Navy wanted you to have a wife, they would have issued you one" was the not-so-facetious and often repeated admonition that underscored the official regulation. The regulation barring marriage for midshipmen was one of the early examples of how the military's requirements impinge on one's personal life.

Thus my first marriage took place on 10 June 1952, immediately after receiving my orders and several weeks before carrying out those orders by reporting to the Amphibious Training Command at Little Creek. At least there was time for a week at Martha's Vineyard, a small island seven miles off the coast of Massachusetts, just south of Cape Cod. It was an appropriately maritime atmosphere.

A new reality set in, however, when I reported to The Amphibious Training Command on 11 July '52. Since I didn't have the money for a housing alternative, my wife stayed in New York City, and I checked into the "bachelor officers' quarters" (BOQ) at the Navy's Amphibious Base at Little Creek, VA. As I recall, it was pretty basic living: a small room, clean sheets, a clothes locker, and a basin. The shower was down the hallway. There was of course no air conditioning, an uncomfortable circumstance that anyone who has spent a summer in Norfolk can readily appreciate. The Amphibious Base endorsement of my orders summed it up in unambiguous and terse terms:

Subj: Orders

1. Adequate government quarters and mess facilities are available for yourself, but not for your dependents if any.

A Unique Curriculum

The school at the Amphibious Training Command was where the basics for delivering military force over hostile beaches were taught to newly-commissioned naval officers. It was my introduction to "The Gator Navy," the nickname taken from one of nature's nastiest amphibians, the alligator.

The courses involved the rudiments of the logistics, tactics, equipment, and doctrine involved in the delivery of U.S. Marines and their equipment across a hostile beach. There was a lot to communicate, and it was all delivered "fire hose style." It all added up to the complex process of amphibious warfare—sometimes called expeditionary warfare—that had been developed during World War II. What was being taught were the basic lessons learned the hard way at such crucial World War II amphibious invasions as Fedhala and Algiers in North Africa, Gela in Sicily, Salerno and Anzio in Italy, Normandy in France, Attu in the Aleutians, as well as Guadalcanal, Tarawa, Iwo Jima, Leyte, Okinawa and other previously-unknown islands in the Pacific. In basic terms, I was learning the Navy's way of delivering heavily armed U.S. Marines, in ill humor, to places and at times that are inconvenient to our nation's enemies.

The course also included my introduction to the specialized boats that were an integral part of the Navy's amphibious warfare technology and tactics of the time. Foremost was the ubiquitous 36-foot LCVP (Landing Craft for Vehicles and/or Personnel). The shallow-draft LCVP was manned by a coxswain, an engineman and a seaman. The latter was generally referred to as "the bowhook," since he was frequently positioned on the bow with a boathook. The LCVP could carry 36-39 fully-equipped Marines, or a jeep pulling a water tank, or a 37-mm cannon.

At the time, the LCVPs were constructed of plywood, with quarter-inch steel armor on the sides of the hull providing dubious protection for the troops from small-arms fire and shrapnel. It must be noted at this point that the boat's coxswain was the one person in an LCVP who had virtually no protection from the combat hazards involved in putting troops ashore on a hostile beach.

The LCVP had a single 225 horsepower diesel engine, a steel bow ramp which was lowered when the boat's bow grounded on the beach, a protected propeller, and a specially designed spoon—shaped bow that facilitated a straight-on landing and a straight-off pull back from the beach. The LCVPs and other special amphibious craft were designed to be lifted on or off ships with booms or special Welin Davits that handled nests of three boats each. The Welin Davits could lower an LCVP in sixty seconds and could raise one in 90 seconds. Loading and offloading the boats required a lot of skill, and accidents during the process were not unknown.

Proper handling of the LCVPs in the water also required an extremely high degree of boat handling skills on part of the coxswain, especially during the grounding on the beach and withdrawal after offloading. During those few minutes, a boat could easily be broached by the surf and the currents running along the beach. During an operation, broached boats on the beach were bad news, since they became a major obstruction for subsequent incoming boat waves. In addition, pulling a broached boat off the beach inevitably damaged one or all of the boat's skeg, propeller, and propeller shaft. Damage to any one of those items was guaranteed to make the ship's carpenter and boat repair people very unhappy.

The LCVPs were amazingly functional craft but they were completely open to the elements. Their crews and the embarked troops were thoroughly soaked in rainy weather and even by the spray thrown up on clear days and in moderate seas. And because of their special design to accommodate landings on a beach and their relatively small size, they did a lot of pitching and rolling. In summary, the last thing in the mind of the LCVP's designers was crew comfort.

The basic LCVP design was created by Andrew Jackson Higgins, a rough, outspoken boat builder from Louisiana who overcame resistance from the irascible, then-Chief of Naval Operations to design and mass-produce the series of basic amphibious landing craft that became the backbone of the U.S. Navy and Allied amphibious capabilities of World War II.

Higgins, a self taught designer and manufacturer, had to fight a tough bureaucracy to get his designs accepted for production. Both his personality and design approach epitomized the pragmatism of the early European settlers in America, people who had to deal with life's challenges in new and practical ways. Their solutions usually lacked sophistication. They just worked well.

Higgins, who overcame the many challenges in his career with iron determination, once said: "I don't wait for opportunity to knock. I send out a welcoming committee to drag the old harlot in."

I was going to spend a lot of time in Andrew Jackson Higgins' boats during the next two years. It wasn't going to be comfortable, but it would be interesting, and improbably, sometimes even a perverse kind of enjoyment.

Setting up Housekeeping

About the time the Amphibious Training Command assignment ended—plus a two-day fire fighting course tacked on after the amphibious course—my former wife and I were able to set up a place to live in Norfolk, which was *Sarasota's* home port. Our first "home" consisted of a bedroom with kitchen privileges in the home of a retired Navy chief petty officer. Fortunately the chief, his wife, and two young daughters were welcoming and sympathetic to the financial realities of a couple living on an ensign's modest pay.

The completion of the amphibious course also was the point at which I bought my first car, a small, durable, second-hand British Anglia. The car cost me $750. It wasn't exactly luxury travel, but it did its job during a two-year period, covering a lot of miles between Charleston, South Carolina and New York City.

It was only a short while until an affordable (barely) apartment was located in Norfolk's Oceanview neighborhood. The Oceanview Apartments were occupied almost entirely by young Navy couples from around the country. Arguably the most important feature of the apartment, something that didn't show up in the lease, was the informal support network that operated quite effectively among the residents.

The network was particularly important for the wives whose husbands were away for weeks or even many months at a time. The network became especially active a few days before each payday, when household funds could get very tight. If one of the wives was down to her last ten dollars and someone else was flat broke, the "someone else" got five dollars of your money, no questions asked.

The system was a kind of fraternity/sorority, except it was non-exclusive to the degree that everyone in the Oceanview Apartments was an equal member, and there was no waiting period to join the network. You were a member from the moment you moved in.

The system was an informal variation of "The Navy takes care of its own," a concept that I was beginning to absorb. It represented the way people should look after one another, not because it was their job or because it was required, or because it made a good impression, but because it was the right thing to do. And for the group of Navy people in the Oceanview Apartments, it also was simply the natural thing to do.

My two years of active duty in *Sarasota* fell between the ship's two Mediterranean deployments, so the longest continuous period I was at sea was probably about seven weeks. But there were numerous two, three, and four weeks at sea along the way.

While *Sarasota* was in Norfolk, we operated with three duty sections. That meant that during the periods when the ship was in port, I was able to get home two out of three nights and was usually able to get two out of three weekends at home as well. It wasn't the kind of routine young married people usually experienced, but despite its inconveniences, it had some pluses. You made good friends fast and there was a geographic dispersion among the people that added an extra dimension to the relationships.

One of the reasons those relationships were important had to do with Norfolk being a Navy town. It was not exactly a friendly community for young Navy couples. The city wanted the jobs and revenue stream that the Navy brought to the community, but its permanent citizens were not in general enthusiastic about the Navy people, most of whom came and went, after tours that lasted only a few years. In general your social life, such as it was, did not extend into the civilian community.

A Momentous Weekend

In the spring of '53, *Sarasota* went into the Charleston Naval Shipyard for a repair period. At the time, my wife and I were expecting our first child, and on weekends when I had liberty, I drove up to Norfolk. I would leave the ship at 1600 on Friday afternoon and drive for about eight hours, getting to Oceanview around midnight. On Sunday evening, I would leave home around 2100, get back to the ship around 0500, clean up and show up for quarters for muster at 0800 Monday morning. There was not a lot of sleep involved, but that was a general state for the entire two years I spent on active duty.

On Friday May 1st, I made my usual drive up to Oceanview and on Sunday afternoon, before I began the return trip to Charleston, Sue decided that the baby was imminent. I immediately drove her to Portsmouth Naval Hospital, where she had been going for prenatal care. After an examination, we were sent away, with the suggestion that we have dinner and come back later. The process of having babies at a major U.S. Navy hospital involved extremely good medical care, but it also was pretty casual in its approach to normal births in those days.

We returned after dinner and a long delivery process began. I had called the ship to get an emergency extension on my weekend liberty, and I settled down in the hospital waiting room, alternately reading and dozing. It was a long wait.

Very early Monday morning on May 4th, Joseph F. Callo III arrived. As I remember, he weighed in at about ten pounds. Then, after a very quick visit with mother and son, I was back on the road and headed for the Charleston Navy Yard and *Sarasota*. The whole process had been pretty much of a blur, but during the eight-hour drive back to the ship, the importance and joy of the event displaced my fatigue.

The birth of my first child certainly had not been a big deal to the Navy. And there was no family around to lend support. On the other hand, there at least had been a rational accommodation by my ship that had made it possible for me to be present for the event. And that accommodation was achieved with a telephone call, notwithstanding the Navy's all-encompassing bureaucracy.

When I climbed *Sara's* gangway in the Charleston Navy Yard, crossed the quarterdeck, and reported my return to the ship, I was expected to pick up on my work routine immediately. There were a number of sincere congratulations from shipmates as I made my way about the ship, but no one suggested that I was entitled to even the slightest break in my shipboard responsibilities. It was strictly "business as usual." That was the Navy way, and it was what the job and the ship demanded. That might seem uncaring in today's world where sensitivity to everyone and everything is common. But for me the situation was actually liberating.

The tempo and focus in the ship were not one iota different. As I crossed the quarterdeck, I had immediately stepped back into a world of never-ending, four-hour segments shaped for watchstanding, with a heavy load of administrative work woven in along the way. There was little time for sleep and no time for self-sympathy. But, based on the weekend's events, I knew that I was different in a very positive way. That's what counted for me.

CHAPTER SEVEN
GETTING TO KNOW SARA

I don't like work—no man does—but I like what is in work—the chance to find yourself. Your own reality—for yourself, not for others—what no other man can ever know.

Joseph Conrad 1857-1924

I had walked up the gangway to report onboard USS *Sarasota* at the Naval Operating Base in Norfolk, Virginia in the early morning of 5 August 1952 and served in her for slightly less than two years. The final endorsement on the basic orders that had been delivered to me upon commissioning was, considering the impact on my life, remarkably understated:

Subj: Orders

1.You reported aboard for duty this date.

Sara

Sarasota lacked the ferocious aspect of destroyers, cruisers, battleships, and aircraft carriers. From the pier, she appeared to be just another haze-gray Navy ship. Even her nickname "Sara" lacked panache. She was built on a basic merchant ship hull and her decks were crammed with 26 amphibious craft, along with the cranes and Welin Davits that were used to rapidly launch the boats for an amphibious operation and recover them after the operation was over.

In addition to the living spaces for the crew of approximately 300, there were "accommodations" for 1,500 U.S. Marines. The latter were generally embarked over the gangway at Morehead City, North Carolina. For final delivery, the Marines, with their weapons and basic gear, climbed backwards down debarkation nets rigged over the ship's side roughly thirty feet into amphibious craft that were rising and falling while simultaneously rolling right and left. Once fully loaded, the boats drove through frequently choppy seas and delivered the Marines over whatever beach was involved in the operation. The ill humor that built up in the process was probably just what was needed when the bow ramp dropped and the Marines stepped (sometimes waded) ashore.

Sarasota wasn't new and she couldn't be described as graceful, but if you studied her, you began to realize that she was an extremely efficient fighting machine. She was designed for a very specific job and was, in fact, every inch a warship.

After you lived with her a little bit, you also realized that she had a special beauty that sprang from her relentless functionality. She was at her best when they piped "Away all Boats!" *Sarasota* could do her complicated job of offloading and delivering Marines in an over-the-beach assault, which persistently illuminated the *really* big question, could you do yours?

Sara's Pedigree

Sarasota was built in Richmond, California, launched on 14 June 1944 and commissioned in the U.S. Navy on the same day. She was one of many hundreds of amphibious assault ships that were designed to deliver troops across a hostile beach. During World War II she earned three battle stars, and her logs contain names that evoke visions of some of the most difficult and important amphibious assaults of that war: Hollandia, Bougainville, Lingayen Gulf, Zambales, Leyte, Okinawa, and Ia Shima.

By the time she was decommissioned in August 1946, *Sarasota* had delivered uncounted thousands of U.S. troops across beaches throughout the Pacific Theater, more often than not while facing enemy fire. Then, in February 1951 during the Korean War, she was recommissioned, assigned to the Atlantic Fleet Amphibious Force and homeported at the Navy's Main Operating Base in Norfolk, Virginia. It was about eighteen months after *Sara* was brought back into service that we met. She was decommissioned for a second time in September 1955, a little more than a year after I was detached from her crew.

When she was deployed overseas or on a major training exercise, *Sarasota* carried an assault group of 1,500 fully equipped U.S. Marines, or on rare occasions, U.S. Army infantrymen, and a small portion of their mechanized equipment. Generally she operated as half of a two-ship unit, along with another ship of similar size and design, designated an AKA. The companion AKA carried the bulk of the APA troops' mechanized equipment—up to and including light tanks—along with the equipment's operators. The two ships in tandem delivered a battalion landing team with its accompanying jeeps, trucks, light tanks, and associated combat gear.

In major amphibious operations, many pairs of APAs and AKAs would be combined, along with other types of specialized amphibious ships and supporting combatant ships (destroyers, cruisers, etc.), to make up the full assault force. The process of getting the Marines down the debark nets, into the boats, to the beach, and then across the beach at the right place and time was, to put it mildly, complicated. And the whole process was often carried out in less than ideal sea conditions.

Weather, equipment problems, and human error were the first enemies to be dealt with before a single Marine crossed the beach. A successful amphibious assault was a truly amazing accomplishment. It was a complex event that was possible only because of the techniques and technology that had been developed and honed during World War II, plus the skills of the people who had to make it all come together within required parameters of efficiency and safety.

It should be added parenthetically, that today's amphibious forces involve radically different ship and assault craft designs, smaller ship numbers, and the ability to reach far beyond a beach with air cushion vehicles, helicopters and "tilt-engine" aircraft. Today's expeditionary forces move faster, have greater flexibility, and pack a much greater punch than the forces of the 1950s with which I was involved. But the basic objective remains unchanged: deliver heavily armed Marines, in ill humor, at times and places that are inconvenient for America's enemies.

My new home-away-from-home was 455 feet long, 62 feet wide and cloaked in U.S. Navy haze gray. She was armed with a twin 40-milimeter gun on the bow, a similar emplacement aft and a single five-inch gun on the stern. It was immediately impressed upon me, however, that the ship's "main battery" consisted of her 26 landing craft and the Marines they delivered.

My initial welcome to *Sarasota* was perfunctory: after a few brief introductions, I was shown to my living compartment. That was about it; that was my introduction to the two most formative years of my life. The process was short on conversation but long on implications.

My personal space in the ship measured about fifteen by twenty feet and it contained two double-decker bunks, two steel lockers, a small fold-down desk, a small sink with a mirror, and two combination safes for classified documents and our 45-calibre side arms. Each safe was presumably to be shared by two officers. During my tour, they were mostly used to store our "45s," which, according to my first firearms instructor, were designed to hit hard enough to put down a charging cavalry horse. I must confess in passing that, in my two years in *Sarasota,* I was never once attacked by someone on a horse.

Naturally, as a newly assigned ensign to the ship, I was assigned an upper bunk. As I recall, there was about ten inches of space between my face and the steel overhead in the compartment. I left more than a little bit of head skin on that overhead. The communal shower was—I was getting used to the arrangement— down the passageway.

Fortunately, the Navy had a unique way of avoiding any sense of overcrowding in its shipboard living quarters. Between watch standing and the average maintenance and administrative work load, the only time you were in your living compartment was when you were sleeping, and that was not a lot of time.

Good News, Bad News

My initial duty assignments in the ship turned out to be good news. I was assigned the basic responsibilities of assistant boat group commander, amphibious salvage officer and assistant third division officer. That package of three jobs could not have been better for someone interested in small boats. To the Navy's credit and contrary to popular wisdom, they do frequently match an individual's assignment to his or her qualifications.

The boat group included the maintenance and operation of all of the ship's 26 amphibious craft. Within the boat group, the amphibious salvage officer's primary responsibility was keeping the beach clear of broached and otherwise disabled boats during an amphibious landing. In the latter case, the amphibious salvage officer's main "work place" was in and around the surf, a difficult work environment in a 36-foot LCPL, which was a stripped down version of the LCVP.

The third division was a basic unit in the ship's deck force, with the responsibility for the maintenance and handling of boats and cargo. The division—consisting of boatswain's mates and seaman training for that rate—also was the largest in the ship, with approximately 50 enlisted personnel and two officers.

It was a tough group, and was in fact a far cry from the all-volunteer force of today. Members of the deck force were sometimes referred to by other members of the crew as "deck apes." But only rarely was the reference made in the presence of a member of the deck force—and *never* twice in their presence. It was not unusual at the time for several members of the division to have had the distinction of hearing a judge give them a choice between jail and enlisting in the military. As I said, that Navy was a far cry from today's all-volunteer force.

Said another way, *Sara's* deck force was not a particularly cerebral environment, but there was a basic intellectual honesty to it that has been difficult to recapture in my more cerebral non-

Navy life. It was a blunt world: know your job, do your job, don't run your mouth, and as the Frankie Valli song says, "walk like a man."

During a full-bore operation when all of the boats were involved, there would have been seventy-plus sailors in the boat crews. The boat group commander and third division officer was Ensign Fay Lossing, a Naval Academy graduate from Jackson, Mississippi. He too was newly commissioned and had arrived at the ship only a few weeks before I did.

On the face of it, a Naval Academy graduate from the South, someone who was aimed at a military career and who was more thoroughly trained in Navy matters than I was, might not have been the best combination with a Yale NROTC reserve officer from The Bronx, a "short timer" in Navy vernacular.

The potential for an abrasive relationship certainly was present. But what actually developed was a good working relationship and almost as quickly a friendship. I give Fay a lot of credit. He took a positive approach to what could have been a touchy combination and it worked to our benefit and that of the ship.

There was, however, one serious problem associated with my initial duty assignments: the first lieutenant. The first lieutenant was the department head responsible for the boat group and all three deck divisions. He was a lieutenant, and only the operations officer, executive officer, and commanding officer were senior to him in the ship. To a brand new ensign assigned to his department, he was an eminence from the top of Mount Olympus.

Sara's first lieutenant also was a former merchant marine officer who had been through World War II in the Navy's Pacific Amphibious Force, which gave him considerable credibility. The difficulty was that he had a special dislike for Ivy Leaguers and reservists. So my case was a matter of double jeopardy, and he quickly made those prejudices clear by singling me out for several unusual assignments.

A Key Point

Probably the most noteworthy of those assignments involved a number of medium-sized corrugated cardboard boxes, perhaps there were five or six, that were filled with an assortment of keys. The boxes of keys had been in one of the ship's holds when she was recommissioned. My assignment was to find the lock in the ship that matched each key, and then tag the key. There could have been a thousand keys in the boxes. The mathematics of trying each key in each lock were mind boggling, and the chances were good that there actually were no locks that matched up with many or perhaps even all the keys.

I was pretty sure the first lieutenant was pulling my chain, but challenging him did not seem to be an option at the time, and it would have been a coup to match even a few keys to their locks. I figured that there had to be a way to resolve the situation.

Then one night after dinner, as I was sitting alone in the small deck department office, trying to come up with a practical way to attack the problem, Chief Boatswain Kelly walked in. "Boats," who had been in the Navy for more than 30 years, had worked his way up through the enlisted ranks to earn his warrant officer commission as a chief boatswain. He asked what I was up to. I explained. He frowned and paused for a moment, obviously reaching for a way to solve the problem. At least, that's what I thought. Then he asked, with what seemed to be anger, if I would like some help.

I knew that a warrant officer with thirty-plus years of Navy experience would have to be a help. When I answered in the affirmative, "Boats" picked up one of the boxes and said, "Take a box and follow me." He walked out of the office and along the passageway that lead to the main deck. He stepped to the ship's rail and dropped the box over the side and into the water below. Then he turned to me and said, "Do that with the other boxes," and walked away.

Stunned I followed his advice, and several days later I learned that he had subsequently gone to the first lieutenant, and notwithstanding the fact that the first lieutenant was his boss in the ship's chain of command, he told him in clear language to cut out the crap.

The incident was an early learning lesson for me that illuminated two important things about the Navy's culture. One was that there were unwritten rules about authority that were just as important as the written rules. In this case, the unwritten rule was that authority was not to be exercised for entertainment purposes, not even when the victim was a raw ensign.

Part two of the lesson was that long experience in the Navy imparts its own special kind of authority. Technically, Kelly was the junior officer in the deck department. Even a newly-commissioned ensign was officially senior to him in the chain of command. But his many years of experience gave "Boats" a standing that every officer in the wardroom recognized and honored. It gave him all the authority he needed to put a stop *unofficially* to something that was not in the ship's interest.

The first lieutenant got the point, and I got the learning experience. That was OK with me.

It took a few months, but eventually the first lieutenant and I arrived at a reasonable working relationship, thanks to Chief Boatswain Kelly's eyeball-to-eyeball, cut-the-crap approach at a key point in my assignment. The incident was the first of many lessons about the Navy's unwritten but very important rules.

Watch Standing

> Morning Watch 0400-0800
> Forenoon Watch 0800-1200
> Afternoon Watch 1200-1600
> First Dog Watch 1600-1800
> Second Dog Watch 1800-2000
> Evening Watch 2000-2400
> Middle (or "Mid") Watch 2400-0400

Following breakfast the first morning after my arrival, I looked at the wardroom bulletin board, which was an interesting combination of official information and humorous "commentary"—the latter always anonymous—on the official information. It was one of the many ways humor made grinding situations tolerable.

Much to my surprise, my name was listed on the in-port officer of the deck watch bill. There was no briefing and no indication that it was an under-instruction assignment. It was my introduction to one of the Navy's approaches to breaking in new officers: throw them into a job and see if they "swim." The role of the Officer of the Deck is described in the *Watch Officer's Guide,* an unofficial publication. [6]

> The officer of the deck (OOD) in a naval ship occupies a unique position. Nowhere in military or civilian life is there a parallel to the range and degree of responsibility that is placed in the hands of the OOD. As a direct representative of the captain, he acts with all of the authority of command, and next to the captain and the executive officer is the most important person in the ship.

The specifics of the OOD's responsibilities and authority are spelled out in official navy instructions, but in layman's terms, the OOD is in charge of the ship while he or she has the OOD watch, and that involves a lot of responsibility. I was about to discover how the magnitude of that responsibility sharpens one's focus and compresses a learning curve. On the other hand, it doesn't do much for the nerves.

Somehow I got through that first in-port OOD watch, largely through the down-to-earth and low profile guidance of the boatswain mate of the watch. God and petty officers who grasp the concept of the public good do look out for new ensigns.

It wasn't long before another and larger challenge appeared on the wardroom bulletin board. One evening before we were to get underway my name appeared on the OOD *under way* watch list. This time it was identified as "under instruction." There was good reason for the under instruction aspect: the OOD underway is responsible for the operation of the ship under infinitely more dangerous circumstances than during an in-port watch.

When *Sarasota* was steaming, the OOD was responsible for 6,783 tons of government equipment worth many millions of dollars and more than 300 crew members of inestimable value. When deployed or when involved in a major training exercise, there would be the lives of an additional 1,500 U.S. Marines involved. A wrong decision or even a small mistake while underway could be disastrous.

For the next four months whenever *Sarasota* was underway, I stood OOD watches under instruction. Then I was deemed qualified to stand a "top watch" underway, and I became one of the few junior officers who were qualified as underway OODs. There was a significant measure of status to the selection, and I have to admit I was impressed with the mark of confidence on the part of my seniors that it represented.

I remember the sense of responsibility I felt the first time I spoke the specific—and only—words that indicated that I accepted the full responsibility for the ship from my predecessor OOD: "I relieve you, sir." It was the moment I felt a crossing over; I was at that point really part of *Sarasota*. I consider it the *moment* when I really grew up.

With the new status, there was a large measure of additional stress. There generally were four officers in the underway OOD rotation, and on some occasions there were only three. When standing one-in-four or one-in-three when we were steaming, sleep was a premium item. About three to four hours a day, on average, was about it. And just to keep one's mind occupied, you were expected to do your administrative, training, maintenance, and other routine work when you were not on watch. It was a time when I began drinking coffee, a lot of very strong coffee.

The Sounds of *Sara*

Being under way at sea and out of sight of land for days at a time is a distinct experience. There is a sense of detachment from life as we know it on land, and days and nights run together. Time is parceled out in four-hour segments, with the end of each parcel noted by the appropriate number of ship's bells. The under-way routine takes over ones' life. Day and night lose the sharp delineations they have on land, and sleep becomes a sometime thing, to be snatched a few hours at a time, day or night. You become an operating part of the ship and that defines—and justifies—your existence for the duration of the voyage

Patrick O'Brian called attention to the feelings in his book *HMS Surprise:* "This life, with its rigid pattern punctuated by the sharp imperative sound of bells, seemed to take on something of the nature of eternity." [7]

During at-sea periods, the sounds of the ship take on special meaning. They seem more acute, and in their own way, they contribute to the feelings involved in being detached from the normal sensory cues that dominate life on land. There is, for example, the steely clang of a steel water-tight door being closed and dogged. Similarly there is the distinctive echo of footsteps on the ship's steel ladders. Puntcuating the day, there are the periodic messages emanating from the ships announcing system, with each announcement preceded by the sound of "Attention" piped by the bos'nmate of the watch.

Voices are generally subdued, and verbal exchanges are clipped, especially on the bridge, where there are few extraneous words. There is also the constant, almost imperceptible hum of machinery interwoven with the throb of the ship's main engines transmitted through the steel decks and bulkheads.

Most pleasing are the sounds of the sea, such as the periodic splash of the water thrown up by the bow or the subtler rush of the water as it slides back along the ship's hull. Finally there is the sound of the wind in the rigging, usually humming, but on occasion screaming.

Cumshaw

The word "cumshaw" derives from a phrase in the Chinese dialect of Xiamen and translates to "grateful thanks." It is believed that the term originally was picked up by the British Royal Navy in China in the 19th century. In the U.S. Navy, it has become a term that describes "informal procurement." Sometimes there is barter involved, sometimes not.

A lot of ships had a cumshaw artist, and make no mistake, it was an art. In a bureaucratic system as complex as the Navy's there often is a significant time gap between when something is needed aboard a ship and when it can be secured through the system. That's when the talents of the cumshaw artist are invaluable.

I have no idea whether or how one trained for such a specialty, and there were no written rules on the subject of cumshaw. But there were several unwritten ones. One is ethical and immutable: cumshaw is never used to secure personal items. Another rule was that the process must never deprive another ship or unit of something that it *really* needs. The latter is of course a judgment call that sometimes can lead to hard feelings. The final rule is that it was used with discretion.

Sarasota's cumshaw artist was a third class boatswain mate; I'll call him "Zed." Everyone in the ship knew about Zed's special role. He was a minor celebrity of sorts. Yet he was a loner. I never saw him go ashore on liberty with anyone, and he seemed to have no close friends among *Sarasota's* crew. He didn't talk much. Most of the time, he just smiled at you. Zed's skills made him important beyond his status as a third class petty officer, and his talents as a cumshaw artist gave him a special standing with his division officer and the first lieutenant. I never saw him stand any of the normal boatswain's mate watches.

When Zed left the ship during working hours, you knew something was up. Generally he was on foot as he went down the pier, but almost always he returned to the gangway in a vehicle with a driver. It might be a jeep or it might be a truck, depending on the size of what he was bringing back to the ship.

On one particular morning right after quarters for muster, Zed was seen walking down the pier of the Naval Operating Base in our homeport of Norfolk. The word that there was a replacement part required for some of the cargo-handling equipment. We were getting under way in a few days and there was wasn't time for the normal procurement process. Normally Zed would be back within a few hours. This day he didn't return until mid afternoon, when a flat-bed truck pulled up to the gangway. Zed jumped out holding a box that would have been about the right size for the replacement part. Obviously it was mission accomplished.

But wait, there was more. Within a few minutes, a small work detail was at the truck. They slid a canvass cover off something on the truck bed and hooked it on to one of the ship's booms. The something was a compressor the approximate size of a Volkswagen "Bug." With astonishing speed the compressor was hoisted aboard and positioned carefully on deck. Instantaneously a welder appeared with his torch, and the compressor was firmly secured to the deck.

Anyone who has served in a steel ship knows that the process of chipping paint from areas that are beginning to show rust and that need repainting is both ongoing and onerous. It was normally carried out with a hook-shaped steel tool that was swung like a hammer or with a hammer with a special chipping edge. The process was tedious, noisy, and usually assigned to the most junior enlisted men. But suddenly things would be different in the entire forward half of the ship. The compressor was hooked up by hose to a small pneumatic jack hammer. The work of many could now be done by a single person, and it could be done faster by one man than an entire work detail.

We went to sea with our compressor and for several months it was a boon to the lowliest, but then came a materiel inspection. As the inspectors went about their initial topside inspection, they came upon the compressor. There was no appropriate answer to the question: "What the HELL is this!" The shock among the inspection team was palpable, and their surprise was followed by comments such as, "You guys have to be kidding!"

The inspecting team was unequivocal: the compressor was declared to be in excess of the ship's equipment allowance and had to be removed immediately. It was gone the same day. But Zed's reputation in the ship—undoubtedly even beyond *Sarasota*—was fixed forever. And we wondered where the "excess" compressor went next.

God on the Mess Deck

There was no chaplain assigned to *Sarasota* on a regular basis. There were, however divine services in the ship every Saturday and Sunday while we were under way. The services were conducted on the mess deck by members of the ship's company, and they were well attended. I don't remember ever hearing a single sermon during those services, but I do remember that they filled a need for me and apparently for others.

The experience of self-administered religion had a surprising effect on me. It was something beyond the conventional Roman Catholic Church services with which I grew up. It was the beginning of identifying God in my own mind, rather than in external terms. It wasn't a rejection of religion or the Catholic Church, both of which are part of defining God. But those institutions are not the end game. It was a breakthrough of sorts for me and started me on an intellectual quest that is ongoing.

Too Young to Die

I was being pushed hard physically and mentally, and even though the war of the time was being fought in Korea and not in the Atlantic, there was a degree of stress and danger in our operations and training in the Atlantic and Caribbean.

The day-to-day danger was exemplified by the accidental death of a friend during a so-called routine boat operation. Dick Muller and his wife Debbie lived in the same Oceanview Apartments as my first wife and I. They were friends and part of the mutual support system among the apartment's residents.

Both Dick and Debbie were from The Bronx and Dick was a graduate of the New York State Maritime College at Fort Schuyler, also in The Bronx. He had been commissioned at the same time I was and was assigned to USS *Mount Olympus,* an amphibious command ship homeported in Norfolk. When we were both off duty at the same time, we hung out together.

The *"Mount O"* was in Norfolk a lot more than *Sarasota* and most of the other amphibious ships based there, and Dick took a lot of barbed kidding about how lucky he was to be assigned to a ship that was "welded to the pier." As it turned out, luck was not really on his side. One day, he was in a boat that was being hoisted aboard by a Welin Davit. It was a routine operation that junior officers in amphibious ships did hundreds of times. On that day on that ship, however, the davit malfunctioned. When its lifting cables snapped, the boat was dropped and Dick was fatally injured.

I was one of two officers informally elected to attend the funeral in New York City and provide support to Debbie, who was pregnant. Dick's death was the first of a contemporary friend that I would experience during my lifetime, and I learned a lot about how people behave when confronted with an unanticipated death. In most it brought out the best. In some it brought out the worst. Dick's case was not an exception, but the most important thing was providing some support to Debbie.

The Gig Affair

Every U.S. Navy ship of significant size has a captain's gig, a designated boat used for the captain's transportation and only in special situations for other purposes. In a very real sense, the appearance of the gig and how it's handled by its crew represents the captain and the ship. In most ships, the gig is extremely well maintained and smartly handled. Amphibious ships, such as *Sarasota,* were different. The captain's gig was also the amphibious command boat, the boat used by the boat group commander during operations. That meant it took a lot of wear and tear and looked pretty much like the rest of the boats in the boat group in terms of outward appearances.

Fay Lossing and I got the bright idea that we would do something special for the "old man." We couldn't change the exterior of his gig in any way. From the outside, she had to look just like any command boat in the Amphibious Force. But we figured that didn't mean we couldn't do something to spruce up the interior, and we figured that would really please the captain.

We got our division's chief petty officer and the division's leading petty officer, who was a first class boatswain's mate, involved in the plot. They agreed that it was a nice idea for the skipper, and that we should make it a surprise for him.

The gig was usually at the top of a stack of boats on number one hatch. That meant that no one would be able to see what we were doing with the gig's interior until we were finished.

For several days the work went on. We came up with some white canvass cushions for the bench seats and a few of the experienced hands in the division created some macramé to tone up the inside of the cabin. We also found a few places in the interior where we could scrape away the grey paint and produce some varnished "brightwork."

The finishing touch was the repainting of the interior. Somewhere in the back of the boatswain's locker we found some pale blue paint, strictly non-regulation, but a real change from the navy haze gray that had covered the gig's interior.

When the surprise was finished there was just one more step. We had to show the finished product to our boss, the first lieutenant. It was a challenging climb up the stack of boats and into the gig and we led the way. As the first lieutenant climbed over the cockpit coaming and stepped into the gig's cabin, we couldn't wait to see his reaction.

He stepped into the cabin, blinked, and said, "This looks like the inside of a whorehouse, change it back."

Working in the Surf

During operations, my job as the amphibious salvage officer was to keep the beach clear for incoming waves of boats. The main problem was broached LCVPs. If an LCVP coxswain didn't keep his boat straight on to the beach, it inevitably would be broached by the surf. That meant that instead of having his bow on the beach, with his stern in deeper water and aimed seaward for backing off the beach, his boat was resting in the sand and parallel to the edge of the beach. In that position, the boat was stranded, and it was my responsibility to get it off the beach, hopefully with a minimum of damage.

My salvage boat was an open LCPL. At 36 feet in length, it was the same length as an LCVP. There was no bow ramp on the LCPL, however, and she was more maneuverable than the LCVPs. The crew of the amphibious salvage boat was the same as the other landing craft: a coxswain—often referred to as a 'boat driver"—plus the engineman and the "bowhook" who helped handled the lines.

Operating in the surf was a tricky business. Small mistakes could leave the salvage boat itself broached, something that made beachmasters and the boat group commander cranky and the salvage team grossly embarrassed. There were times when I came close, but fortunately during my two years of boat operations in *Sarasota* that never happened to me.

The main reason it never happened was a third class boatswain mate by the name of Morrell. He was the salvage boat coxswain for just about every operation in which I participated. Morrell was a quiet man, perhaps a bit older than most third class boatswain mates. He always seemed to be somehow separated from the rest of the men in the division. He was a bit of a "loner."

Morrell also was a master when handling the salvage boat. He could sense exactly how far he could push matters while maneuvering to tow a boat off the beach. Time after time, he maneuvered the salvage boat into a precarious position in order to get a towline over to a broached boat. And just when it looked like disaster was inevitable, he would gun the engine, spin the wheel, and the boat would virtually leap out of its dangerous position, take an even strain on the towline, and slowly drag the broached boat off the beach and into deep water, where it could move off to its mother ship for another run.

There was a lot of extremely difficult physical work required in the amphibious salvage process, but more than anything, it was a matter of teamwork and knowing one's job. And for *Sara's* salvage boat, that process centered on a quiet third class boatswain mate with an uncanny instinct for the sea and the knowledge of exactly what he could accomplish with his boat and its crew.

The CIC Gang

After standing underway officer-of-the-deck watches for a number of months, I also qualified as an underway Combat Information Center (CIC) watch officer. There were some significant differences between the two watch assignments. The underway OOD stood his watch on the bridge with the helmsman, quartermaster of the watch, boatswain mate of the watch, port and starboard bridge lookouts, phone talker, messenger of the watch, and the Junior OOD. It was generally something between very busy and very, very busy on the bridge. It was not a casual scene.

In contrast, the CIC was a small compartment, roughly fifteen feet by twenty-five. The center of the space was occupied by a special plotting table. On the bulkheads was electronic equipment, including several radio units. There also were several Plexiglass status boards and a variety of cables running along the bulkheads and the overhead.

The key piece of equipment in the CIC was the surface radar (SG-1B) repeater, with a circular screen about the size of a large dinner plate. A constantly revolving electronic sweep illuminated contacts as small luminous dots. There was also an air search radar (ANSPS6-C) that was used in selected circumstances.

When underway, a radarman operated the equipment and interpreted what the screen was showing. There was a lot of technical and intuitive skill involved in his watch. In a rough sea, for example, it could be difficult picking out a ship among the "sea return." We had good radarmen in *Sarasota,* and one who was particularly skilled was a third class petty officer from Brooklyn, Charlie Amato. He is the only member of *Sara's* crew I still am in touch with, and we regularly exchange e-mails.

Underway in a formation or during an operation, the CIC was extremely busy. But when steaming independently, the CIC functioned as a navigation aid if there was land within the range of the radar. It was also used to track any ships that were within radar range. There was less minute-to-minute pressure than there was while standing an OOD watch.

While steaming independently, we spent a lot of time identifying ships up to roughly twenty miles away and determining constant ranges and bearings. With that information, it was possible to plot a contact's course and speed and determine how close it would come to *Sarasota*. Our radar equipment was pretty basic stuff compared to the radars in use today, but it did the job.

During normal steaming there were only three people in the CIC: the watch officer and two radarmen. And because the space was so tight, you spent a lot of the watch sitting down. It was an "inner circle" of sorts among the various under way operating teams in the ship. On a really quiet watch, there might even be some casual conversation.

In an e-mail exchange, however, Charlie Amato reminded me that, even when steaming independently, there could be some lively moments during a routine CIC watch. He wrote of an otherwise quiet midwatch:

While CIC watches could be routine, you never knew when you might get a distress call over the TBS (talk between ships), which was a radio communication link among both military and civilian ships in the area. The TBS in *Sarasota's* CIC was never turned off while under way and it was monitored constantly.

One really stormy night we were steaming north of Cape Hatteras, North Carolina, under a pitch black sky. You could tell there were unusually heavy seas running by the intermittent vibration in the deck. The vibration was generated each time the severe pitching of the ship caused the top of her propeller to emerge from the water. Each time the propeller emerged, it sent a brief vibration through the entire ship.

Around 0200 it was quiet in the CIC as we went about our work, using various ranges and bearings to points along the distant shore to help track the ship's position. Suddenly, the TBS barked: "Ship below us, we can make out your lights, identify yourself." The voice went on to identify himself as an officer leading a four-plane group of

Banshee fighter aircraft that was low on fuel. Apparently they were having problems with their navigation. They needed a bearing and distance to the Naval Air Station at Norfolk, Virginia.

We quickly gave them the information they needed and they moved off into the night with a crisp "Thank you." The entire incident took only a few minutes, and in the heavy weather, the planes never were sighted. But you can be sure there were four very relieved pilots heading off for the Naval Air Station, at Breezy Point, Norfolk.

Perhaps the biggest advantage to standing CIC watches was that the CIC had its own coffee pot. In contrast, during an OOD watch on the bridge, the coffee had to come from the galley or wardroom. In addition you constantly were busy, and you were always on your feet. Those were not circumstances conducive to having a cup of coffee.

During a CIC watch, you just poured a cup of coffee and set it down beside you. Particularly during the midwatch from midnight to four AM and the morning watch from four to eight AM, the coffee was a big factor in staying awake. There also was a psychologically comforting aspect to having the cup of coffee beside you as the watch wore on.

There was a nice tradition in *Sara's* CIC: you *always* put on a fresh pot of coffee for the oncoming watch. I have to admit, however, there was one down side to that ritual. While we were steaming, the pot was never washed. That meant at least seven pots of coffee in every 24-hour cycle, for as long we were under way. By the time we set the sea and anchor detail at the end of a period at sea, the hot coffee was still welcome, but the taste was more than a little exotic.

C-Rations

Boat operations could extend over long periods. It was not unusual to be in the boats from sunrise to sunset, or even longer. On some training operations, we wouldn't get back to *Sarasota* for several days. Those stretches of boat operations raised the issue of chow. For a while we were provided food from the ship's general mess. That meant a steady diet of sandwiches sent out periodically from the ship in one of our boats. In theory that didn't sound too bad.

In practice it was very bad. Inevitably, by the time the sandwiches reached the individual boats, they were soggy, often soaked in salt spray. While working hard physically and under a certain amount of stress, eating soggy sandwiches—particularly fried egg sandwiches soaked in salt water—can lead to a certain amount of surliness among boat crews.

So Fay Lossing and I took the matter up with the ship's supply officer. After all, the welfare of our boat group crews during operations was a prime responsibility. Fortunately, there was a solution: C-rations. "C-rats" were not gourmet food by any means, but they were a huge improvement over what we were getting. They consisted of a variety of small, individual-portion cans of items such as spaghetti and meatballs and franks and beans; small cans of fruit, such as peaches, pears, and fruit salad; candy bars, and cigarettes. The items were packaged in corrugated boxes that contained enough to provide a meal and snacks for two or three people. If a boat had four or of five boxes of C-rations, there was enough food for several days.

There was a major bonus to the C-rations. We quickly discovered that the cans for the main course items—after a small puncture in the can top with a marline spike—could be strategically placed in contact with the boat engine manifold for a period of a few minutes, and voilá, hot food!

The problem with our solution to the chow issue was the supply officer. In blunt terms, it cost him more from his supply account to provide C-rations than it did to provide soggy sandwiches. The issue was resolved, however, after several very tense meetings. There were angry exchanges but no overt threats by either Fay or me—that I can remember.

The Boats

There was a love-hate relationship with the amphibious craft carried in *Sarasota*. Almost all of the officers hated them. When you were in one you were usually wet, often cold, and invariably uncomfortable. Fay Lossing and I liked them for different reasons. For Fay, they were a means to expand and display his naval leadership qualities. For me they were an opportunity to learn about small boat operations and learn some lessons in leadership, particularly about making decisions on the basis of the situation and facts at hand. Those lessons would cut across a lot of activities in my civilian life.

The greatest fringe benefit of being involved with the boats, however, was that they were the means for us to be on our own for extended periods of time. While we were in the boats, we were physically separated from our senior officers in the ship. We had to rely on our own initiative and there was a special satisfaction in that.

During boat operations there were operational orders that established in general terms what we had to do and how we were to do it. There also was radio contact with *Sarasota* that provided further control over what we did. But the physical separation from the ship was liberating. There were a lot of moving parts in an amphibious operation and literally thousands of small decisions that were critical and that were up to us individually. The boat operations were a special dimension to our duties, and we liked that, notwithstanding the extra pressure and effort that were involved.

It should also be mentioned that there was a special benefit to Fay and me as a result of our boat operations. It was a benefit that generated a lot of envy among our colleagues in *Sarasota*. On returning to the ship after a particularly rough day in the boats, the ship's doctor, "Doc" Bartholomew, would issue a shot of brandy to each of us "for medicinal purposes."

Today the over-the-beach amphibious operations of 50 years ago have been expanded exponentially with a capability for faster, deeper, more telling strikes using helicopters, air cushion vehicles, and tilt-rotor aircraft. And for basic, across-the-beach delivery, the LCVP has been displaced by faster, longer-ranged, better protected Marine Expeditionary Fighting Vehicles.

The vehicles are launched from flooded welldecks of high-tech ships that have been designed from the keel up to facilitate the delivery of Marines faster and more efficiently than in the past. The thousands of LCVPs that were the ubiquitous personnel carriers of the post-World War II Navy and the scenes portrayed in newspapers and black-and-white theater newsreels are gone.

There are no ships of the same class as *Sarasota* left in today's U.S. Navy. They have long since been replaced by ships that combine the functions of several of the previous generation of amphibious assault ships. In the evolution from the amphibious force that I knew, the hitting power, tactical reach, and strategic flexibility of the Navy's expeditionary warfare capabilities have all increased many fold. Typical of this new force are the USS San Antonio-class ships with a flight deck that can handle helicopters and the "tilt-engine" Osprey aircraft, along with air-cushion vehicles and a wide variety of modern landing craft.

But there's no doubt that the days when a very young officer could leave the mother ship and control his own "mini-fleet" of amphibious craft are gone, but not forgotten by those of us who served in the "Gator Navy" of the Korean War era.

CHAPTER EIGHT

GETTING TO KNOW MYSELF

The mind is its own place, and in itself
Can make a Heav'n of Hell, a Hell of Heav'n.

John Milton

One of the most challenging aspects of my two years in *Sarasota* was the deep, ongoing loneliness I felt. I was surrounded by competent and well motivated people; some were even friends. My duties were challenging, interesting, and important, and I was succeeding in carrying them out. My first fitness report from *Sara's* captain was evidence of the latter. That initial fitness report pointed out that, despite my inexperience, I was an officer with potential. The fact that I was serving my country gave special meaning to what I was doing.

Yet with each passing day and even as my competence grew, I felt more and more isolated. Despite being constantly involved with people in intense ways, I was quite simply alone. Years after my tour in *Sarasota*, I heard singer Neil Diamond capture the feeling in the phrase: "I'll be what I am: a solitary man."

Approximately ten years after leaving active duty, I tried to revisit those feelings by getting them on paper. What emerged was a description of a young officer coming off an under-way midwatch with a compression of feelings that grew from deep fatigue and feelings of profound isolation. For some reason, I wrote about what I remembered of those feelings in the third person. I suspect there was a reason my remembrances came out that way.

But life went on: day by day, watch by watch. And I was learning important things, at times in brilliant flashes but mostly in little bits and pieces and in unsuspected times and places. And the lessons learned were made more vivid by my emotionally compressed shipboard environment. That's the way it is at sea, where you are expected—no, required—to get things right the first time. Do-overs are as uncommon as a full night's sleep.

Elements of Leadership

Arguably the most important thing I was learning in *Sarasota* was leadership, and lesson one was that leadership is more art than science. There are many different leadership styles that can be effective, and the proof of that was right before my eyes, among the commissioned officers and petty officers of a ship's company.

There were no training sessions on the subject, but there were constant opportunities for learning in *Sarasota* on any given day. And it became clear quickly that there was a strong correlation between leadership and concepts and the U.S. Navy culture. What those cultural elements added up to was a collection of unofficial but basic rules, informal but definitely not optional requirements for effective leadership. The rules didn't spring from official U.S. Navy documents or the Uniform Code of Military Justice. And despite being unofficial, they are immutable. Those unwritten rules are based on a tremendous body of experience, and they have evolved over centuries. They came from the likes of John Paul Jones and a long line of warfighters—most of whom never became famous—who succeeded Jones and his fellow leaders in the cobbled-together Continental Navy of the American War of Independence.

One of the most interesting things about those special rules is that they also became relevant in my civilian life, despite their being clearly counter-culture in that a non-navy arena. They represent guides to behavior that are not common in today's non-military world, where "taking care of number one" has become a dominant way of life.

The rules include the following:

- Take care of your people. You are not only given authority over your division, your boat crew, or even a working party, you are given the responsibility for their safety and well-being, and their safety and well-being are more important than your own. In a military bureaucracy, especially when circumstances are stressful, taking care of your people in that way can be a challenge. It is, however, an absolute requirement, arguably the most important of all unwritten rules of leadership.

- Demonstrate loyalty to those senior to yourself. The loyalty you receive from those you command will be in direct proportion to the upward loyalty towards your seniors that you demonstrate.

- Don't hang out with those you command. Inevitably, you are going to have to give unpopular—sometimes *very* unpopular—orders that will be undermined if those you command believe that they can resort to friendship to avoid the onerous orders. That does not mean avoiding socializing among those you command. It's a fine but important line.

- Praise in public and criticize in private. Over time, this quality will be recognized and appreciated by both those you command and those in authority over you.

- Admit your mistakes and take immediate action to correct them. It's too easy for a person in authority to find a scapegoat when something goes wrong, but that inevitably becomes apparent and compromises morale and efficiency.

- Be consistent and firm in your leadership and pay close attention to the most junior and inexperienced people over whom you have authority. Some day one of them will hold your career in his or her hands. Someday one of them might hold your life in his or her hands.

- Be apparent. It's important to delegate authority, but it's equally important to be seen frequently by those you are leading.

- Don't judge people by externals. People will surprise you. Often the least likely person based on externals will be the person who will really come through under pressure. This admonition works two ways. It applies to those who are junior to you and to those who are your seniors.

- If you disagree with your superior officers, voice those disagreements behind closed doors. And what transpires in the conversation behind the closed door remains there.

In addition to the foregoing, there were two additional unofficial requirements that emerged quickly in *Sarasota*. These requirements that were narrowly focused on shipboard routines, but that are also, in a way, roughly transferable to civilian life:

- Always show up to relieve the watch fifteen minutes before your watch begins. The officer you are relieving should have plenty of time to brief you on the things you should know before taking the responsibility, and nothing is more irritating than being relieved late after a difficult watch.

- Never discuss women, politics, or religion in the wardroom.

One of the noteworthy things about the above rules was that as I was learning them from actual experience in *Sarasota*. Another noteworthy thing was that I began remembering hearing a number of the unwritten rule as a very young child. Those recollections of childhood were remembrances of the rare occasions when my father discussed his service as a U.S. Marine Corps sergeant in the American Expeditionary Force in France during World War I.

The Pif Paf Pouf

There were less profound times during my two years in *Sarasota*. For example there was occasional liberty in interesting places that broke up the long stretches of fatigue and stress. One was the Pif Paf Pouf, a funky lounge bar in San Juan, Puerto Rico, a place where you could laugh at what was going on around you and at times even yourself.

It was a time in San Juan when—believe it—there were only two large resort hotels: the new Caribe Hilton and the older Condado Beach. The flood of new hotels, with their neon glitter and gambling casinos, had not yet begun. In fact, there were some at the time who maintained that the new Hilton would never survive. There could, according to them, never be enough business and tourism in San Juan for more than one large hotel.

It also was a time when San Juan's Old City still had the Spanish colonial aura that remains a part of the heritage of many of today's Caribbean islands. There were the ramparts of El Moro that helped repulse Sir Francis Drake in 1595, El Convento Hotel, which was a former Carmelite nunnery dedicated in 1651, and the narrow streets paved with blue hued cobblestones that came to the New World as ballast in Spanish galleons. It also had remnants of the poverty that went with the colonial era.

I have no idea how long the Pif Paf Pouff had been around, but on the occasions I was in San Juan in '52, '53 and '54 it was very popular for a young crowd of locals, tourists, U.S. Navy people assigned to the then-Tenth Naval District in San Juan, and Navy people ashore for liberty from visiting ships.

What really made the Pif Paf Pouf memorable was the entrance, a 20-foot, twisting slide that was the only way in. That entrance introduced a nonsensical note, something that challenged for just an hour or so the palpable weight of responsibility-tension-isolation of my steady routine. The entrance was as nonsensical as the bar's name, and it guaranteed that everyone entered laughing.

The Pif Paf Pouf was written up in *Life* magazine, and I remember getting a copy of the article in the mail from my father. Of course the key photo was of an attractive young woman ending her slide in considerable disarray. He wrote that he was glad that I didn't hang out in places like that. I am still not quite sure whether or not his comments were tongue-in-cheek, but the older I got the surer I was that they were. He was too smart for it to be otherwise.

Sitting at the bar and watching the patrons arrive—especially those entering for the first time—was a lot better than just sitting at a bar. It was a fairly harmless way to have a drink or two with a couple of shipmates. At least it was most of the time.

There were those inevitable occasions, however, when arguments would develop over such things as the parental lineage of guys from other Navy ships that were in port, or the chronic lack of sensitivity among "zoomies" (the second half of the friendly term sometimes used to identify naval aviators). But those were all family differences that were the result of temporary misunderstandings.

In hindsight there were much better ways to spend one's time in San Juan. And over the years I have managed to get to know that city on a much higher plane. But when you are in your mid-twenties, handling more responsibility than most people deal with in their lifetime, there was something genuinely recreational, even therapeutic, in having a few drinks and more than a few laughs at the Pif Paf Pouf. It was a place where, at least for a little while, you simply couldn't take yourself too seriously.

Mail

I don't think anyone who hasn't served in the military can imagine how important an old fashioned letter was before e-mail changed the whole personal communication equation within the military. And I believe the importance of those analog-era letters was particularly acute for those with sea duty. It was an essential link to the people you cared about and who cared about you. Each letter was a brief suspension of the tyranny of distance that separates love from love.

On the other hand, not getting a letter when there was mail call compounded the sense of isolation from things less stressful and those loved. It was, in fact, a rejection that added to the sense of loneliness.

No less a naval hero than Britain's Admiral Lord Nelson—victor at the Battles of the Nile, Copenhagen, and Trafalgar, where he established a century of British naval dominance and shaped the course of history from the decks of his ships—reflected the importance of mail in his writings. One notable example appears in a brief letter to his wife, written during a dangerous combat operation at Calvi, Corsica on 8 July 1784. There is a poignancy in the letter from the hardened warfighter, written unselfconsciously and in his plain-talking style: "I long to hear from you, for a post has arrived without a letter...I am very busy, yet own I am in all my glory: except with you, I would not be any where but where I am, for the world." [8]

Maelstrom

In 1953 *Sara* went through a hurricane. We had just returned from a training exercise and had barely gotten our dock lines secured in Norfolk when word came through that there was a major hurricane headed our way. Alongside a pier is not a good place for a ship in a hurricane, and *Sara* was quickly assigned to a Navy-designated hurricane anchorage in lower Chesapeake Bay.

In retrospect, I'm convinced that the ship probably would have been safer alongside the pier, as undesirable as that might have been. And comparing notes with other officers in ships ordered to ride out other hurricanes at Navy-designated hurricane anchorages in the Chesapeake, I learned that others concur in that opinion.

When we reached our assigned anchorage it became clear that we were in bad company. We were surrounded by other amphibious ships, which would not normally be a problem. But the surrounding ships included many LSTs, the notorious, box-like, and unseaworthy landing craft that carried tanks, trucks and other heavy equipment used in amphibious assaults. The slab-sided, shallow-draft LSTs turned out to be a special problem in the coming hours.

As the storm mounted and night came, the captain took over on the bridge, which meant he, not the OOD, was in command of the ship. In navy terms, "the captain had the con." I was among those assigned to the bridge watch that night.

Sara's commanding officer at the time was not popular in the wardroom. He was introverted, gruff and had been given an uncomplimentary nickname to match the officers' perception of him. And it's safe to say that he would have been no one's first choice to guide the ship through what was coming our way that night.

As the storm mounted to full hurricane force, *Sara*—with her single engine helping to take the strain off the anchor chain—rode reasonably well for a while, diving headlong into the seas that attacked with steadily increasing violence. Again and again she dove and shuddered under the pounding, smashing force of the storm. As the storm mounted, it became clear that the greatest danger to *Sara* was from other ships, especially the LSTs. Because of the great "sail area" of their large flat sides and relatively shallow draft, the LSTs were prone to dragging their anchors. As they drifted rapidly out of their positions, there was a real danger of them actually colliding with other ships and tangling anchor chains in the process.

At one point an LST started dragging her anchor and the reports of the direction of her movement from the CIC's radarman were unequivocal; the LST in question was heading straight for us. Somehow the captain maneuvered *Sara* just enough for the LST to barely miss us and slide by, disappearing back into a black maelstrom, where she no doubt menaced other struggling ships. Once clear of the danger from the LST, attention shifted back to the mounting threats from the wind and sea.

Someplace above us there were stars—perhaps even a moon— but where we were there was only blackness, violence and new depths of fatigue. The atmosphere in the wheelhouse was weighted, filled with an immense and formless threat. The loaded atmosphere hung on everything and everyone. The captain, helmsman and the others on the bridge eventually seemed congealed into a slowly undulating mass.

The hurricane howl threatened to demolish thought. Gusts of wind struck the ship with gigantic, jarring impact. It was a strange and frightening feeling, something that contrasted sharply with the usually smoothly connected, rhythmic motions one becomes used to in a ship at sea.

I remember wondering at one point how each of us would tell about the storm—if we made it—and who we would want to tell about it. But as the storm grew, there was only a single, shared purpose among us: help *Sara* fight the hurricane.

At first you only felt it in your guts; it was becoming more and more difficult to keep the bow headed into the wind and the seas. The bow was slowly being forced farther and farther off the wind, and as the wind and seas smashed *Sara* more and more from the side, she rolled farther and farther. It was a sickening feeling, and with each roll of the ship, it took longer and longer to start rolling back.

Then it came. *Sara* rolled past any point she had reached before. She groaned and her groan became a scream as she resisted pressures and forces that only nature could compound. The ship paused and hung on the edge of destruction for what seemed like eternity. Everyone on the bridge was clutching something to keep from sliding across the deck. She waited. We waited.

Then, slowly *Sara* recovered from the paralyzing roll, and gradually the engine and the rudder began to force the bow back into the wind. The extreme rolling was eventually replaced by the familiar and welcome headlong diving into the wind and sea.

No one spoke for a while. We all knew where we had been. And we had each been there alone.

Epiphanies at Sea

That long night fighting a hurricane in 1953 taught me two very important lessons. The first was a true understanding of the monumental power of a hurricane, something that could only be fully understood when face to face with a hurricane at sea, where there was no place to retreat and no fallback position. Your life depended on your ship and your shipmates, and I realized that at times it had been a near thing.

The second lesson involved our captain. During the hours we struggled for survival, he never faltered. His orders to the helmsman and to the engine room were delivered calmly and without hesitation. He consistently demonstrated great seamanship and confidence in his own abilities—and ours. There were no wasted words, and there were no histrionics, and I don't think he ever raised his voice. His attitude and manner set the tone for everyone in the wheelhouse.

After the event, it was clear that there was no one in the ship who could have matched his leadership and professional competence in the crisis. I'm sure there were a lot of private reevaluations of the captain going on among the ship's officers.

In the morning the storm abated, the sun came out, and we set about cleaning up the ship and reestablishing normal routines. There were a few LSTs strewn around us in the anchorage that had not been there the night before, and a number that had been there the night before were gone. The captain immediately reverted to his previous self, a thoroughly unpleasant, standoffish and bad-tempered person. He had not changed one bit. But I was wiser.

I realized that during the crises, the captain's social persona didn't matter. And his lack of popularity among the officers was absolutely meaningless. What mattered was his ability to understand a violent and rapidly changing situation and to make the decisions that would get *Sara* and her crew safely through the night. It was a lesson that was applicable to subsequent situations in life, both Navy and civilian.

Perhaps the most visible change after the hurricane was the attitudes about the captain among the officers. The attitudes were radically different. I never again heard his nickname used. He was from that point on always referred to as "the captain."

Esprit de Corps

Over time in *Sarasota*, I slowly began to learn about that thing called *esprit de corps*. There weren't any lectures or manuals on the subject, I just absorbed it, hour by hour and day by day.

It was a matter of fraternities, in the literal sense of the word. The innermost fraternity was your division in the ship. No matter what the problems might be within your division—every division had problems—you knew it was still the best division in the ship.

The next fraternity was the ship, and beyond *Sarasota*, no dumb-ass better denigrate her. She was part of you; you were part of her. And so on the rings expanded: amphibs were better than other Surface Navy communities and certainly better than those outside the Surface Navy. The final ring included the other military services. Of course the other armed services were OK but not as good as the Navy.

That part of Navy culture that involves *esprit de corps* might be considered divisive or overly competitive by outsiders, but it is not. It's a matter of pride in yourself and the people and things on which you have come to depend. And it is that pride that is part of the unique character of the U.S. military. It begins with yourself and then moves outward in expanding rings and is part of the matrix of American traditions that add up to the exceptional performance of the U.S. military in exceptional circumstances.

Those traditions transcend a lot of things: draft vs. all-volunteer force issues, radical changes in technology, massive changes in social morés, and even the military's sometimes less than perfect civilian leadership. If we ever blot out that pride in self that expands *outward* we will have eliminated a force multiplier that has carried the day in some of America's most important military crises.

The Letter

Humor in many forms helped to relieve the stress in *Sarasota*. Usually it was benign, and very often it was self-deprecating. On the other hand, sometimes it was aggressive. And sometimes it was absolutely bizarre.

One extreme example of the latter involved a fellow junior officer. I'm going to call him Bob. The first lieutenant called him "the man with a size eight hat and a size aught brain." It wasn't really that he was dumb. Bob simply was other-worldly. His focus always seemed to be somewhere else, and that was a quality that wasn't generally appreciated in an environment where proper focus and safety went together.

Like a number of the other junior officers in the wardroom Bob had been recently married, and his wife, I'll call her Dottie, had the same detached attitude as Bob. But they were a good match, indifferent to the jibes of others, and clearly very much in love. In fact, it's fair to describe Bob as love-struck.

Bob and Dottie lived in the same Oceanview Apartments previously described, and they were very much a part of the informal mutual support system that operated among the young Navy couples there.

At one point *Sarasota* was involved in an extended training exercise in the Caribbean. We probably were away on the exercise for a month. Because there were no opportunities to visit a liberty port, a special liberty was arranged at one point during the exercise on one of the small islands used in the operation. The deal was that a liberty section was taken into the beach in one of the ship's LCM boats. Ashore, those on liberty could at least swim and have a beer or two that was provided by the ship.

There was a tiny village on the island, and at one point, some of the local inhabitants came down to the beach with a small horse that they offered for riding along the beach. The charge to ride up the beach and back was fifty cents.

Bob was part of the liberty party and he was one of the few who took advantage of the opportunity for the impromptu horseback riding. It was a harmless enough way of trying to break the shipboard routine, but after the liberty Bob made a big mistake and wrote to Dottie about it. A portion of his letter went something like this:

> We haven't had any liberty for three weeks, but yesterday we at least had a chance to get into the beach to swim and have a beer. While we were there, some of the locals brought a horse to the beach that we could ride for fifty cents. But you had to keep kicking the horse to get any real action. Anyway, it was better than sitting around in the ship.

Bob's handwriting was exceptionally bad and it wasn't unusual for Dottie to get together with some of the wives to try to decipher

Bob's letters. In this instance, the process produced a disaster. After struggling mightily with Bob's handwriting, the word "horse" was finally mistranslated to "whore."

Naturally Dottie was very upset and none of the wives could figure out why Bob would have written such a cruel letter.

When *Sarasota* returned to Norfolk several weeks later, those of us living in the Oceanview all arrived home at about the same time. As usual, Bob was the most outwardly eager to get home.

Almost immediately, Dottie's screaming was echoing through the building, punctuated periodically with the crash of breaking objects. It took about thirty minutes for the screaming and crashing to subside, presumably when Bob was able to calm his wife down enough to clear matters up.

The next morning, when Bob showed up at the ship, He behaved as if nothing had happened. It was difficult to determine whether we were dealing with a tragedy or a comedy. In that regard there was a certain resemblance between the situation with Bob's letter and life at that point. We left it that way.

Standing by

The U.S. Navy is known for its rules and regulations, In fact, they're omnipresent. But at times there are accommodations within those restrictions that help to make life a bit more livable. One such custom is that of "standing by" for a shipmate. I don't know how it began, but the first commanding officer of a ship who decided it was an OK practice deserves at the very least a medal.

When you were in the duty section you were not permitted to go on liberty. Generally *Sarasota* had three duty sections. That meant that even when we were in our homeport of Norfolk, those in the duty section were not permitted liberty on one night out of three and one weekend out of three. The U.S. Navy-wide rationale is that there has to be a sufficient number of people aboard to get the ship under way at all times.

The same rule was applied in liberty ports, which differed only in that liberty in ports other than our homeport generally expired at midnight, rather than 0800 the following morning.

For married officers with wives and families in Norfolk (which was mostly the case) it meant that every third night was spent aboard ship. That was far from an ideal routine for the married officers.

The informal accommodation was that if you could get someone to "stand by" for you, you could go on liberty and spend the night at home. Since I was married and Fay Lossing was not, we were able to swap "stand bys" with one another from time to time. Fay would stand by for me on occasion in Norfolk and I would reciprocate for him on occasion in liberty ports. We didn't keep records and it was not a precise one-for-one situation, but it worked out pretty evenly over time.

The custom of "standing by" for a friend or colleague was not a big deal, but it's typical of how sailors take care of one another, and it reflects an attitude that is not always dominant in society. In *Sarasota* it was routine.

Comeuppance

After I had been in *Sarasota* for about a year, I had begun to be reasonably comfortable about being able to do my jobs. Then one day, I heard something very interesting about LSMRs, large landing craft configured as rocket launching ships. Their executive officers were lieutenants junior grade, and sometimes even senior ensigns, and I got the bright idea that I would like to finish out my active duty as the XO of an LSMR.

The first step was to write a letter requesting transfer to an LSMR. I crafted a masterpiece, citing every inch of my experience and qualifications in *Sarasota,* and started it on its way through the official chain of command to the Bureau of Naval Personnel.

The first endorsement on my letter would have to come from my present commanding officer. He was a good captain, friendly, firm and a good seaman, and he had given me a promising first fitness report. No problems there, I figured.

The same day I had initiated my letter, in fact within about an hour of the time I started it on its way, I was sought out by the messenger of the watch, who had instructions for me to report immediately to the captain. Ensigns did not get called to the captain's office in the normal course of things.

When I entered the captain's office, he had a strange expression on his face. His opening line was, "Callo, what's this request for a transfer all about?" Then it dawned on me, the captain thought I wanted to get off his ship because of some kind of problem I was having.

I assured that captain that I had no problems in the ship, and I simply wanted to go to an assignment where I would have more responsibility. His expression softened slightly, and I thought I even saw the hint of a smile. At that point, I figured my transfer was a sure thing

"Sit down, Callo," were his next words, and I sat. He looked at me for a few seconds, and again, I thought there was the flicker of a smile. Finally, he looked at me with a captain's basic stern countenance and said: "Callo, you haven't begun to figure out what's going on in *this* ship. You're not going anywhere."

I left, and I'm sure the next stop for my letter was in the proverbial "round file." [9]

The Crossing Over

Although ensigns are commissioned officers, they are the lowest of the low in that group, primarily for their obvious lack of experience. And that status was clear every minute of every day while I was an ensign assigned to *Sara*. You were given significant responsibilities very quickly, at the same time, you were constantly on trial, and it was assumed by almost everyone that you really didn't know anything.

Someone once wrote, "chief petty officers have a way of making the title 'ensign' sound like a four letter word." And just in case your low status might slip your mind at some point, you were reminded of your lowly standing by your senior officers at least three times a day. The three reminders were built in to your meals, since at the officers' seating places at wardroom tables were arranged by seniority beginning with the executive officer (the captain ate his meals in his own quarters). The only officers seated below the ensigns were the commissioned warrant officers (there were three in *Sarasota*), but they had a special status of their own based on their number of years in the Navy.

The fact that promotion from ensign after eighteen months was almost automatic was some consolation.

When the promotion came, the shift from a single gold bar for your collar device to a single silver bar and the addition of a narrow gold stripe over your ensign's stripe wasn't much of an external change. But notwithstanding the lack of a dramatic insignia and striping change and the fact that the advancement to lieutenant junior grade was virtually automatic didn't diminish the event. For one thing, you had an undeniably difference presence as a lieutenant junior grade, and you knew that with the silver bar and additional "skinny stripe," others took you more seriously.

The difference between being commissioned as an ensign and being promoted to lieutenant junior grade was the difference between being recognized for your training and being validated for your performance.

Goodbye *Sara*

Sarasota was no beauty queen. Every one of her men knew it, but none thought less of her because of that. Her paint never completely covered her age or her scars. She could be dangerous, and she had ways of making you know yourself—intensely and truthfully—in quiet moments and in wild moments.

She was steel-cold and never gave you anything for free, but she could take you to amazing places within yourself. She could turn a youth into a man, fast. Most of her men gained strength through her, and it was a special strength no one could ever take away. She could also break a man—terribly, completely.

Sara's men relied on her totally, and over time, they realized that she relied on them too. They justified each other. Her men understood her importance, and in hot, man-hugging sunshine and in blue-black starlight, she was a constant.

Her relationships went very deep. It was a mysterious thing. She took her men to sea and back. It was a process older than history, one that has been discussed and written about endlessly, but never fully defined.

There was absolutely no sentimentality in my official detachment from my ship. The heart of my orders was written in blunt Navy-speak:

> "When directed by your commanding officer in May or June 1954 you will regard yourself detached from duty at your present station and from such other duty as may have been assigned to you."

As I walked down her gangway for the last time and away from *Sara*, I knew we would never be together again. It was a strange feeling. She had been my world for the better part of two years. It was where I was. We had been through a lot in a few years. There had been stress, but there also had been the special beauty that is experienced only at sea in a good ship. And the stress had been shared with a good crew.

Sara tested me frequently and severely, and I had passed her tests, not with a perfect grade, but with a reasonably good mark, and yes, with some luck too. Shortly after I left her, she was again decommissioned, and this time she wasn't put into a reserve fleet for possible recommissioning in the future; she was scrapped. In unofficial Navy terms, she was converted into razor blades.

But as long as I live, I will remember her feel, her basic tempo, and her deep, throbbing beat while underway at sea. My internal rhythm had become a part of hers. Her rhythm had been absorbed into mine, and it was all inside of me as I left. It could never be lost.

CHAPTER NINE
FROM SARA TO SARA

All nature is but art unknown to thee,
All chance, direction which thou canst not see.

Alexander Pope

In May of 1954, after completing my two years of sea duty in *Sarasota,* I returned to civilian life. I had a wife, a one year old son, and a just-born second son. My military obligation required that, as part of what was referred to as the "Ready Reserve," I be available until 1958 for recall to active duty. On the other hand, I was not required to affiliate with a reserve unit or perform any annual training duty during that period of availability for recall.

In any event, my intention was to get started on a civilian career in the advertising business, with as few outside distractions as possible, but a chance meeting altered my approach to getting involved with activities outside family and business.

A Victim of Circumstances

I don't remember exactly how I met John Goodman, but I know it was something that was not planned. John had served in the U.S. Navy during World War II and was, when I met him, the advertising manager at American Oil Company. As I recall, our common naval service somehow created the circumstance of our meeting, and when John learned that I was working in an advertising agency, he lit up like a recruiting officer at a school career day.

It seems that there was a volunteer (no pay) U.S. Navy public affairs unit in New York City that John thought might be of interest to me. I explained at some length and probably with some emphasis that I had just served my two years in the Atlantic Amphibious Forces as a surface warfare officer and really didn't know anything about U.S. Navy public affairs. For good measure I pointed out that I had a family to support, full time.

Like all good recruiting officers, John didn't push too hard. He did point out, however, that the unit had people working in business areas related to my chosen civilian career field. If I chose to, he suggested, I could think of it as a professional society. The end line is that I was susceptible enough to buy into his suggestion that I check out the navy reserve public affairs unit.

What I found was a group of people working in civilian jobs related to public affairs, which, in Navy terms, included three general categories of mass communications: community relations, media relations, and internal relations. There were people working for a publisher, a daily newspaper, a TV network, the public relations department of a major company, and in other mass communications fields.

The men and women in the unit had served their country, returned to civilian life and then found an opportunity, through the Navy Reserve public affairs unit John was talking about, to continue serving in a way that was related to their civilian careers. And they did it as true volunteers—without pay. [10]

As it turned out, two of the best friends I developed in the years to come were people whom I met in that navy reserve public affairs unit. Both were naval aviators who were no longer eligible to fly in the Navy; one was George Heinemann, a producer at NBC-TV, and the other was Art Ward, the head of a major audio production studio in New York City. In any event, I was beginning a second phase of my naval career. All of my reserve assignments brought me in contact with sailors, and those assignments also widened my experiences with the sea.

Sara II

I began attending the meetings, which were held at the Third Naval District headquarters at 90 Church Street in downtown Manhattan, and I continued through 1955. Around the middle of '55, I was promoted to lieutenant, and towards the end of the year, an unusual opportunity turned up: the Navy was looking for a reservist for a special, three-month assignment in the Pre-commissioning Detail of another ship nicknamed *Sara*. In this case it was USS *Saratoga*.

Saratoga was the second ship of a new class of large-deck aircraft carriers, and she was under construction in the former Brooklyn Navy Yard. Her prospective commanding officer was then-Captain Robert Stroh, a naval aviator.[11] The assignment was for a public affairs officer, and it would be for 90 days.

The more I thought about it, the more the challenge drew me in. Although it was contrary to my plan to concentrate on my civilian career, I put in for the assignment, and within a few days, I had my orders and was back in uniform.

I've wondered over the years why I did what I did. Maybe it was that it was a one-of-a-kind assignment for a reservist. Maybe it was because I missed the special challenges I had faced during my two years in *Sarasota*. Perhaps it was because I missed the friendships I had formed during that tour of active duty. And maybe it was because one of my seniors in my reserve unit told me I was too junior for such a "big" assignment. In any event, it was one of the better decisions of my life.

Before I had time for second thoughts, I received my orders and reported on 3 January 1956 "for duty in connection with the fitting out of U.S.S. SARATOGA (CVA-60) at the New York Naval Shipyard, Brooklyn, New York." [12]

A Special Leader

As soon as I cleared the inevitable paperwork and reported, I had my first meeting with Captain Stroh. He was cordial, but there was something about him that said you wouldn't want him for an enemy. As I recall, he didn't ask me about my credentials in U.S. Navy public affairs. And that was good, since they were virtually nonexistent. He did ask me about how I intended to go about my assignment. I described some of the more obvious possibilities and then a few things that would have been considered "out of the box." I came away feeling that he was amused by my high expectations, but that he also was pleased that I was aiming high. I was encouraged by the latitude he seemed to be giving me.

Then he laid out, not the specifics of what I was to do, but a few basic guidelines. Most important: the crew and the ship were always to come first in anything that I did—*always*. And I would report directly to him, which was an unusual situation for a reserve fresh-caught lieutenant in an important command and with a senior captain clearly ticketed for important responsibilities in the Navy. Finally, he explained that it would not be necessary for me to keep him informed of details of my efforts, but there were to be no surprises for him as a result of what I did.

In short, my orders were to do good for the ship and the Navy, to not run scared—and *no surprises*. These were obviously requirements not listed in my written orders, but they were my real orders. I was beginning to learn that there was a level above the ever-present Navy bureaucracy, a place where you are expected to think and to deliver for the command to which you are attached. It was the place where the real Navy lived, and I liked inhabiting it.

It was hard to believe. In an organization known for hierarchal structure, I was reporting directly to a senior captain. In a situation where his future career was very much on the line, I had been given virtual *carte blanche*. It was not only hard to believe; it scared the hell out of me. I couldn't wait to do good things for *Saratoga* and Captain Stroh.

Under Pressure

During the three months-plus that followed I worked extremely hard. I had no staff, and twelve-hour days with seven-day work weeks were the rule. And given the approaching commissioning date, there were virtually no opportunities for do-overs if mistakes were made. In fact by the time the commissioning was imminent, I was on the verge of a physical breakdown. But help arrived in the nick of time in the person of another reserve lieutenant, Frank Allston, who was assigned to *Sara's* Pre-commissioning Detail for his two weeks annual reserve training.

Frank jumped into the breach and kept all of the projects I had initiated on track, while I pulled myself together. Frank was a 1952 NROTC graduate from the University of North Carolina who was in the early stages of a brilliant career in corporate communications when we met in that spring of 1956. At that point he was working in the advertising department of General Electric.

In addition to his outstanding civilian career, Frank went on as a naval reservist to become a rear admiral in the U.S. Navy Supply Corps, and it was a special—and unanticipated—coincidence that we both reached flag rank. Frank and his wife Barbara remained friends over the years, and he presided at my Navy retirement ceremony, almost thirty years after we met. That's the way U.S. Navy friendships usually work out.

A Very Big Day

Saratoga was commissioned on 14 April 1956. It was the end of the construction and fitting out of the ship and the beginning of her career as a commissioned ship of the U.S. Navy. To cap a series of solid public affairs achievements during the run-up to the commissioning, there were two particularly noteworthy events associated with the commissioning ceremony. First, on the day before the commissioning CBS TV did their entire morning show, then known as *The Morning Show*, from the ship. Will Rogers Jr.

was the host of the show at that time, Ned Kalmer did the news, and Pamela Good was the weather person.

As the show progressed, there were commentary and interviews that illuminated the ship's mission and basic daily operation. It was a unique and particularly interesting piece of morning TV programming, and from the Navy's point of view, it was an effective way to get the story of the ship's capabilities and mission to the general public. Most important, it made the crew feel good about their ship and themselves.

There were alternating producers for CBS's morning show at the time, and the producer assigned for the *Saratoga* show was Shad Northshield. It was clear that he was amused by my "we can do that" attitude as each production problem surfaced and was resolved, and over the years Shad and I became friends.

On several occasions, he was a guest lecturer at the college classes in mass media that I taught part time in the communication arts program at St. John's University in New York. Getting to know Shad, who was highly respected in the TV industry for, among other achievements, his outstanding documentaries, was an unexpected and long term byproduct of my *Saratoga* assignment. Our friendship was also representative of the kind people with whom I have gotten to know because of my U.S. Navy Reserve career.

The second particularly notable media event associated with the commissioning was the start-to-finish national coverage of the commissioning by ABC TV. As with the CBS show, it was a matter of not knowing what couldn't be done. In another similarity with the CBS *Morning Show* the day before, the ABC TV coverage helped make Sara's sailors feel good about themselves and their ship.

In hindsight, it also was clear that because of the ground rules established by Captain Stroh, which gave me credibility in the ship beyond my rank or experience, I was able to get commitments from two national TV networks before anyone could say it could not or should not be done.

Loyalty Down

Based on my orders, I was scheduled to be detached from the Pre-Commissioning Detail of *Saratoga* the day before the commissioning on 14 April. When we finally focused on that timing, I assured Captain Stroh that I would be aboard on my own time for the commissioning. I wasn't about to walk away before the job was done.

At that point, the captain called in the administrative officer and asked him why I was being detached the day before the commissioning. The admin officer explained that by law reservist could serve only 90 days on temporary duty without causing major problems in the administrative system. It was a reality, he explained, based on the laws related to the mobilization of reservists. The ninetieth day of my duty was the day before the commissioning; thus I had to be officially detached on that day. It was a classic example of government bureaucracy at work.

Captain Stroh looked at the admin officer and said something like: "I want Callo to be part of the ship's company on the day the ship is commissioned." There was no further discussion, and at that point, I realized what was going on. If I were a member of the ship's company on the day of the commissioning, I was technically a "plank owner," an official member of the crew on the day a ship is commissioned.

What Captain Stroh did that day sealed my high opinion of him as an outstanding leader, and I still have my plankowner's certificate with his hand-written message:

With much appreciation for your indispensable assistance in getting "Sara" commissioned and off to a great start—
Warm personal regards and best wishes,

Robert Stroh, Captain, USN.

Along with all of the things I learned about leadership when working for Captain Stroh, there was one more thing that I learned during the very last days in *Saratoga's* Pre-Commissioning Detail:

III

I shouldn't believe it when told that "the system" makes doing something good impossible; there's always someone who can help you make that something good happen.

In the perspective of time, I've realized something else: working for Captain Stroh had a lot to do with me continuing a U.S. Navy Reserve career. Working for him had reinforced my opinion in the high quality of Navy people, and was a significant factor in my continuation as a Navy Reserve officer beyond my legal obligations in the Ready Reserve.

An End and a Beginning

The commissioning of *Saratoga* was the end of my assignment and the beginning of her life as a commissioned ship of the U.S. Navy. During 38 years of service, *Saratoga* was involved in 22 deployments to the Mediterranean, a combat deployment to the Western Pacific in '72-'73 during the Vietnam War, combat operations against Libyan attempts to exclude U.S. ships from areas of the Mediterranean, the capture of the terrorist hijackers of *Achille Lauro,* protection of U.S. citizens during various crises, support of military actions during Operations Desert Shield and Desert Storm, and scores of other situations in which she directly supported U.S. national interests and U.S. citizens around the world.

My part of *Saratoga's* career was minuscule compared to those who manned her and flew from her decks in the dangerous situations that marked her life. But my brief assignment, although tiny, was still a part of the whole, and it was significant enough for me to identify with her important contributions over the years to America's safety and the protection of her citizens.

A Wrenching Encounter

The last time I saw *Saratoga* was in June 1998, forty-two years after I walked down her gangway following her commissioning. She was laid up near the former Philadelphia Navy Yard, as part of the Navy's inactive fleet. It was an unexpected meeting. At the time I was standing a helmsman's watch in the recreation of Captain Cook's square-rigged bark *Endeavour*. I was part of the working crew for her transit from Philadelphia to New York.

We were easing down the Delaware River from Philadelphia toward the Atlantic in a light rain, with just a whisper of a breeze and bare steerageway. I was concentrating hard on maintaining our course in the channel.

At one point I happened to glance at the shore to starboard. We were passing the anchorage where many of the "mothballed" ships of the inactive fleet were moored. My eye caught the transom of a large aircraft carrier; I was stunned.

The name traced in steel across her transom was USS *Saratoga*. There were streaks of rust running through her name. An ugly web of cables held her motionless. She was surrounded by ships in various stages of deterioration, sitting in murky waters in a gray drizzle. She was crewless, lifeless, abandoned. It couldn't have been more than a minute or two before we were easing around a bend in the river and she disappeared.

She was gone. It was an unsettling goodbye.

CHAPTER TEN
IF NOT ME, THEN WHO?

Victory is reserved for those who are willing to pay its price.

Sun Tzu

Following my assignment in the Pre-Commissioning Detail of USS *Saratoga*, I again returned to civilian life, which coincided with the arrival of my third child Mary Ellen and a move from an apartment in The Bronx to a house in Croton-on-Hudson. The house was about 35 miles up the Hudson River from New York City. My focus was back on my family and my advertising career.

An Attitude Adjustment

Following my *Saratoga* special assignment, however, there was an important change in my thinking about the U.S. Navy Reserve. I had begun to see it as an ongoing effort, rather than just the fulfilling of a short term commitment. As part of that attitude shift, in 1959 I requested a change in my official Navy specialty from surface warfare to public affairs.

The primary reason for the request was the rapid advances in technology in the U.S. Navy. It would have been increasingly difficult to keep my surface warfare skills up to date. In addition, my work in advertising would contribute toward some of the skills required for a Navy public affairs specialty.

One of the negative byproducts of the shift to a staff designation was that put some distance between my reserve activity and direct contact with the sea. On the other hand, I would still be actively involved with the Navy and the group of people I had learned to respect.

Not long after my decision, there was major event that reinforced my choice to continue my involvement with the U.S. Navy Reserve. That event was the Vietnam War and particularly the anti-military attitudes the War engendered. During the Vietnam War, my commitment to the U.S. Navy Reserve grew in direct proportion to the rise in anti-military attitudes among so many individuals and groups in the country. The worse the hate-the-military cries became, the more convinced I became that my continued involvement as a reservist was important. When asked by incredulous friends why I would want to stay associated with the military when I was not obligated to, my answer always began with: "If not me, then who?"

Speaking Up

During the Vietnam War, I even went so far as to make talks at local high schools in support of the military. They were disturbing experiences. There was, however, one thing that made the talks worthwhile. At the end of the sessions and the acrimonious Q&A follow-ups, there inevitably were a number of students who approached me, usually self-consciously, to thank me for bringing a very different view of the U.S. military to them. The students often went on to say that I had provided a view that contrasted sharply from everything they were hearing from their teachers and from the media on a daily basis.

In addition to the talks at schools, I became a frequent interviewee on the Barry Farber late night syndicated radio show that was broadcast on AM radio station WOR in New York City. Barry Farber was and continues to be a brilliant radio personality and his shows were shaped by his rational and balanced approach to the emotionally charged issues of the time. One of the positives about those appearances was that, based on Barry's handling of the show, I ended the sessions considerably smarter than I had started them. The occasional e-mails that Barry Farber and I still exchange are a happy reminder of his unique talents as a broadcast journalist.

An Extra Dimension

One of the most important aspects of my post-*Sarasota* and *Saratoga* reserve affiliations was that my reserve career added a dimension to my life that would have otherwise been missing. On an ongoing basis it opened a window to the strategic role of sea power in geopolitics. It gave me a broader perspective of the sea than I had developed during two years at sea in *Sarasota*. British author Peter Padfield expressed one particular view of how profound the sea has been in our history and way of thinking, as well as how it affects our own lives and times:

> Maritime supremacy is the key which unlocks most, if not all, large questions of modern history, certainly the puzzle of how and why we—the Western democracies—are as we are. [13]

Over the course of my periodic active duty assignments as a reservist, I was exposed to a wide range of situations that enhanced my awareness of how sea power was affecting the security and prosperity of America. For example a reserve assignment with the U.S. military mission to the United Nations advanced my understanding of how international treaties and agreements are part of a global geopolitical dynamic that has significant impact on our daily lives. An assignment in the office of the Chief of Naval Operations gave me insights into the special leadership qualities of the people leading the world's most powerful navy. In another instance, an assignment with the U.S. Navy Construction Battalion Center in Davisville, RI gave me insights into planning for a mission to Antarctica.

Assignments with operating forces, such as the staff of Commander Sixth Fleet, expanded my understanding of the strategic importance of the Mediterranean to U.S. security and the importance of forward deployed naval forces in advancing U.S. interests around the world. An assignment on the staff of Submarine Group Two furthered my understanding of the strategic and tactical facts of life in the U.S. Navy's "Silent Service." A strategic studies assignment at the Naval War College brought me in contact with some of the most promising officers of the Navy, Marine Corps, Army, Air Force and foreign militaries. And an assignment in the office of the Oceanographer of the Navy helped me to connect basic scientific knowledge to military capabilities.

On and on it went for more than 30 years as a U.S. Navy Reserve officer, with each assignment, each challenge expanding my knowledge of different aspects of sea power, while also demonstrating there was more to learn about the geopolitical aspects of the world's seas.

Extra Dimensions

They say that travel is a fringe benefit that goes with a U.S. Navy career, and my experience proved what they say. One example was my assignment with the staff of Commander, U.S. Sixth Fleet in the spring of 1970. It was a time when the Cold War was in full swing, and my assignment was professionally interesting, but there were also some personal, non-military aspects to what I was doing that have stuck in my memory.

At that time the Sixth Fleet staff was embarked in USS *Little Rock*, which was homeported in Gaeta, Italy. I had one day off during my two-week tour and decided to use the day to go to Rome. I had never been there, and I was anxious to take advantage of the opportunity to visit. Gaeta is about 125 miles south of Rome and I decided to take the train.

Aboard the train I found myself in a compartment with a young couple with several small children. Quickly I was adopted. The magic word was "American." They spoke no English and I spoke no Italian, but we somehow managed to communicate. Words like "bambino," "familia," and "New York" combined with gestures and facial expressions that reflected good humor made for a surprisingly enjoyable conversation. When we parted at the station in Rome, it was as if we were blood relatives. The experience must have been transformational for me, and I must have actually taken on the look of a Roman during my experience on the train. As I walked away from my adoptive family, I was stopped to two Italian nuns asking me for directions.

I spent the entire day walking through the ancient city, and apart from the tourist sites there were two aspects of my visit to Rome that still stand out. The first was lunch in a small neighborhood restaurant. The food was outstanding and the fact that I spoke no Italian and the waiters spoke no English only seemed to add more good humor to the day.

The second thing I particularly remember from my day in Rome is sitting in a sidewalk café on Via Veneto in the late afternoon, enjoying an espresso and watching the passing scene. It seemed the ideal way to "process" what I had absorbed.

"You first, Captain..."

My reserve assignments were varied in interesting ways. In some instances, for example, the mode of transportation had some unusual aspects. A special assignment with the U.S. Navy's Second Fleet in 1977 was an example. The assignment involved producing a short film about the people, missions, and significance of the U.S. Navy's Second Fleet. It was basically an internal communications piece for the men and women attached to that force. I had a group of six Navy film specialists assigned to the project, none of whom I knew before the morning we met for three day's shooting aboard the missile destroyer USS *Dahlgren*. We rendezvoused for the assignment at the former U.S. Navy base at Roosevelt Roads, Puerto Rico.

There was a cameraman, an audio man, and four technical assistants in the group. I think the oldest might have been twenty two or twenty three years old. At the time, I was in my forties and was a captain. There was a bit of awkwardness as we introduced ourselves—nothing really unusual, just a natural hesitation when a team that has been operating as a unit is suddenly assigned to a fast-moving project with a leader they have never met.

The shooting was scheduled aboard *Dahlgren* during a period of missile training, possibly fifty miles or so out in the Atlantic. I had lined up a helicopter flight from Roosevelt Roads to the ship. On paper it was just "another Navy day at the office." In fact it turned out to be somewhat more.

My initial assumption was that we would be put down on a helicopter pad aboard the destroyer. Then I learned that there was no heli pad on *Dahlgren*, so we, along with our equipment, would have to be lowered on a cable onto the ship's small fantail. Fortunately it was a clear day. The bad news was that it also was windy and there were heavy seas running.

On the way out to the ship, we were briefed on the disembarking procedure by a member of the heli crew. It was pretty straightforward. A harness was slipped over your head and under your arms. The harness was hooked to a cable. You sat at the edge of the helicopter door and slid out. You were then winched down until you were on the deck.

When we got over *Dahlgren*, one of my crew—probably all of nineteen years old—looked up, smiled benevolently and said: "You first captain." It was one of those small but defining moments, seemingly unimportant but filled with implications. If I had hesitated, it would have bent my relationship with my team. I knew better, stood up, got into the harness, hooked on, sat at the edge of the heli door, and on "go" from the heli crewmember slid over the edge.

The helicopter was perhaps forty feet over the destroyer's stern. The pilot was having some problems holding his position in the gusty winds, and the ship was rolling and pitching significantly. The surface I was headed for was rising and falling about ten feet, while simultaneously rolling from side to side. The heli also had some vertical and horizontal motion of its own. When I first touched the deck, it immediately dropped out from under me. When it returned, the jolt was as if I had hit the ground after jumping out of an upper story of a building.

I was still in pretty good shape, so I managed to complete the drop standing, possibly even making it look as if I did that kind of thing every day. My harness was unhitched and I moved aside for the others and our gear to be lowered.

One of the first things that I noticed as we gathered our gear and went about our assignment was that we were working as if we had been together for a long time. It quickly did become "another Navy day at the office." The situation also was an example of how human relations adjustments at sea are more than a little unpredictable and more than a little out of the ordinary.

Exit

It would be wrong to omit some comments on my retirement from the Navy Reserve. It was of course a matter of some personal satisfaction to have reached the rank of rear admiral. That satisfaction is, however, diluted by several realities. Among the most important is that there are a lot of factors involved in being promoted to admiral, and many of those factors are beyond your own abilities and motivation. Seeking and getting challenging assignments along the way, what the Navy's needs are at given points in one's career, and being in the right place at the right time all enter into the process.

Through my promotions to the rank of commander, I tended to think that advancements in rank were, to a very significant degree, rewards for accomplishments. By the time I was promoted to captain, however, I had begun to realize that it was not so much a reward as a matter of the Navy having more challenging assignments for me and consequently giving me the additional authority needed to get the job done. The main factor in a promotion had become less a matter of what had been done and more a matter of what needed to done. The title "admiral" and the additional authority connected to it were not a reward but a means to an end.

Role Models

Since there is no school for learning how to be an admiral, I was fortunate in having a number of outstanding role models who were career naval officers. There was Admiral John ("Profane") McCain, Naval Academy graduate, submarine officer, former Commander-in-Chief Pacific, and member of a distinguished U.S. Navy family that includes his son Senator John McCain and his grandfather Admiral John "Slew" McCain, who was a World War II naval aviation leader.

I first met Admiral McCain when I was a lieutenant, junior grade, and over the years I worked on a variety of projects that again brought me into contact with him. Those contacts gave me an opportunity to realize the incredible dedication he had to his country and to the U.S. Navy. They also demonstrated how colorful adjectives can be used to clarify a point.

There also was Admiral Joe Metcalf III, a Naval Academy graduate whom I had the privilege of knowing during the latter part of my career. When I first met Admiral Metcalf he was Deputy Chief of Naval Operations for Surface Warfare. Previously, he had commanded the joint U.S. military rescue operation in Granada in October/December 1983. During the Granada operation, Admiral Metcalf led a hastily assembled, joint services U.S. force in an operation that rescued many innocent Americans and for which there was no prepared plan. He had the ability to focus on what was really important in terms of the interests of his country and fellow citizens, no matter the situation or the distractions, and in that context I benefited from my friendship with him.

Vice Admiral Bob Dunn is a Naval Academy graduate and one of the Navy's leading combat pilot veterans of the Vietnam War, when he flew 500 combat missions. As the Chief of the Navy Reserve, he was my reporting senior during much of my final tour as a reservist. My initial meeting with Admiral Dunn was in 1983. We discussed my new reserve mobilization assignment as Deputy Chief of Information and Director of the Navy Reserve Public Affairs Program. He asked what I hoped to accomplish in my new job, and after I responded, he established an unbureaucratic reporting relationship. I simply was to write an informal letter to him each month, describing what I was doing. It was an approach that demonstrated his confidence in my abilities from the start of our relationship, and it facilitated my ability to focus on the essentials on my job, rather than paperwork.

Rear Admiral Bruce Newell was the Chief of Naval Information during almost all of my tour of reserve duty as the senior Navy Reserve member of the Navy's Public Affairs community. He also was a Naval Academy Graduate, a Surface Warfare officer, and a qualified nuclear propulsion officer who had held significant commands at sea, including command of the nuclear powered cruiser USS *Bainbridge*. He also had served as the Navy's Chief of Legislative Affairs. Admiral Newell consistently demonstrated that he had a "One Navy" approach to the relationship between the Navy's active and reserve components. That was critical in my new assignment. We remain friends today.

One of the most important role models in my career as a reservist was Rear Admiral Sig Bajak. Sig was fellow reservist who was an executive at NBC-TV. He was also a Naval Aviator and at one point he commanded a Naval Air Reserve anti-submarine warfare squadron. At another point, when I was commanding officer of a reserve unit in New York City, he was my reporting senior. Sig was very low key and he also was very wise in the ways of the U.S. Navy. I tried to listen a lot when I was with him and learned a lot in the process.

And although I never knew him well, I was privileged to have served as a young officer while Admiral Arleigh Burke was the Chief of Naval Operations in the late 1950s and early 60s. It was Admiral Burke, who earned a reputation as a destroyer commander and squadron leader during World War II, who once observed that the main difference between a good naval officer and a great naval officer was about ten seconds.

Maintaining Perspective

One of the best lessons in how to maintain perspective as a flag officer that I ever received came from Rear Admiral Norman "Bulldog" Coleman, a fellow reservist from Colorado. Bulldog was a few years older than I was, and he was recently retired from the Navy when I was promoted to rear admiral. He wrote a nice letter of congratulations to me on my selection for flag rank, and it was the last few lines of that letter that have stuck with me. He wrote: "Finally, remember two things. One, hit the track running, because it will be over before you know it. Two, as an admiral, you ain't never going to hear the truth again."

There was a conversation with my wife Sally that serves as a sort of bookend with Bulldog Coleman's wisdom. Sally and I were sitting in our living room, discussing my imminent retirement from the Navy Reserve. She commented on how much I was going to miss the challenges and the people with whom I had been involved. I agreed that they would indeed be missed, but that it was a matter of turning over a new page in life and learning new things.

Sally's response was, "You know, you're right about the importance of learning new things, and the first new thing you are going to have to learn is how to take orders again."

PART III
SAILING
WHAT I LEARNED IN BOATS

Chapter Eleven
The Dyer Dinghy

For one thing, I was no longer alone; a man is never alone with the wind—and the boat made three.

Hilaire Belloc

When I returned to civilian life in 1954 the focus was on my family and getting a career in advertising started. It was probably five more years before I was able to even think about sailing. And by then there was a mortgage on a house in Croton-on-Hudson, about thirty-five miles from New York City, and a growing group of kids. Joe had been born in 1953 and Jim was born in 1954. Mary Ellen, my third child, was born in 1956 and Kathleen, my fourth, was born in 1958. Patricia arrived in 1962. It was an astonishing experience to welcome each of them into the world, and dealing with each of the five maturing personalities was a joy and a challenge.

With the house, I had joined the ranks of the millions who commute to and from New York City each day. The trip by train along the Hudson River and into Grand Central Station provided productive thinking time, but it also was time consuming.

The Dinghy

The answer to reestablishing my contact with the sea, despite the financial demands and time limitations of those years, was a 10-foot Dyer sailing dinghy.[14] She was a pretty thing, with a nicely designed fiberglass hull, just a bit of varnished oak trim and a single red sail. There was a minimum of maintenance required, and the only additional equipment I needed was a trailer to get the boat frm its storage spot to the launching ramp. I built the trailer myself with two-by-fours and wheels from a shopping cart.

I thought of naming the boat "Spindrift," which means windblown sea spray, but never seemed to have time to paint the name on the boat's transom.

The Dyer dinghy was boating at its most basic level. Usually I sailed the dinghy by myself, and when you are sailing a dinghy, the only way to get closer to the water is to swim. That special proximity with the water was part of the fascination—and the challenge.

It turned out that the dinghy sailing also provided me with an ideal opportunity for serious thinking. I found that, for some reason, it was possible to focus on the sailing while other matters were being processed in my mind. At a time when the combined pressures of family and job were mounting, a few hours in the dinghy on a Saturday or Sunday were more than enjoyable, they were therapeutic.

During the spring, summer, and fall, the dinghy was kept at Senasqua Park, which was on the Hudson River about a mile from my house in Croton. If I looked out a window at home and studied the wind in the tops of the trees, I could tell quickly if it was a good sailing day. From that evaluation to the time I was wheeling my boat down the concrete ramp and into the water would take no more than twenty minutes.

Once afloat and alongside the pier, it was only a matter of a few minutes more before the rudder and tiller were shipped, the centerboard was lowered, the sail hoisted and the dinghy and I were easing off into the waves to see what the wind and water had to offer that day.

Because it was so small, the dinghy was very sensitive to the sailing conditions of the day. A strong gust of wind that would simply drive a larger sailboat faster could capsize the dingy. Skills like "reading" the surface of the water upwind to know when a strong gust was heading towards the boat were essential.

Watching sailboats upwind also was a way of "going to school" on the wind strength I would be dealing with in a few minutes.

In addition, acute sensitivity to the feel of the tiller was crucial, and there were constant signals transmitted through that medium. In short, there was virtually no margin of error when sailing the dinghy, and in anything from moderate to strong winds, consistent focus was required. The price of a lack of that kind of attention could well be an upside down boat.

The Setting

The sailing area off Senasqua Park—about ten square miles of open water—is called Haverstraw Bay, and it's the widest point in the Hudson River. One of the best features of the River at that point is that the water is still salt water. That gave the sailing much more of the feel of the sea than if it had been a fresh-water lake. The difference between sailing on fresh water and salt water is hard to articulate. But when you get it, you get it.

There is a series of high cliffs along the western shore of the Bay, and backing the Bay along its eastern shore, where I lived, are rolling hills, lush and green in the spring and summer and spectacularly alive with color in the autumn. It was an ideal venue for dinghy sailing. And there was a bonus: a day of sailing in Haverstraw Bay was often capped with a spectacular sunset behind the cliffs to the west.

There were several old wooden barges that had been grounded end-to-end in the shallow water along the edge of the river as a breakwater for Senasqua Park and its small beach. At times after sailing the dinghy for a few hours, I would climb out on the barges and sit quietly, with only my sailbag as company, and watch the sunset. After one such day, I recorded the experience in the journal I had started after my tour at sea with the U.S. Navy:

The strong breeze driving out of the northeast during the afternoon had softened. The day's sun had only a few minutes of life left and faced me like a huge, fiery Cyclops eye. Streaks of thin clouds paralleled the tops of the cliffs on the facing shore, covering portions of the sun. As the sun sank, the clouds went from wispy gray to jet black. The sky behind the cliffs backed the scene with implausible golds and reds.

I've seen a lot of sunsets—in the open ocean, among tropical islands, from pine-rimmed lakes, from aircraft, and from mountain tops—but their fascination never fades. I've thought about that and realized that the raw beauty involved is only half of the enjoyment. The other half is that the sunset introduces the night, and I have always liked the night. Even as a young child, I had not feared the dark.

It's a time of recovery and discovery.

Capsized

The wind and water conditions in Haverstraw Bay can change quickly, but in all the years I sailed there, I only capsized the dinghy once. It was a notable experience, and it was another event recorded in my journal:

It was a fine stiff breeze, and I was enjoying it to the fullest. Then I was in the water so quickly, I hardly realized what had happened. I had been tearing along on a port reach when a gust hit. I slacked the sail a bit and started to ease up into the wind. The gust intensified. The outer tip of the boom dipped into the water. Instantly a wave broke over the stern, and the boat was swamped.

When I cleared the water from my eyes, my first thought was for the boat and the equipment—basically a couple of life-preserver cushions—which had already begun to float away in the choppy water. The floating items were gathered quickly and tied to the stern of the boat, several inches of the port side of the transom showed above water. The boat was actually on her side and a bit down by the bow, with the mast and sail just below the surface and the port quarter showing above the water.

'This mess is going to be a bitch to tow,' was my initial thought. The first thing was to get the sail down. I couldn't quite reach the cleat where the halyard was secured, so I had to dive—only a few feet—to get to the cleat. The halyard seemed iron-hard in my hands as I worked the line underwater.

It took me three tries before the halyard was free. Slowly I worked the sail down the mast slot until it was almost free. Two more short dives and the sail was free at all points. I was getting tired but still working within myself.

I didn't notice the small outboard skiff until it was almost on top of me. It took a few minutes to convince my two "rescuers" that I was OK. Then the sail and the loose gear went into the skiff. Next I went underwater again, this time to get my bow line and secure it to the skiff.

As they began to tow the boat, it continued to lie on its side and the forward motion actually was tending to submerge the boat even farther. Dragging the mostly submerged dinghy through the water was putting a tremendous amount of strain on the bow line and the small ringbolt to which it was attached. It would not do.

We stopped and I went back into the water. After several dives, I managed to get the bow line off the ringbolt. I then took it to a lifting ring attached to the transom, and we resumed the tow, this time the dinghy was being dragged stern first. It was slow, but nothing tore lose and eventually we reached shallow water and a small beach.

Once on the beach, I was able to get the centerboard up the rudder unshipped and the boat righted. My first step was to spread the sail on the sand and to begin drying it—and me—in the sun.

It took about ten minutes to bail the boat dry, and I then sat on the beach to rest. I was happy to have gotten the boat to shore without damage. When the sail was dry, I got the boat out into shallow water, got in and quickly got the centerboard down, shipped the rudder and tiller, rehoisted the sail, and sailed off.

There was still a fine stiff breeze and I enjoyed it to the fullest on the way home.

Nobody's Perfect

One of the most positive aspects about the dinghy was that it provided an opportunity to teach my children how to sail. Because of the dinghy's smallness, all lessons were one-on-one. There was one particularly noteworthy session with my daughter Mary Ellen.

The normal routine for sailing the dinghy began with rolling the boat down the concrete ramp in its trailer and then paddling it over the short distance to the floating dock. At the dock, the sail was bent on and the centerboard lowered and the rudder shipped. Normally, within minutes I would have shoved off the dock, hauled in the sheet, and sailed way.

Until the boat was actually shoved off from the dock, it was essential for the sheet to be unsecured. On the day in question, all of the preparations went smoothly, until just before getting into the boat. At that point there was a particularly strong gust of wind. The mainsheet snagged and the gust actually capsized the boat at the dock.

The incident became known among my children as "the day Dad dumped the boat at the dock." And it was always repeated with a broad grin.

Going No Place on Purpose

There was something about my sailing in Haverstraw Bay that occurred to me after my first few ventures out in the dinghy: I was never sailing *to* anyplace. There was no destination for the sailing except to return to my starting point at Senasqua. In the years that I sailed the dinghy in Haverstraw Bay, I never put foot ashore anyplace but the place where I started—except for the day I capsized the boat.

When sailing the dinghy, I wasn't trying to *get* anyplace. The sole purpose of what I was doing was to *sail*.

Under those circumstances, I could take exactly what I wanted from the wind and the water. If I felt like reaching before the wind for a while, I could do that. If I wanted to beat into the wind for a while, I could do that. There was a special sense of liberation in those circumstances. I could get together with the boat, the wind, and the water any way that I wished and the circumstances encouraged.

That sense of liberation contributed to my ability to use the dinghy sailing as thinking time, and in its way, the dinghy sailing helped me to think through some difficult times. By 1975, my first marriage was in serious trouble and by 1976, my first wife and I were separated. It was a time when I found survival in and at my work.

I didn't realize it at the time, but while sailing alone in the dinghy in Haverstraw Bay my small boat had been a refuge. She had become a private place of sanctuary and renewal.

CHAPTER TWELVE
BRITISH VIRGIN ISLANDS I

A very peaceful and hopeful place that should give all adventurers great satisfaction...

Captain N. Butler (circ. 1637)

My discovery of the British Virgin Islands in November 1976 came at a time when I was living alone on East 49th Street in New York City in an efficiency apartment. I had just completed an exhausting assignment as line producer for a new, thirteen-episode children's series at the NBC TV network called *Muggsy*. After eight months of fourteen-hour days and seven-day work weeks shooting on location and editing back at NBC in Rockefeller Center, I was ready for a major break—not just a relief from physical fatigue, but something that would repair an overstressed mind.

During production of the children's TV series, the technical director for the production, Heino Ripp, had casually mentioned a new kind of sailboat chartering operation that he had tried out. And as production on the series was winding down, I got more of the details from "Rippy." What he described was a special approach to cruising (in contrast to racing) sailing that was beginning to emerge in the British Virgin Islands. It was called a bareboat charter. In those days it was a new concept, but subsequently bareboat chartering has become a worldwide phenomenon for sailors who want to do some serious cruising sailing without devoting the time and money to boat ownership.

This different approach to sailing involved chartering a nicely designed and well maintained boat that was provisioned to the charterer's individual order and that you walked away from when your cruise ended—all at about the cost for the same number of days at a good hotel in the Caribbean. That combination, plus the fascination of the relatively unknown British Virgin Islands, sounded like a perfect arrangement for me at the time. So I decided to give it a try, along with my friend and boss at NBC, George Heinemann, and another friend, Sally McElwreath.

Beyond Expectations

The first leg of our journey, the flight from New York City into San Juan, was routine. On the other hand, the second leg from San Juan into the British Virgin Islands' Beef Island Airport was definitely not a routine matter. It involved a small, single engine plane, with one of the five passengers sitting in the copilot's seat. The pilot looked, and acted, like a character from a Humphrey Bogart movie.

The flight east past St. Thomas and St. John islands didn't last much more than thirty minutes, and it ended with our plane banking sharply and then dropping down perilously close to a mountainside for our final approach. The landing on a heart-stoppingly short runway ended abruptly at the water's edge.[15] It was an attention-getting arrival at a place that I would return to many times over the years, a place where most things were done on "island time."

What I found in the British Virgin Islands, which are located just east of St. John and just north of latitude eighteen, was unspoiled and exotic. The sea was omnipresent; it dominated sight and mind.

A Mix of History and Astonishing Beauty

The Islands' known history began with the Arawak and Carib Indians, who had gradually moved northward from the Orinoco basin of South America. That early history then expanded when Columbus became the first European to find the area during his second voyage of discovery in 1493. The Islands were subsequently colonized by the Dutch, Spanish, French, Swedes, Danes, and ultimately the British, and names like Cabot, Drake, and Hawkins and legendary pirates such as Morgan, Blackbeard and Mary Read are 'writ large' in the area's history.

The mini-sea at the center of the fifty-plus islands is known as the Sir Francis Drake Channel. Only twenty or so of the islands are occupied and some of those that are occupied count no more than a score of inhabitants. The local architecture was strictly low-rise and was very comfortable with its environment.

The largest of the British Virgin Islands is Tortola, a Spanish word meaning "land of the turtle dove," and it's roughly eleven miles long and approximately three miles wide at its middle. It tapers to narrower points at each end. A main road hugs the south shore of the island and runs from the Beef Island Airport at the east end to the Sopers Hole anchorage at the west end of the island. From the airport, we traveled the main road in an open jitney-type bus, wending its way between Tortola's rugged and mountainous interior on our right and the beckoning sea to our left.

The names of Tortola's settlements I passed on the way, along with other places I would come across while sailing in the area, unleashed my imagination: Fat Hog's Bay, Maya Cove, Brandywine Bay, Sea Cow Bay, Nanny Cay, Pockwood Pond Fort, Frenchman's Cay, Sopers Hole, Smuggler's Cove, Apple Bay, Shark Bay, Rogue's Point, Pull and Be Damned Point, Throw Way Wife Bay, Mother Hagal Bay, and The Last Resort, the latter being no more than a single-story restaurant with a reputation for raucous entertainment perched on a miniscule island not much larger than the building that occupied it.

The construction of the buildings along the road from the airport was a mixture of reinforced concrete, wood, and stone. Later I would learn that some of the Islands' stone buildings were built with the ballast taken from the holds of the sailing ships that brought the first European settlers and the first African slaves to Tortola.

A relaxed conversation with the jitney driver began my education on the unique culture—initially based on sugar plantations and now focused on tourism—we were entering. And that education continued with the same driver and others on subsequent trips to the BVI.

Clusters of vivid tropical flowers punctuated the roadside panorama that continued to slide past us, but when all was said and done, it was the sea and the boats and ships—ranging from sailboats to small inter-island ferries and small cargo ships—that dominated the sense of place I was absorbing.

After a final blind curve along a cliff that dropped straight into the sea, the road quickly dove back down to sea level, and we were delivered to Caribbean Sailing Yachts, which was at the time one of the two bareboat charter companies in the BVI. The CSY base was located in a single, two-story building at the edge of Road Town, the BVI's only real town and coincidentally its main harbor.

After check-in at the base, my first day in the BVI was capped with an outstanding dinner at a small, nearby restaurant called Maria's, where Maria told you in person what was available that night and then cooked and served the meal herself.

The Briefings

After breakfast the next day, the first order of business was a chart briefing by Simon Scott, one of the sailors who pioneered bareboat chartering the in the BVI.[16] The briefing began with a very quick oversight of the BVIs. Tortola, we learned, had been the BVI's capitol since 1741. It was also pointed out that the BVI's second largest island is Virgin Gorda—Spanish for "fat virgin." The name was given to the island by Christopher Columbus in 1493, probably after three or four glasses of Madeira. Virgin Gorda is about ten miles long. Mountain peaks dominate its north and central sections, and its main feature for sailors is Gorda (or North) Sound, where charterers had three options for an anchorage: Drake's Anchorage, the Bitter End and Biras Creek.

Since that initial visit, a fourth area for charterers to overnight was established at Leverick Bay.

The entrance to Gorda Sound is guarded by a large, dangerous reef that is just below water level. It was casually pointed out that the channel into Gorda Sound was completely unmarked by any buoys or other navigational aids, and in fact, the same was true for all of the anchorage entrances in the BVI. The lack of any navigational aids in the area added one more adventurous dimension to the sailing, and it was a special aspect of the BVIs that has been missed since the addition of buoys to mark a number of the area's more threatening approaches to anchorages. And as it turned out, during daylight the channel into Gorda sound was not too difficult to spot as it was approached. At night without buoys it would have been virtually impossible to see.

The briefing went on to describe the other anchorages used by charter boats, ending with the third largest island, Jost Van Dyke, named for the seventeenth-century Dutch pirate who operated from a base there. At the time we first sailed to Jost Van Dyke, there were five overnight and day anchorages along the Islands south shore. Like Tortola and Virgin Gorda, Jost Van Dyke is mountainous, but it's much smaller than those two islands, measuring only about four miles in length. A special feature of Jost Van Dyke described in the briefing was Foxy's Bar in Great Harbor, where Foxy and his guitar held forth long into the night.

Two additional features ashore on Jost Van Dyke included Abe's by the Sea in Little Harbor, which over the years has become a personal choice for the BVI's best island-style chicken and lobster, and the Soggy Dollar Bar in White Bay, named for the bar patron who swam ashore from his boat for a beer.

One of the main points emerging from our briefing was the variety of the anchorages and marinas scattered among the many Islands. Some are relatively large and have shops and restaurants ashore; others are small and isolated from land activity. Each anchorage has a story to tell. Some of the stories are part of the BVI's written or oral histories. Some are told by the anchorages themselves, when one is really paying attention. Marina Cay and Little Harbor on Jost Van Dyke are examples of the latter

There also are countless beaches and scuba diving sites. The best known of the dive sites is The Wreck of the Rhone, named for the British Royal Mail steamer that was caught between two of the BVI's smaller islands in a vicious hurricane in 1865. The ship had found refuge in Great Harbor, Peter Island and as the eye of the storm passed over, her captain decided to make a dash for the relative safety of the open sea. It was a bad decision and as the full fury of the storm struck again, the ship was hurled onto the rocky western shore of Salt Island, where she broke up and then sank, with the total loss of her passengers and crew.

Later in the course of that first visit to the British Virgin Islands, I met George and Luana Marler, who were professional divers, and who were at that time operating a dive school in the British Virgin Islands. They were very familiar with the *Rhone,* and in 1978 I wrote a foreword for their book about scuba diving at the site:

> Ships are like people in many ways, for example, sometimes they become better known after death, and it is the quality of their death that gives special meaning to their lives. As nature took her back, *Rhone* assumed a new beauty. She became a brilliant display piece of marine life. Now with the advent of underwater photography and scuba diving, more and more people have learned to look at *Rhone*—and learn.

The Marler's book *The Royal Mail Steamer Rhone* can still be found in the British Virgin Islands' dive shops and recently George and Luana published a new, expanded edition of the book.

Under Way

Because I had not sailed in the BVIs before, CSY required that I take a local skipper with us. It was agreed, however, that he would be put ashore as soon as he was confident of my ability to handle the boat and the local conditions. Immediately after the chart briefing, we were introduced to the local skipper who would be with us. He was a pleasant, no-nonsense Englishman named Alan Allmark.

Alan and his wife were on their way from England to Australia in a 30-foot sailboat. At that point they were spending a few months in the BVI, before moving on through the Caribbean and Panama Canal to the Pacific Ocean. Alan took us through a thorough boat briefing aboard the boat we would sail and live in for the next eight days, a sturdy but graceful 34-foot sloop named *Breezin' Up*. Then we were ready to go.

Breezen' Up was secured stern to the pier with an anchor off the bow. Alan slacked off the stern lines and his first order was, "Joe, I'll have the anchor up now." It was a line I'll never forget, for the tone with which it was delivered as well as its implications. Allan's tone was clipped, and there was no doubt what he wanted or about when he wanted it. In addition the general implications— considering the pleasure I would experience and knowledge I would gain in the BVI in coming years—were immense.

In moments we were free of the land. We left the base on our engine and within ten minutes we were clear of the harbor and had set our mainsail and genoa. The surge of the boat as the engine was shut down and the wind took hold of her was special. The memory of my feelings at that moment is still clear.

For the next two days I got to know *Breezin' Up* and the local sea conditions, and after two days of sailing and two successful anchorings, we put Alan ashore. I assume that he and his wife eventually reached Australia safely, and I have a feeling that they might still be on their way to somewhere in their boat even today.

Daily Discoveries

During that first bareboat charter, we overnighted in a wide variety of different anchorages each night. The unique beauty among the different locations was astonishing, and each had its own personality. Some, like the U-shaped anchorage at The Bight at Norman Island and Little Harbor at Jost Van Dyke, were sheltered by surrounding hillsides that created a sense of calm isolation. Others such as Manchioneel Bay were more open, more boisterous, and provided dramatic vistas. And there was Marina Cay, nestled behind a reef at the end of a long bay. The anchorage was swept by the prevailing winds but the reef that broke down the waves being driven into bay. The result was a refreshingly cool and pleasantly calm overnight. For a number of years there also was a pleasant restaurant perched at the top of the hill that was Marina Cay. Over the years to come, I also discovered that Marina Cay was the habitat of a resident barracuda that liked to linger under the boats and dinghies in the anchorage.

Most of the evening meals centered on the boat's hibachi that was rigged over the stern railing. There also was a memorable lunch ashore at a small restaurant just off the beach and tucked into a lush hillside at Manchioneel Bay, where Sally discovered shepherd's pie. And just as we had begun to settle into a more basic sailors' routine, there was an astonishing five-star dinner at The Old Yard Inn near Spanish Town on Virgin Gorda. There, over a gourmet meal elegantly presented on an elegantly set table in a candle lit room, we quietly marveled at the profound beauty of the Caribbean corner that we were exploring.

As fascinating as the environment was, it was the first few days of actual sailing that are primary in my memory. I couldn't believe the degree of joy I experience sailing a good boat in the steady 18- 20 knots of wind and in the incredibly beautiful surroundings of the British Virgin Islands. It was discovery of a kind and magnitude I hadn't anticipated and I sailed myself into a state of near exhaustion each day, partly from exertion and partly from the intensity of the experience.

I doubt if Alan was aware of what was really going on with me during the first few days he was with us; he was strictly business and was intent on evaluating my abilities. But I believe that Sally grasped what was going on, and I was glad of that.

Trouble in Paradise

There were some challenges as our initial trip to the BVI unfolded. The most testing occurred about mid-point through the charter. We had begun to feel that we knew *Breezin' Up* and were comfortable in our surroundings. We had spent the previous night at Little Harbor at Jost Van Dyke. It was a small, quiet anchorage, ringed on three sides by steep hillsides and open to the sea on the fourth. It was a perfect place for relaxing and reviewing what we had experienced up to that point.

The next morning we headed to nearby Green Cay, a sandy dot in the cobalt waters, for a morning swim, snorkeling, and a relaxed lunch in the boat. After lunch we left for Cane Garden Bay on the north shore of Tortola, a short, straightforward reach of four nautical miles. What should have been the easiest leg of our BVI odyssey turned into something else.

We left Green Cay on our engine, then as we began to get our mainsail up, the halyard snagged under the masthead light. The obvious solution was to continue on the engine into Cane Garden Bay, anchor there and then sort out the halyard problem.

About halfway there, things took an ugly turn; without any warning the engine quit. Later we learned that a fuel line had clogged, but at the moment all I knew was that I was equidistant between Tortola and Jost Van Dyke with no engine, no mainsail, winds gusting at more than twenty knots and five-to-six-foot seas running.

Luckily I had some sea room, and the next move was obvious: we set the genoa jib, limped back to Green Cay and anchored. I had picked Green Cay, which was about the same distance from Cane Garden Bay as Little Harbor at Jost Van Dyke, because it was upwind. And I had learned at a young age that when there is trouble in a sailboat, it's best to work out the problem as far upwind as possible. Then it was up the mast to free the snagged halyard.

The second attempt at the four-mile transit, this time under mainsail and genoa, was uneventful, but as we approached Cane Garden Bay, I faced a new problem: the narrow entrance to the anchorage was between two submerged reefs that came close to joining at one point but that left a very narrow opening about twenty the thirty feet wide into the harbor. And since both reefs are submerged, it was virtually impossible to define the narrow channel as we approached.

As pointed out in the boat briefing, there were no buoys to mark the channel. To further complicate matters, as we got under the lee of the shore and approached the narrow opening between the two reefs, there was only the slightest suggestion of a breeze and it was an offshore breeze dead on our nose.

After what seemed like an interminable series of extremely short tacks and some intense "reading" of the shallow waters from the bow by George, we ghosted into the small anchorage and dropped the hook.

Our reward was commensurate with our struggle to get to Cane Garden Bay: an idyllic anchorage dominated by a sandy, crescent beach, palm trees and steep, green mountainsides holding it all together. The only interruptions to the natural panorama were two small beach bars, Stanley's, with a signature swing fashioned with a rubber tire hung from one of the slanting palm trees that leaned over the beach in front of the bar, and Jill's about fifty yards along the beach. There was also a deserted rum distillery. All three were tucked into the palm trees and foliage that rimmed the beach.

That evening, after our mechanical misadventures, we had a robust dinner at Stanley's, while watching a spectacular sunset behind Jost Van Dyke. Then we went to sleep to the sound of steel drums drifting out over the anchorage from Stanley's, where some with more stamina danced into the night.

The last time we visited Cane Garden Bay, Stanley's was still there at the center of things, virtually unchanged. On occasion we still go there for the native cooking and wide open, westward-looking location that provides incredible sunsets. Jill's was long gone, unfortunately, and today Cane Garden Bay is rimmed by houses, restaurants and a small two-story hotel that's marked by its chaise lounges and beach umbrellas. The anchorage has been developed a lot, but it's still beautiful. And now there are buoys marking the entrance channel!

The following day the engine was repaired by a mechanic who drove over the mountain from the CSY base in Road Town, and we moved on for the balance of our first trip in the British Virgin

Islands and our last overnight at The Bight at Norman Island, fittingly the anchorage where I began my BVI odyssey.

On 27 November 1976, my final log entries read:

0915 Prepare to depart The Bight, Norman Island, engine won't start, battery dead—no showers—no radio.
0920 Prepare to get underway under sail, wait for heavy squall to pass.
0930 Hoist anchor, under sail for Road Town, starboard tack and starboard reach into Road Town harbor.
1100 Make buoy at CSY under sail, commence check-out.
1200 Secure.

On that final day, *Breezin' Up* and the local weather seemed to be a little contrary, but my interpretation was along different lines. I chose to think that the boat and the weather were telling me "Don't go."

The Ultimate Test

On the flight home, there was a lot to sort out in my mind about my first sailing experience in the British Virgin Islands. There was the exotic beauty of the place, the warmth of the British Virgin Islanders, the special challenge of sailing in an area with absolutely no navigation aids, dealing with the mechanical problems in the boat, and the incredible variety of the individual anchorages.

Gradually another aspect of the experience began to dawn on me: spending a week in a boat with other people requires a lot of adjusting. The close quarters and inability to escape the confines of those quarters can create frictions. Personal idiosyncrasies that might be amusing, even charming, in an office or in a house can become major irritants in the tight confines of a boat, where there is no escape. Of greatest importance there has to be an ultimate authority on sailing matters, particularly on issues that relate to safety. Sailing is very, very enjoyable, but it's not a game. And it's definitely not safe without basic rules of behavior.

At the same time, however, eight days living in a boat can demonstrate positive traits, such as patience, control of one's emotions under pressure, and the ability to react immediately to fast-changing circumstances. Those were things that rose above congeniality, and they were things about a person that might never come into play under routine shore-side circumstances.

Years after that first trip, Sally summed up how spending time in a sailboat can expose a personality with exceptional clarity: "Spending a week in a sailboat with someone is a pretty good measure of whether or not you could get along in a marriage." And so it would eventually be.

Chapter Thirteen
Hurricane Frederick

An horrid stillness first invades the ear,
And in that silence we the tempest fear.

John Dryden (1631-1700)

In March 1979 Sally and I were married, and later that year we decided to buy a boat. A new boat was not in the budget, but we found an affordable alternative in a second-hand boat with a good pedigree. Her name was *Carmali*. We were told the name was a combination of parts of the first names of the original owner's children.

Carmali had been part of the Caribbean Sailing Yachts bareboat charter fleet for several years and was the same class boat as *Breezin' Up*, the first boat we sailed in the British Virgin Islands. She was also the first boat of her class to come off the production line at Bristol Yacht Company in Providence, Rhode Island, a company with an enduring reputation for building very good fiberglass boats.

Carmali had a white hull and cabin. She was slightly more than thirty-four feet long and had a beam of ten and a half feet. Her lines were graceful, with an aggressive bow, a gentle and pleasing sheer and flat transom. She was a near-perfect combination of grace and strength, both of which had been proven as a charter boat. Her cockpit and cabin were accented with enough varnished "brightwork" to add character and warmth to her overall look. Her sail plan was perhaps slightly undersized for her length and draft, but she was sturdy, went well in all conditions, and could sleep four pretty comfortably. And she was affordable.

Since we had sailed other boats of *Carmali's* class, we knew her basic characteristics, and that was another factor in our decision to buy her. She was designed by well known sailboat designer John Alden, who had coincidentally designed the boat in which I learned to sail, and was an ideal boat for a couple cruising in the West Indies. I quickly learned to love her, notwithstanding the circumstances of our initial meeting on September 1st 1979.

Taking Possession

When we flew to Tortola to take possession of the boat and get in a few days of sailing, Sally and I were accompanied by my son Jim, who was twenty-five years old at the time, and my stepson R.J., who was thirteen years old. Jim was an experienced sailor, having delivered boats to sites ranging from Florida to the Great Lakes for a number of years. Both were physically strong, and as we planned our trip to the British Virgin Islands to pick up the boat, we had no idea how important their strength would prove be.

There was a sense of excitement as we left New York City on the flight to San Juan, the first leg of the trip to the BVI. But the excitement was tempered by the knowledge that there was a hurricane named David headed in the general direction of San Juan. Hurricane David arrived at San Juan at about the same time we did. I believe we were the last flight to make it into Muñoz Marin airport before it was closed.

As a result we spent several days at San Juan's historic El Convento Hotel waiting for Hurricane David to pass through, the city to recover, and the airport to reopen. Despite the fact that there was very little food and no electrical power in the Hotel, we looked upon Hurricane David as a temporary inconvenience. It was just another aspect of the adventure of buying a boat. All we had to do was wait Hurricane David out and then get on to the British Virgin Islands to take possession of *Carmali*. At least that's what we thought.

There was no question that we were safe within the sturdy walls of the 17th century former convent that had withstood

Caribbean hurricanes for more than three centuries. Consequently we took advantage of the circumstances to appreciate our place of refuge. As Hurricane David did its thing, we took the opportunity to walk the halls and study the interior details of El Convento. The structure's graceful arches, courtyard-facing balconies, ancient wooden beams, and handcrafted tiles spoke of the days of Spanish colonialism, a time when religious missionary fervor teamed with imperial ambitions in a drive for discovery and riches in the New World. It was impossible to not feel the presence of those who had reverently walked the same corridors three hundred years ago, and the sense of peace within the former convent's walls contrasted starkly with the violence outside its confines.

When the San Juan airport reopened, it was total chaos, and as we scrambled from airline counter to airline counter, we were unable to find a flight into the British Virgin Islands. After many hours checking and rechecking the small airlines that served the region, we managed to book a flight aboard a small, single engine charter to St. Thomas. At that point, we were at least going in the right direction.

The airport at St. Thomas was even more chaotic than the one at San Juan, and it was a true test of our collective patience. But with admirable equanimity, we were finally able to scout out an inter-island pilot who was willing to get us to the British Virgin Islands. Ragged but happy, we got to the airport at Tortola, caught a taxi into Road Town and the CSY base, and with great anticipation we picked up our "new" boat.

The next morning we shoved off from the CSY dock and began sailing. After a full day of sailing with good wind and crystal clear skies, we learned that there was another hurricane, this one named Frederick, headed in our direction. Before David had struck, the BVI had not experienced a hurricane in 25 years. Now the second hurricane in a week was a real possibility. Notwithstanding the weather issue, we left CSY, sailed up Sir Francis Drake Channel and after a brief stop at The Baths on Virgin Gorda, we wound up at Marina Cay and the east end of Tortola.

The following day we made the very short transit through Camanoe Passage and down the north side of Tortola, heading first for Green Cay and then eventually around the west end of Tortola towards Norman Island. The sailing conditions were perfect, with mostly clear skies and wind in the 18-20 knots range. *Carmali* was in her glory and we thoroughly enjoyed the sailing. As we progressed, however, our regular weather checks on the VHF radio were dampening our spirits.

That night, we anchored at The Bight in Norman Island. There were not a lot of boats in the anchorage, which gave me an uncomfortable feeling. Clearly the news of the oncoming hurricane was spreading, and boats were already heading for shelter. As we tracked the storm, however, it appeared that we had about twenty-four hours before its arrival, and we still had hope that the storm would make a course change towards the north and miss us.

My log for the second of September shows that we had a problem getting the anchor to hold in the Norman Island harbor, and we actually wound up setting two bow anchors before settling in for the night. The difficulty anchoring was a hint of the challenges that were heading towards us from the southeast.

Early on the morning of September 3rd, we checked the weather on our radio and found out that Frederick was continuing to head straight for us. We also radioed the CSY base to discuss our options, and they suggested that we head for Hurricane Hole in St. John. That was the closest protected anchorage—only five and a half nautical miles away—and from the earliest days of the age of sail, Hurricane Hole had been used by seamen during hurricanes.

Unfortunately there was an immediate complication; the engine would not start. We finally gave up on the engine and cleared the anchorage under sail at a little after 0900. We took a quick look into Hurricane Hole, and I didn't like what I saw. For one thing the relatively small anchorage was already crowded with boats. Some of the boats were secured by a bow line tied to the surrounding mangrove trees, plus a stern anchor in the opposite direction. That kind of setup suggested to me that there were going to be loose boats flying around the anchorage when the storm hit.

And finally, since I had never anchored in Hurricane Hole, I wasn't familiar with such things as where the best holding ground for an anchor was.

I decided to head back to Road Town where I was familiar with the surroundings and figured we had just enough time to get there and get ready for Frederick. With the wind at 25 knots or better we were able to make Road Town and the charter base on a hard-driving beat to windward that didn't involve a single tack. By late morning we were back at a permanent mooring at CSY, and preparations for the storm, which was scheduled to arrive around sunset, began.

The first thing was to resolve the engine problem. Fortunately Jim knows a lot more about diesel engines than I do, and eventually he was able to start the engine by jumping two terminals with a screwdriver blade. We succeeded in putting a charge on our batteries, and that meant that we would have electrical power in the boat for light, notwithstanding the balky starter. As it turned out, we had electrical power in the boat throughout the storm, while all power on Tortola was lost as the storm increased in violence during the night.

Next was the issue of how the boat would be moored. We picked up a CSY permanent mooring in their anchorage area and also set our main anchor off our bow. Our spare anchor was set off our starboard quarter to prevent the boat from slewing, which was one of the things that puts repeated shock pressure on lines, cleats, shackles and other equipment. Then everything in the boat was securely stowed or lashed down.

As we finished our preparations, I suggested to Sally that she and R.J. spend the night ashore at the CSY base, while Jim and I stayed with *Carmali*. The response was a look—first surprised and then ominous—from Sally, followed with a pointed "Why would we want to do *that*?" I realized that the question was better left unanswered, and the four of us dinghied out to *Carmali* and braced for the storm to arrive.

How do you do, Frederick

By 1700 all four of us were ready and waiting in *Carmali*. The air was oppressive. It was eerily quiet, except for the wind, which was building steadily, and the rain, which was beginning to sting as it hit our faces. By 1800 the wind was steady at 50 miles per hour and gusting to 90. As darkness fell, the sound of the wind mounted to a constant roar.

By 2000 the gusts had reached 100-plus miles an hour and were slamming in to us like runaway freight trains. *Carmali* was beginning to feel very small, but she was riding with confidence to the permanent mooring and our two anchors.

The combined sound and physical impact of the wind gusts began reminding me of something. It took a while for me to figure out what, and then it came to me. It reminded me of my midshipman's cruise in USS *Macon*, where my assignment was as one of the gun captains, and the feeling in the gun turret when we fired a round from one of her eight-inch guns. It was the feel and sound of compressed and then suddenly released violence that you felt in your gut and that was almost beyond comprehension.

For hours the storm hammered the boat, and at first I worried about the cascade to catastrophe that would begin if a critical cleat or chock was to rip out or if one of mooring lines was to part. But *Carmali* took the pounding hour after hour and never faltered. I began to comprehend her strength and that gave me confidence. She was not only good-looking; she was *tough*.

As the wind shifted it came time to adjust our mooring and anchor arrangement. The anchor line to our bow had to be taken to the port quarter. The anchor line that had been secured at our starboard quarter had to go to the bow. It was time for firm grips, very strong backs and no mistakes. That was when I was thankful for the sheer strength, steady nerves, and mental focus of Jim and R.J.

By 0200 confidence had largely overtaken apprehension, and at one point Jim and I sat on the foredeck for awhile in the wind and rain, watching a most astonishing display of sheet lightning. At intervals, the lightning illuminated everything around us for an instant, including the mountainsides surrounding Road Town harbor and the lower profile of Peter Island, roughly three miles away on the other side of Sir Francis Drake Channel. Our struggles and discomfort were worth the show. When Jim and I talk about the unique light show provided by Frederick that night, the communication is more in our eyes than in our words.

One of the unusual aspects of the night was how little conversation there was among the four of us. And whatever talk passed among us was subdued, calm, and mostly related to *Carmali*. There was a lot of listening and thinking and an overriding sense of just waiting to see what Frederick was delivering and how *Carmali* was answering the storm's challenges.

Beneath that calm, however, was my constant mental process of evaluating the state of the boat as the storm progressed: should the bow anchor line be slacked a bit? What affect would that have on the effectiveness of the anchor off the quarter? How rapidly was the wind direction shifting? Was that last gust that hit us stronger or weaker than its predecessors? Are the gusts hitting at shorter intervals? How long before sunrise? On and on the mental process went, hour after hour as the storm hammered *Carmali*. One thing that never came into question during the thought process was the unfaltering competence of my shipmates.

One of the things that has always fascinated me is how efficient conversation usually is in a boat. In my own case, I believe it's because I am always listening and sensing. During Hurricane Frederick, that tendency was intensified. I was, for example, constantly listening to the wind to gage it by its sound. And I also was listening for the sharp Crack! that would mean that a line had parted or a piece of equipment had broken under its strain.

I also was constantly focused on the boat's motion. Was it beginning to roll more violently? Was I feeling an alternating jerking that meant that a line or lines were not taking a steady strain but were being stressed more dangerously by periodic, concentrated stress?

In my memory, the calm and subdued tone that pervaded *Carmali's* cabin during the night was all the more striking, in light of the violence that was steadily ripping things apart outside our boat and randomly distributing them around Road Town harbor and the Tortola countryside.

There was one noteworthy casualty as the storm began to wane: Jim's favorite shirt. Between the rain, oppressive humidity, and heavy exertion, Jim's shirt had become pretty soggy. Then he came up with the idea of drying it out in the galley oven.

The idea of having a dry, warm shirt to put on did have its appeal, so we paid close attention as Jim began baking his shirt. Unfortunately, there were no instructions on the oven for drying shirts, and as could have been guessed, Jim's favorite shirt was seriously overcooked.

Aftermath

By the time the pitch blackness began to dissolve, the wind started to abate. The ferocity of the storm had passed, and around 0700 we were picked up by a dinghy from the charter base and taken ashore for some hot coffee. *Carmali* was safe; we were safe. As I sat in the CSY dining room, looking at the sky where the building roof had been and out over the disarray in Road Town harbor, the hot coffee began pulling things back into something approaching normalcy.

Our first cruise with *Carmali* had been a strange transition: first sailing in perfect conditions, then hurriedly preparing the boat as nature wound itself up for mega violence, then finally experiencing the slowly building exhilaration of coping with the extreme circumstances of the hurricane. All of which played out against an extraordinary combination of beauty and violence from the sea.

The aftermath of the storm lacked any of the inherent beauty of the storm itself; it was just ugly. Roads were washed away and in many places blocked by fallen trees and mud slides. There was no electrical power on the entire island of Tortola. The normally crystal clear, cobalt water of the harbor was a dirty reddish brown from mud washed down from the mountainsides, and it was filled with floating debris, everything from large tree branches to empty plastic bottles and an occasional piece of outdoor furniture.

It was a disturbing scene, something that told of the sudden suffering ashore, something that contrasted harshly with Road Town's normal undercurrent of low-key charm.

In fact the island was paralyzed, and it was days before Tortola and the surrounding islands began to show signs of recovery. We had a sad departure from a place we had come to love for its beauty and the character of its people. At that point in time, those people were staggering in devastation and widespread dislocation. But there also was our confidence in the character of the British Virgin Islanders and their ability to regroup and rebuild.

Time proved our confidence was well placed. When we returned to the BVI in June of '83, it was almost as if Frederick had never happened.

When I asked Jim, usually a man of few words, for some of the things that he remembered about Hurricane Frederick, he picked up the narrative when we first knew for sure that Frederick was on the way:

> The first thing we did was sail over to St. John to take a look at Hurricane Hole, where CSY suggested we ride out the storm. It was already crowded with boats and clearly not a good situation for nasty weather.
>
> When we go back to Road Town and CSY it was really quiet, but I can remember hearing the halyards of all of the boats in the anchorage clanging especially hard on the boats' masts. It was like a wild drumbeat, warning of what was coming. To this day I think of that hurricane when I hear a halyard banging on a mast.
>
> Before we got our mooring and anchor lines really set up we were getting a wild ride. The boat seemed more like a bucking horse than a boat. The big problem with what was going on at that point was losing my railroad trainman's cap over the side.

I also remember how eerie it was to sit out on the deck at one point during the storm. It's hard to put into words what it was like to feel the power of the storm.

When I got back to Croton, Frederick had turned up the coast and already been there ahead of me. He left his calling card. There were trees down all over the place, and there were no lights in that area of Westchester County. None of my neighbors could believe that I had ridden out the hurricane in a boat in the British Virgin Islands.

I also asked R.J., another man of few words, for his recollections of Hurricane Frederick. This is what he wrote:

Here are a few of my mental snapshots of those amazing days. When we flew into San Juan it had been raining all day, and Hurricane David was arriving at about the same time. My stepbrother Jim and I got to know each other very well as we sat out David in El Convento Hotel in San Juan.

After David passed, we worked our way into Tortola, got aboard *Carmali,* and started sailing. But after only one day, it was clear that Hurricane Frederick was heading right for us. We decided to get back to the CSY charter base, and when we arrived, the base staff was very busy preparing for the storm. Jim and I actually helped them get some of their boats out to the moorings and secured for what was coming.

As we worked to get *Carmali* set up at a mooring, we could hear a lively hurricane party of charterers starting at the small, two-story CSY hotel. People were drinking, dancing, and you could hear the noise throughout the anchorage. I was thirteen years old at the time, and the partying seemed a bit out of place to me, but we went about our business.

We had decided to ride out the storm in the boat, and we settled in onboard *Carmali* and waited.

As the hurricane built, we kept the VHF radio on, and at one point during the night, we heard a skipper attempting to find a protected harbor where he could ride out the storm. After a while, he went silent, and we never heard from that boat again.

During the early stages of the storm, all of the lights went out on shore, and the partying at the CSY hotel ended abruptly. We found out later that the hotel had lost its roof.

We were getting rocked pretty good in the boat, and I had my first experience with the feeling of being seasick. Jim and I wanted to get out on deck, but we had to be secured with improvised lifelines to do so, and no one was allowed to go topside alone. We did get topside a few times to adjust the anchor setup, but we were too busy to do any looking around.

During the night the air was thick and heavy, and when the eye of the storm passed over, it got strangely quiet. The backside of the storm didn't seem as bad, and I remember actually getting some sleep. I also remember my mom making deviled eggs more than once. That helped to keep our spirits up.

In the morning after the storm had passed we went ashore to look around. The devastation was bad. The first thing I noticed was that the roof of the CSY hotel was gone. We walked around the town for a while, and anything that was not solidly constructed was gone. I felt really sorry for the people who didn't have much to start with; they had nothing left.

Hurricane Frederick worked its way up the U.S. East Coast after hitting the British Virgin Islands, and we got back home to New York City right after it had hit there. In our neighborhood in Forest Hills, there were a lot of big trees down, but it was good to be home.

There were lessons, some learned and some reinforced, from Hurricane Frederick. One was the importance of timely and unambiguous decision making under pressure. For example, it was clear that there was no time for hesitation about where to ride out the storm or how to best secure the boat in the anchorage. Handling the shifting of lines demonstrated to critical importance of teamwork. There was absolutely no chance of accomplishing what we did that night in the screaming wind, driving rain on the pitching and rolling deck of *Carmali* without the total cooperation and coordination of the three of us involved in that operation.

It also became clear over time that there is a bonding process among individuals who have shared danger. There is no doubt that the shared experience during Hurricane Frederick on the night of 3 September 1979 brought Sally, Jim, R.J., and me closer together.

CHAPTER FOURTEEN
CARMALI TO THE FORE

The islands are clustered and offer exhilarating but short passages in sight of land, with a wide choice of anchorages...somewhat more challenging than the Virgins.

Cruising Guide to the Leeward Islands

In 1980, after our brief adventure with Hurricane Frederick in our then-newly purchased boat, *Carmali*, we had decided to move our boat from the BVI to St. Maarten. Part of the reason for the move was to add *Carmali* to a small bareboat charter operation in the harbor of Philipsburg, the capital and main port of St. Maarten. As partners in the charter operation, we had the opportunity to sail our boat for short periods when she was not chartered, usually for about a week to ten days at a time. We took advantage of those opportunities quite a few times over the next few years.

Expanded Horizons

The second reason for moving the boat to St. Maarten had to do with a basic drive for discovery of new places. Our initial sailing trips in the British Virgin Islands had opened a new world of cruising sailing for me in an exotic and welcoming corner of the Caribbean, and by 1980 I was ready to expand those cruising horizons. In addition I was interested in further testing my sailing skills in an area that was not familiar. In a sense I was reaching out to explore "the beyond." Thus the decision to test the sailing grounds surrounding St. Maarten.

The three main islands in the area, often referred to as the Renaissance Islands, include St. Maarten/St. Martin, Anguilla, and St. Barts. All three islands are well within sight of one another, so transits from anchorage to anchorage can be as short as an hour or as long as five or six hours. In that sense they were similar to the BVI. There was one significant difference, however, between the sailing among the Renaissance Islands and sailing among the British Virgin Islands: the transits in the former are generally more of an open ocean variety and thus a bit more challenging.

St. Maarten/St. Martin (at times identified as simply St. Martin) is administered by both the Netherlands and France, with the Netherlands administering the southern half and the French administering the northern portion. Anguila to the north is a British Territory, and St. Barts to the southeast is administered by France. The three-way cultural variety of the area adds a special flavor to the sailing there, and the cluster of three islands provided an opportunity for Sally and me to explore further along the chain that forms the Caribbean's Leeward Islands.

A Sailing Venue with a Lot of History

The first European visitor to the harbor now called Philipsburg was Christopher Columbus in 1493. The town was founded in 1763 by a Scottish captain in the Dutch Navy, John Philips, and it quickly became a significant center of trade in the West Indies. Two historic forts, Fort Amsterdam and Fort Willem, attest to its strategic value during the age of sail.

Philipsburg harbor is relatively large and quite open, and it's perhaps more suited to the cruise liners which anchor at its outer edge and then ferry passengers ashore in motorized tenders than for boats like *Carmali*. When the wind was between north and east, which was most frequently, the harbor was reasonably comfortable for small craft. But if the wind went around to southeast or south, it could become untenable for smaller boats, and in a hurricane it simply was not a place where a small boat could survive.

Our charter operation, called Leeward Islands Yacht Charters, was located on the favored eastern shore of the harbor. The operation was comprised of a finger pier and enough anchorage area for the LIYC "fleet." A first-class restaurant called Chesterfields was at the head of the pier, and Bobby's Marina, at the time the only "full service" marina on the island, was located a short distance to the north and toward the inner harbor area.

Although Philipsburg is pretty big as Caribbean harbors go, it still had the feel of an exotic tropical port when we were first there. The waterfront was rimmed with shops, small restaurants, a church, and small commercial buildings. There also was an intangible quality along the waterfront that was hard to pin down. It could have had something to do with the relatively reserved Dutch attitude of St. Maarten, an attitude that contrasted with the more light-hearted tone on the French half of the island, where for example, a nude beach at Bai Oriental on St. Martin's east coast reflected a significantly more relaxed approach to social mores. If there was a somewhat reserved tone to the people in Philipsburg, that was counterbalanced by feeling that there was a solid quality to their friendliness.

Towards a Place of "Ponds and Marshes"

I can still remember my feelings during the first few minutes, as we sailed out of Philipsburg in *Carmali* and turned northwest along the coast toward Marigot Bay on the French portion of the island. My log says we had a 12-15 knots wind on our starboard quarter, and I got far enough offshore to take full advantage of the wind, while still benefiting somewhat from the slightly calmer seas in the lee of the St. Maarten coastline. It was an enjoyable balancing act and *Carmali* was liking the conditions a lot.

For me, it was a dream come true: on the wheel of my own boat, heading for a tropical harbor I had never seen before, the wind over my shoulder, and Sally with me in the cockpit. As we settled in on our course, Sally looked at me, smiled and asked, "How do you like your new boat?" I didn't answer; she knew. We didn't talk much for the next hour.

By the time we had rounded Point Basse Terre and then Point Plum for a short return beat back towards Marigot, it had gotten squally. The approach to Marigot harbor is wide open, however, which was helpful under the conditions. There was plenty of room in the anchorage to drop the hook in a comfortable position, and the anchor was set firmly in a matter of a few minutes. By 1700, we were securely anchored, had tidied up the boat, and had time for a quick dinghy trip ashore to scout the town.

Because we had gone from the Dutch side of the island to the side administered by the French, the first thing to be addressed was customs clearance. We found two gendarmes leisurely patrolling the waterfront on foot, and they looked exactly like their Parisian counterparts. I asked where I could check in to clear customs. My question produced a quizzical look between the two officers and simultaneous shrugs of their shoulders. What followed would have fit a Peter Sellers' movie.

I speak virtually no French and the two gendarmes either spoke virtually no English, or they put on a good act. In any event, by showing them our passports and boat papers and pointing toward *Carmali* in the anchorage, we managed to communicate our desire to check in at customs. By nodding and pointing up a hill to a small building near an ancient fort, they were able, in return, to convey their directions to the customs office.

The procedure was worked out in good humor, and during the process, the two gendarmes managed to make it clear that they thought my passport photo was not very appealing, while on the other hand, they made it clear that Sally's was quite good. I recall hearing "Tres bon" more than a few times. My guess is that our encounter was the most challenging event of that late afternoon in Marigot for the gendarmes. The experience was undoubtedly my most unusual start to a customs-clearing process—and the only one in memory that didn't begin with standing in line.

The town of Marigot was established around 1789 and I was told that its name translates to "ponds and marshes' in English. At the time we were there, however, it consisted of much more than ponds and marshes: a historic fort looking down menacingly on the anchorage, a picture-book waterfront market that teemed with merchants and buyers on Wednesdays and Saturdays, a church, a few upscale boutiques, some less upscale shops, and a number of restaurants, all packed into about twenty square blocks of buildings. The buildings were a typical Caribbean mixture of a few substantial, two-story structures and numerous small but solid one-story buildings, with a few truly old and abandoned buildings sprinkled into the overall mix.

There were two places that clearly stand out in my memory of that first visit to Marigot. One is Les Jardin Restaurant, where we had breakfast early on the morning after our arrival. The entrance to Les Jardin was through a short, narrow, flower draped alley that led to a patio lined by even more flowers—mostly hibiscus and bougainvillea. The alley and patio, in turn, led into a narrow but pleasant dining room that overlooked the harbor.

During a breakfast of eggs, toast and some particularly good jam, accompanied by coffee that stiffened one's spine, we looked out over the harbor and watched *Carmali* loafing quietly at her anchor, among the dozen or so sailboats surrounding her. She looked content to be where she was.

The second place etched in my memory of my initial visit to Marigot was a shop known simply as La Boulangerie, located only a few doors down a narrow cobblestone street from Les Jardin. Once you were within twenty-five yards of the place, it was impossible to miss the aroma that emanated from the small storefront. It was a shop that needed no signage. Once inside, the variety of pastries and bread was surprising for such a modest appearing establishment.

Since storage and spoilage is always an issue in a boat, we restrained ourselves, with some difficulty, and bought a single loaf of bread and a few pastries. Each time we have revisited Marigot over the years there has been a ceremonial return to La Boulangerie, partly for the aroma and partly for the bread and pastries, but most importantly, as a reminder of the sense of discovery associated with our first visit to Marigot.

A Place to Ourselves

Our next destination was Anguilla, a small, flat, narrow island approximately 16 miles long and located north of St. Maarten/St. Martin. Its name derives from *anguila*, Spanish for eel. There was virtually no profile to the island when it was viewed from a boat, and it had the look of a land constantly scrubbed by wind and salt air and constantly drenched by the sun. It clearly would not be a good place in a serious storm, a reality that was demonstrated several years after our first visit, when the island was devastated by a hurricane.

From Marigot we had an easy starboard reach past Blowing Rocks Point and around Anguillita Point. The last leg of our transit was topped off with a rip-roaring starboard beat along the northwestern coast of Anguilla to Road Bay, a palm-lined, crescent beach called Sandy Ground Village. The village consisted of perhaps a dozen buildings set back about fifty yards from the beach's high water mark. There were a few small restaurants, a tiny shop or two, and a police station that, at the time, doubled as the customs office. There also was a concrete town dock that poked out about 100 yards into the anchorage. In later years, the customs office was expanded and moved to the town dock, where it had a full-time customs staff that lacked the informal charm of the local police who had doubled as customs agents.

We were the only boat in the anchorage. We dinghied ashore, checked in at customs, walked the beach, looked for shells for Sally's collection, swam, returned to *Carmali* and just soaked in being in an isolated and spectacularly beautiful spot.

Since that first visit to Anguilla, I have learned something of the island's interesting modern history, which vividly demonstrates how each corner of the Caribbean has a distinctive and invariably fascinating past, something often overlooked when confronted with the consistently astonishing natural beauty of the Caribbean region.

In 1967, Great Britain decided to declare St. Kitts, Nevis and Anguilla an autonomous state to be governed from St. Kitts. Lacking no more commonality with Nevis and St. Kits than having been a British colony, the Anguillans objected, strongly. At one point, with the aid of several mercenaries, they actually mounted an amphibious "invasion" of St. Kitts.

Fortunately, there were no serious casualties, but the Anguillans had made their point. They remained a territory under

British administration and are today virtually self governed. In recent years, the island has sprouted a number of ultra-exclusive resorts that have effected some superficial changes in the landscape—but none in the defiant Anguillan character.

Heavy Going

After a return visit to Marigot, we headed northeast for a small, unpopulated island called Tintamarre, located about a mile off the northeast corner of St. Martin. The transit triggered an unexpected attitude adjustment.

Up to that point, with the exception of the brief beat up the northwest coast of Anguila, we had generally been sailing in waters that were somewhat sheltered from the open ocean. Heading up the northwest coast of St. Martin and turning over the island's northern tip, however, put us in seas that were unobstructed from the time they left the eastern Atlantic until they reached the Leeward Islands. That was a fetch of more than 3,000 nautical miles.

It suddenly was true blue-water sailing, and as we made the turn over the top of St.Martin we were, in the matter of just a minute, in the midst of ten-foot swells, with flying whitecaps whipping off their tops. It was a breathtaking transition, and all of a sudden, our sturdy, thirty-four foot *Carmali* was transformed into our *little Carmali*. I wasn't quite ready for the transition and was somewhat taken aback.

Up to that point I had been impressed by *Carmali's* stiffness in a strong breeze. Her hull was just a bit heavier than the other boats in her production line at Bristol Yachts in Rhode Island, and that would have accounted for her additional stability, But this was heavy going of a different magnitude, and it triggered an appropriate attitude adjustment, which was accompanied by sharp focus on every detail of *Carmali's* reaction. It was immediately clear that *Carmali* was not fazed by the challenges that had caught me off guard.

A Strange Island

Before too long we were in the lee of the small island of Tintamarre and then anchored off the island's beautiful and completely deserted beach. After a lunch in *Carmali's* cockpit, we dinghied ashore and began to explore the narrow beach and the area of dense scrub growth that extended away from the beach and towards the island's interior. As we picked our way through the underbrush we stumbled, literally, over an unusual item: a roughly five-foot by five-foot section of an airplane wing. Our finding triggered subsequent inquiries about the history of Tintamarre, which revealed some quirky facts.

The island was known locally as "Flat Island," and it was not much bigger than the flight deck of a modern aircraft carrier. In fact it had once been an airfield and the base for a one-plane airline called Compagne Aerienne Antillaise that operated from a dirt runway and flew among the islands of the West Indies. In addition, there was a period in the early twentieth century when its Dutch owner proclaimed the tiny island a kingdom, including a single shop and its own currency for some twenty "citizens"!

On the sinister side of Tintamarre's past are the stories that it was a covert German submarine replenishment depot during World War II. This particular part of the island's background comes up often but, to the best of my knowledge, it's not supported by any real documentation. Given the record of German submarines in the area during World War II, however, and the island's isolated geographical position and secluded and shallow coastal stretches, the stories cannot be discounted out of hand.

After our intriguing stop at Tintamarre, we headed toward a nearby anchorage at Bai Oriental on the eastern shore of St. Martin. Finding the anchorage entrance in clear weather was moderately challenging, but the implications of making even a small mistake in the process were striking. The eastern side of St. Maarten/St. Martin is as nasty a lee shore as one could find. Steep and rocky stretches, interrupted towards the north end by ominous reefs, run the entire length of that side of the island.

The points where there are entrances to the two commonly used anchorages along the coast are easy to miss. Any boat that might be driven on to the lee shore of the island by the prevailing onshore winds would be quickly reduced to fragments. The chances of survival for the occupants of such unfortunate boats would be marginal. There were virtually no opportunities for "soft landings" against the lee shore of St. Maarten/St. Martin.

In any event we rode on the back of the large swells sweeping through the unmarked opening into Bai Oriental, with heavy surf breaking to port and starboard. Once in the bay, we made a quick left turn and found a relatively calm spot in the lee of a large reef and a tiny island called Caye Verte. It was a quiet and thoughtful evening as I slowly got my mind around a new level of challenges with *Carmali*.

The Final Adjustment

The next morning we headed out of Bai Oriental, into open ocean conditions and toward St. Barts and its harbor, Gustavia, roughly fifteen miles to the southeast. The swells were big and the wind was in the range of 15-18 knots. My log shows that we were on a port tack the whole way, and slowly I adjusted to the reality that *Carmali* could handle true open ocean conditions. It was strictly a matter of my mental adjustment and ability to use her capabilities competently.

As we sailed on, I was feeling the deep rhythm of the open ocean running through *Carmali*. In a way, it was a reminder of the sense of the profound power of the sea I had experienced while under way in the open ocean in *Sarasota*. Only in a 34-foot boat, I was experiencing considerably more intimacy with the power source. The feelings were thought-provoking.

As we opened the distance from St. Maarten and the menacing cliff of Point Blanche on our starboard quarter, I could see a cluster of rocks, one of which is marked on the chart: "Molly Baday." I've never been able to find the origin of that name, and I'm left wondering what it was about Molly that warranted having an isolated rock in the Caribbean named after her.

The island of St. Barts measures approximately eight square miles of steep hills and valleys, and its airport's single runway allegedly is even shorter and more of a heart-stopper than Tortola's. The island's fourteen beaches form a necklace around its perimeter. Its only large harbor is Gustavia, which is simultaneously a commercial hub for the region and a center for private sailboats and powerboats.

Like so many islands in the Caribbean, its first European discoverer was Christopher Columbus. Columbus named the island St. Bartholomé, after his brother. It was not the Spanish but the French, however, who colonized the island. In 1784 the island was traded to Sweden. In the 19th century, after a series of natural disasters, Sweden sold the island back to the French, who renamed it St. Barthélemy. The island is now clearly French in character, but vestiges of Spanish and Swedish influence remain.

The approach to St. Barts from the northwest has its own unique set of surrounding rocks and tiny islands with image provoking, and principally gastronomical names, including the French words for Barrel of Beef , Groupers, and Sugar Loaf Rocks, plus Bakers, Fork, and, last but not least, Custard Apple Cove.

Almost Cosmopolitan

Gustavia has a small inner harbor, dominated by a busy commercial waterfront and permanent moorings that are used mostly by locals on a full-time basis. Within a 5-10 minute dinghy ride and northwest of the inner harbor, between Fort Oscar and Gros Oslets, there is an outer anchorage for charter and other private cruising boats. A bit farther out of the inner harbor there is another anchorage called Anse du Corossul.

In between the inner harbor and the other options and along the eastern shoreline, there is a concrete quay where boats use a Mediterranean-style mooring (anchor set off the bow and toward the channel and stern secured, with fenders over, against the concrete quay). Although we would use the more convenient "Med Moor" for a future visit, we opted for the outer anchorage and a dinghy run to the town on our first visit to the town of Gustavia.

Gustavia is U-shaped and wraps around the harbor. One of its memorable characteristics is the series of red roofs that dominate the shore area as one enters the fairly narrow harbor entrance. For visiting boats, there is a free-standing Port Office for checking in and out of customs. The process was considerably more business-like than the one with the two gendarmes in Marigot, but nonetheless, a friendly and efficient process.

There were scores of shops and restaurants to be scouted, and even a Tourism Office. In comparison to either Marigot or Philipsburg, two aspects of Gustavia quickly stood out: it was more upscale and it was larger. In comparison, it had a somewhat more continental than island flavor—almost cosmopolitan.

There was, however, one special common denominator with Marigot: one of my most vivid memories of that first visit to Gustavia was a breakfast at a tiny harbor-side café, appropriately called Le Cove. Fresh orange juice, fresh homemade bread, homemade jam and strong coffee constituted the limited fare, and as we ate, we watched the small inter-island freighters being off loaded at a dock across the street. It was a snapshot of Leeward Islands' life that was very different from the more idyllic settings that we had been frequenting in the Caribbean since our initial visit in 1979. It was a reminder of the workaday reality that underpins the exotic islands of the Caribbean.

On the Way Home

With one full day left of our exploration of the Renaissance Islands, we made a quick transit of about five nautical miles to Il Fourche, a tiny, uninhabited island on the way back to Philipsburg. The anchorage has a wide, unobstructed entrance and is sheltered by the long, roughly C-shaped series of hills that form the island. We anchored deep into the northeast corner of the harbor, only twenty-five yards from a small rocky beach. There might have been one other boat in the anchorage.

In the evening the only sounds were the occasional bleating of the goats that occupied the steep terrain ashore and the echoes of the goat's and even our own voices bouncing off the steep hills that formed the perimeter of the anchorage. It was a sharp contrast with the hustling tempo of Gustavia that we had just left behind.

The return to Philipsburg the following morning was uneventful. The winds were light and dead astern, and to make the "downhill slide" more comfortable we covered the approximately fourteen nautical miles in a series of broad reaches. It was a quiet but enjoyable return. I had discovered a new dimension of *Carmali's* capability and had elevated my attitude to take advantage of it.

CHAPTER FIFTEEN
SAILING ON THE EDGE

There's danger on the deep

Thomas Haynes Bayly

While sailing boats ranging from 34 feet to 50 feet in length in the British Virgin Islands, the Leeward Islands, and as far south in the Caribbean as St. Lucia, I have come to understand the unique merger that can be achieved among the wind, the sea and a boat. When all three are working together, it achieves a special triunion, something achieved by getting inside nature, rather than overpowering nature from the outside.

With an 18-knot-plus wind, all sails precisely trimmed and a crisp blue sky, punctuated by friendly cumulus clouds, there's an indescribable exhilaration. It's not a conquest of nature by any means but a joining of nature to accomplish an end. In those moments it's wind, sea, boat—and me in the middle.

Of course there are inevitable, contrasting experiences, times when nature has turned on me, stretching my skill and strength to uncomfortable limits. In those situations, at times brief and at times extended, safety was the main issue, and luck was a wild-card factor.

These are not situations that I sought out. In fact part of being a good sailor is being able to avoid such circumstances. But even the best of sailors must face them from time to time. When faced and overcome, those rough situations add to the wisdom that only intense learning situations at sea can bring.

Marigot Madness

One of the most vivid of those less-that-idyllic events occurred in 1980, when Sally and I were sailing among the Renaissance Islands in *Carmali*. It was our first opportunity to sail alone in the boat since we had purchased it.

It had been a pleasant transit from Philipsburg, running northwest along the attractive shoreline of Dutch St. Maarten and the tip of French St. Martin, then turning northeast around Point Basse Terre and quickly turning northeast to reach the wide opening to Marigot harbor. We were looking forward to settling in for the night in Marigot, that relatively large, well protected and charming French harbor. We were probably about a mile from the harbor when I began to have some serious misgivings.

It had been a typical Caribbean day: dominant sunshine, puffy clouds, good wind, but with the possibility of afternoon squalls. I was beating to windward with the wind out of the east, and for about thirty minutes I had been watching a squall approaching from the northeast. Squalls in the Eastern Caribbean can be intense, but they are not usually overly worrisome. For one thing, you generally can see them coming in the distance, so you have time to think ahead and prepare. The wind inside the squall is generally violent and the rain can be heavy enough to cut visibility to several boat lengths. But as long as you have some sea room, it's usually a matter of shortening sail and riding it out for ten or fifteen minutes, and that's that.

The problem with the Marigot situation was that I didn't have much time. I could have stood off and ridden the squall out where I had sea room. The alternative was to press on to the anchorage. If I chose the latter, it was a race between getting close enough to take in sail, get the engine on, make the anchorage and get the hook down before the squall hit. The storm won the race. And there was a particularly violent result.

I was probably five hundred yards from my goal and almost to the point of taking in sail when I felt that brief, eerie interlude of calm in the few moments before a squall envelopes you in its violence. The wind drops and there seems to be a pause in nature; it's her final warning before one of nature's most serious acts of hostility begins.

The storm slammed into us, hard. It was especially powerful. This was not a run-of-the-mill squall, and it had something special in store for us. One particularly strong gust—my guess is possibly fifty knots or better—actually drove *Carmali* over on her beam ends. That means that the boat had been heeled over nearly ninety degrees, with the mast almost horizontal with the surface of the water. It was a horrible feeling to realize that I was standing on the *side* of the boat's cockpit, with my hand leaning on the cockpit deck.

The boat hung in that position for what seemed like an eternity, but was actually only a few seconds. Another few feet over and the sail would have been in the water, and the boat would have capsized. It would have been what is referred to among sailors as a knock-down.

But we were lucky. In the last instant, the wind spilled out of the sails and *Carmali* righted herself with a sudden and violent motion that would have catapulted anyone not holding on right out of the cockpit. We carried on for a few minutes more and, as the storm abated, we got the sails in and the engine on. Within minutes we covered the remaining few hundred yards or so into the harbor. We let go the anchor, I backed down to dig it in, shut down the engine, and sat in the cockpit staring straight ahead into space.

One of the things I remember about those first moments, as I sat in the cockpit and began to digest what had happened, was the feeling in the pit of my stomach as *Carmali* had hung on her beam ends. It wasn't terror. The event happened too quickly for that. It was shock, shock at what I was suddenly confronting as the boat hung in her precarious position.

The other thing etched in my memory is the look Sally gave me right after *Carmali* righted herself. It communicated an unspoken and impossible to misunderstand message: "Don't *ever* do that again."

It Was a Dark and Stormy Night

In 1989 we moved down the chain of islands that border the eastern edge of the Caribbean for a bareboat charter in St. Lucia. It was a completely new venue for us, and our friends of many years Rear Admiral Bob and Micki Ravitz joined us for the charter. The forty-three-foot sloop that we had chartered was named *Free Spirit*.

For our first night out, we sailed about sixteen miles southwest along the western coast of St. Lucia to an anchorage at Soufriere Bay. The transit was a comfortable reach, with moderate winds out of the northeast. By the time we reached our destination it was becoming overcast and the winds were freshening.

The anchorage was a nicely situated spot, in the shadow of two conical mountains and along the generally leeward shore of St. Lucia. It would have been a pleasant and comfortable overnight under normal circumstances. But our first night would be anything but comfortable.

The mooring situation in Soufriere Bay was new to me. Because the water depth in the anchorage was so deep, those overnighting there did not anchor but instead got a line over to the beach, where it was secured to a palm tree. Then an anchor was set in the opposite direction from the beach. I chose to take a bow line to the beach and use a stern anchor to seaward. That arrangement seemed very logical at the time, since my bow would be into the wind, but it turned out to be a mistake.

I had picked a spot at the north end of the Bay, in the shadow of a cliff, figuring that would be the most protected spot from the swells that were rolling into the anchorage. Initially, *Free Spirit* rode comfortably. I did have some misgivings about the stern anchor, however.

Because the water was so deep, the stern anchor line, with every inch of the anchor line out, didn't have a good angle to it. For an anchor to be properly dug in, the bottom of the anchor line should be pulling as close to horizontal to the harbor bottom as practical, rather than closer to straight up and down from the bottom. The closer the anchor is to being pulled horizontally the better it digs in and holds. Because of the depth of the water, I didn't have the angle I wanted, and with all of the anchor line out there wasn't anything I could do about it.

During the night, the weather steadily worsened. The rain got heavier and the wind kept building. My biggest worry was a shift of the wind direction. The prevailing winds in the area are generally from someplace between northeast and southeast. During the night, they swung around and were westerly, with strong gusts. That meant that the wind was coming over our stern. It also meant that *Free Spirit* was meeting the waves stern first— not ideal by any measure. But by the time it was clear that the wind was shifting it was pitch dark and raining hard. I figured our best bet was to stick it out with things as they were, rather than trying to reverse our mooring setup in those circumstances.

All night the wind kept gusting and the seas, now being driven by on-shore rather that off-shore winds, kept building. Eventually everyone turned in, except me. I stayed up, trying to read and periodically checking the bow line and stern anchor lines.

It was a dirty night. I was in an anchorage I didn't know, in a boat I didn't know, and in my own opinion, moored ass-backwards in a storm. I kept weighing the wisdom of trying to alter my anchoring setup.

The hours went by, punctuated by dozing and rain soaked trips to the bow and stern to check the lines. There was plenty of spray coming over the stern and occasionally a little solid water. But the self-bailing cockpit steadily eliminated whatever water came over the stern.

Between inspections, and as I sat at the dining table in the almost-dark cabin, I had a feeling that I had known before, a sense of profound aloneness. The others in my small world were sleeping, relying on my judgment and skill. It was me and *Free Spirit* in an ugly setup.

As I kept mentally rehearsing what could go wrong and what would have to be done in each eventuality, I knew that the most potentially serious problem was for the stern anchor to start dragging—or less likely, for the stern anchor line to part. In either eventuality, maneuvering on the engine would have been an awkward next step. No matter what, one false move and *Free Spirit* could very quickly become part of the beach.

As the night wore on, I continued my watch. And little by little, I realized that *Free Spirit* was up to the challenge. She stood up to every blow the storm delivered and did her job, wave after wave and gust after gust.

By morning the wind had dropped considerably. The water in the anchorage was filled with tree branches, cocoanuts, a few dead birds and other debris, the calling cards of "a dark and stormy night" in Soufriere Bay. My log entries for the following morning were brief and wonderfully mundane:

> 0915: Sally, Bob, Micki go ashore to explore sulfur springs
>   and waterfall—heavy overcast with showers.
> 0915-1015: run engine to charge refrigerator.

It was shaping up as "just another day in Paradise," and for that I was thankful. And now I knew *Free Spirit*. That was a good feeling and I savored it.

Rough Riding

In the Virgin Islands, Leeward Islands and Windward Islands, they're called "the winter winds." They aren't associated with storms. In fact they are generally associated with clear weather. They are very strong—reaching 50 knots—and they last for days. When "the winter winds" are blowing, pleasure boats mostly stay in their harbors. On one occasion, I sailed on such a day. It was sailing on the edge.

It was in January of 1993 and once again Sally and I were sailing out of St. Maarten/St. Martin. This time it was in a 44-foot boat called *Vera*. We were sailing with a friend, Larry Heely. When we arrived at the charter base, located at Oyster Pond, we learned that we were arriving close behind a stretch of "the winter winds." The harbor had been closed for three days. We were to be among the first boats allowed out. We might have even been the first boat out.

The anchorage is on the east side of St. Martin. Before becoming a charter boat base in the late 1980s, it was known as an almost perfect hurricane hole, with a short but treacherous entrance that only local sailors were able to navigate. Oyster Pond is aptly named, since its waters are pond-like and there is virtually no wind in the harbor.

Despite being on the windward side of the island, the narrow entrance of the tiny harbor is shielded by two high points of land that protect the anchorage from both wind and waves, one jutting out from the east of the narrow entrance channel and one from the west. The two slightly offset points are probably not more than fifty yards apart. After leaving the dock area, a quick right turn clears both points of land.

The channel just outside Oyster Pond is marked by three spar buoys that curve left through a field of mostly submerged coral heads. Charter skippers are warned in their briefing that they must pass the buoys to port at a distance of no more than twenty-five *feet*. There was absolutely no maneuver room as one passes the spar buoys.

As we prepared to leave the dock, I was warned that our exit might be "a bit boisterous," and for the first and only time sailing in the Caribbean, I got everyone into lifejackets before leaving the dock for an initial departure. The tone of the warning added to my sense that this departure would be different.

We left the dock, as always, on the engine and quickly got our sails up in a small "turning circle" just inside the "throat" in the channel. Sheets were left sufficiently slack and we continued on the engine. As I had my first look outside the harbor, I was suddenly introduced to huge swells rolling towards the shore outside the harbor. The swells were at least 10-12 feet high, double the size of what I had experienced leaving Oyster Pond on previous occasions. The swells had been building up during the winds of the past several days, and as they reached the shore, they gathered themselves and crashed onto the cliff to the left and the rocky coastline to the right. We were in fact in the middle of a maelstrom.

In a blink we had gone from a pond to a heaving rollercoaster ride. There was no room to maneuver and no option but to power on through the curling swells, some of which had begun breaking over *Vera's* bow and washing over the cabin roof. I had my hands full, but out of the corner of my eye I could see Sally staring intently at the oncoming swells.

In a minute or so we were clear of the buoys and in the open sea. The mainsail and genoa were trimmed quickly, the engine was shut down, and we headed off on a rollicking reach with ideal twenty- to twenty-five knot winds for our transit to our first anchorage. As I leaned back and started to enjoy the day, I looked over to Sally with a strained "See, that was easy" smile. But there it was again: the "don't *ever* do that again" look.

Dark and Stormy Night II

Cooper Island in the British Virgin Islands and its anchorage in Manchioneel Bay usually make for a picture perfect overnight. The Island is a single, long, foliage-covered hill with a ridge running along the top. On the land side, the Bay is mostly edged by a thin strip of sand backed by palm trees. A small dinghy dock pokes into the anchorage, as does another small dock used by the scuba diving boat based at Cooper Island.

The anchorage runs southwest-northeast on the western side of the island. At the northern end of the anchorage there is a high, rocky point of land, called Quart-a-Nancy Point, which has led to endless speculation on the derivation of the name. At the southern end there is an offshore rock called Cistern Point, where the snorkeling is outstanding.

In July of 1993, we stopped at Manchioneel Bay with Emily, one of our granddaughters. Our boat was a 47-footer named *Espadone,* out of the Sunsail charter fleet based in Soper's Hole in Tortola. After a relaxed dinner ashore at the Cooper Island Beach Club, we dinghied back out to *Espadone* and settled in for the night at one of the anchorage's permanent moorings.

Around nine o'clock the wind began to freshen; an hour later it was blowing a minor gale, with gusts probably in the range of thirty-five to forty knots. The permanent moorings in the anchorage were designed for heavy weather and we were moored with a double bridle to the mooring line. It was a bit uncomfortable but not necessarily a worrisome situation. And the wind was not onshore, so even in the unlikely event our mooring failed, I probably would have had enough sea room to maneuver and get one or even two anchors set.

The circumstances were enough out of the ordinary, however, for me to stay up during the night and check our mooring line and bridle periodically. *Espadone* was rolling and pitching and tugging very hard at the mooring, but as long as nothing gave out, there wasn't a need for serious worry.

As time passed, I began to wonder what it was that kept me from my bunk? Was it an overreaction to the circumstances? Was it an exaggerated sense of my own importance? Or was it simply the wind buffeting *Espadone* and howling in her rigging? What was bothering me?

As I sat in the cabin, with only the small red light over the chart desk providing illumination, my mind poked down annoying channels. Periodically, Sally joined me to see if I was alright.

Probably around 5 AM, when I had just about decided to turn in for at least a few hours before starting another day, I suddenly began to hear voices above the noise of the wind, and they were quickly getting louder. I went on deck, and looming on our port side was a fifty-foot boat with a number of people scrambling about her deck. Clearly she was dragging her anchor—and rapidly. Worse, she was dragging down on *Espadone's* port side, periodically swinging dangerously close to us.

My initial remedy was obvious: get some fenders over the port side to prevent damage to the boats' hulls and make sure our rigging didn't snag as the fifty-footer and *Espadone* came together. Within seconds, Sally had joined me on deck and the fenders were positioned quickly.

Next it was a matter of preventing the fifty-footer from crossing our bow and fouling our mooring line with his anchor line. As we fended the other boat off and she began to swing away from us, I heard her engine kick on and rumble, and she slowly moved forward, taking the pressure off her anchor line. It was a close call, but the incident was over in a matter of minutes. Our "visitor" continued moving his fifty-footer forward, taking in anchor chain as he went. Eventually he moved off in the dark to find another spot, where he could get his hook down again, hopefully more securely dug in this time.

By daylight the wind had dropped and things again were peaceful in Manchioneel Bay. After breakfast, it was almost as if the night before hadn't happened, except for the reinforcement of a conclusion drawn a long time ago: when the weather and your boat are telling you something that you can't quite understand at the time, pay attention. Eventually the message will become clear.

CHAPTER SIXTEEN
BRITISH VIRGIN ISLANDS II

We hoisted sail and stood toward the distant shore, happy with
one of man's oldest wonders, the way of a ship with the sea.

Captain Alan Villiers

Sailing is a joy just about anyplace. In the British Virgin Islands, however, the venue brings something very special to the experience, something that challenges easy descriptions. Yes, there's the lush, tropical foliage with its saturated colors and the brilliant cobalt and turquoise colors of the sea. And there's the out of the ordinary look of everything for someone who grew up in The Bronx. But there's also something beyond those externals: the individual quality or spirit of each anchorage and the tremendous variety they represent. It's something special that you feel when you have an opportunity to absorb the tone and tempo of a place.

Then there are the people, an evolving and complex ethnic mixture of black and white and just about everything in between, with a cross blending of professional and blue collar workers. And it's all interwoven with a kaleidoscopic mix of different Caribbean cultural strains that have come together over time to create the entity that is the British Virgin Islands.

Still discernable in that mix is the British cultural influence imbedded in the 18th through 20th centuries, when the BVI was a part of the British Empire. For instance, cricket remains one of the most popular local sports, and British Broadcasting

Corporation programming and newscasts are blended into the local radio schedules.

A Change of Emphasis

Although it was fascinating to discover new sailing areas and different Caribbean cultures as we expanded our sailing southward to the waters around St. Maarten/St. Martin and St. Lucia, sailing in the Caribbean gradually became a matter of more than discovery. It also became a matter of appreciation, a way of reaching a fuller understanding of what I was experiencing. And there was clearly a correlation between that process and age, for whatever that's worth.

At the turning point of appreciating an expanded experience, which occurred about a dozen years ago, we made the British Virgin Islands the regular locale for our sailing trips. That's where it started for me thirty years ago in *Breezin' Up,* and over time the BVI had come to feel like a home away from home. It's a place I had come to know and understand. More important, it was a place that had come to know and understand me, and that's what sealed the renewed relationship.

As the years of sailing in the West Indies progressed, my attitude about the size of our boats also evolved. Initially I preferred boats that were between thirty-four and forty feet in length, primarily because Sally and I sailed alone, and that's an ideal size for a couple. After the first five years or so, however, we began sailing with friends and family, and we incrementally advanced to boats up to and including fifty footers.

The bigger boats not only accommodated the larger groups, they were also more comfortable in heavier going, and we got to where we were going a little faster, especially in heavy conditions. That meant we had more time to absorb the subtleties of our destinations. In the process, shaping our itineraries became more relaxed. One of the results was that "Let's stay here for another night" started to replace "Where do we want to go tomorrow?"

A Little Place

One of the distinctions among the BVI anchorages is between those where there is "action" and those that could be described as the "little places," where there isn't much to do except to just be there. Little Harbor at Jost Van Dyke is an example of the latter, and it's a place to which I am increasingly drawn.

The anchorage is a shallow U-shape that can accommodate about a dozen boats. Steep hills form the sides of the tiny harbor and an assortment of low trees and shrubs are silhouetted against the sky at the tops of the hills. The silhouettes form a line of imaginary shapes that can be conjured while sitting in the cockpit of one's boat in the late afternoon with a cup of tea or under a canopy of stars with a cup of coffee.

The open end of the small harbor faces south, with a spectacular panorama view towards the West End of Tortola and St. John in the distance. In the harbor there are three restaurants, and not much else. The restaurants include Sydney's Peace and Love, Harris's Place, and Abe's by the Sea. As I have increasingly come to enjoy Little Harbor, so too have I come to increasingly enjoy Abe's. Dinner reservations and menu selections are made by VHF radio from your boat and the menu selections are not complicated. Chicken, ribs, fish of the day, and lobster are the basic options.

The weathered, one-story, once-white wooden building is perched at water's edge, and the side of the restaurant facing the anchorage is pretty much wide open. The cooking is generally limited to barbecue-style. The meals are served in large portions, and they are accompanied by quiet and genuinely friendly attitudes from the staff. Beer signs and a wide array of both weathered and fresh postcards from former visitors cover the wall.

Dinner at Abe's by the Sea is uncomplicated and devoid of pretense. The people there simply present themselves and the place as what they are: quiet, honest, basic, welcoming—the antithesis of the virtual constructs of so much of the world beyond. Its calm simplicity makes Abe's a place of more than one kind of nourishment.

A Private Place

The anchorage at The Bitter End in Gorda Sound contrasts sharply with Jost Van Dyke's Little Harbor. It's big, and it's also the location of the Bitter End Resort. Ashore there are several small shops and a tiny market with limited provisions and freshly baked bread and pastry that's delivered by ferry from Tortola in the pre-dawn. There also are restaurants at The Bitter End Resort and Saba Rock. The anchorage is well protected, but it benefits from a steady—at times edging towards lively—breeze that blows over a long, low reef that breaks down the seas as they approach the anchorage. In the evenings, the anchorage is also swept by Island music, sometimes melodious and sometimes raucous and always enjoyable.

The real attraction that has made the Bitter End another new favorite for me, however, is a small beach that can't be seen from the anchorage. The beach is on the northeast side of Prickly Pear Island, the southern portion of which backs The Bitter End anchorage. It's completely out of sight of the mooring area, and to reach this beach requires a ten-to-fifteen-minute dingy run around the tip of Prickly Pear and then between that island and the south side of privately owned Eustatia Island.

The dinghy run requires picking one's way through the reef area, and that, plus the fact that it cannot be approached from the land side, may account for the fact that I can never remember being there when more than one or possibly two other dinghies pulled up on the beach.

At the south end of the beach, there's a cluster of rocks that makes for interesting snorkeling, and walking the beach with Sally in the nicely balanced warmth of the sun and cooling of the breeze, while searching for interesting seashells and small pieces of coral, is gently absorbing.

It's the remoteness, however, and the knowledge that there is virtually nothing between the beach and the western shore of Africa that gives it a special quality of detachment. There's a sense of "this is my place" when I'm on that beach.

A Sailors' Hangout

Soper's Hole is a crossroads for sailors, and it contrasts with both Jost Van Dyke's Little Harbor and Gorda Sound's Bitter End. Located between the western tip of Tortola and a small island called Frenchman's Cay, it's a stopover for sailors going from the north side of Tortola to the south side and vice versa through a narrow passage called Thatch Cut. It's also the port of entry for the high-speed ferries coming from St. Thomas. For the visiting sailors it's a place to replenish food supplies, refill fresh water tanks, do some shopping, and take a break for a meal ashore. It's also a customs entry point for the boats coming from St. Thomas and St. John to the BVI.

The dinghy dock, known as Pusser's Landing, is the hub for the comings and goings and is always crowded with the inflatable, outboard dinghies that are the sailors' connections between their anchored boat and the shore.

Within steps of Pusser's Landing is the two-story Pusser's building with an upstairs restaurant, a waterside café and a bar that features a drink fashioned with rum, pineapple juice, coconut cream and orange and aptly named a "Painkiller." There's also Pusser's Company Store, which is well stocked with its trademarked clothing for sailors and its justly-renowned British Navy Pusser's Rum, a robust, dark rum variant that is a true stand-alone among rums.

At both the Pusser's restaurant and store there are members of the staff that I have gotten to know over the years, and there are invariably catching-up sessions that rise to the level of mini family reunions at both places. In the case of the restaurant, one of the waitresses has a son who has advanced from early school to college during the time we have known one another.

Just beyond the dinghy dock and Pusser's Landing, there are clothing shops, a supermarket, a jewelry shop, a small café, a dive shop, an ice cream parlor, two marinas, and a specialty shipyard where there always seem to be several boats with the appearance of having long and interesting histories under repair.

One of the secrets known only to those who know the Soper's Hole anchorage well is Kelly's, a single-story, aged building that has survived hurricanes but looks as if it would disappear in a strong breeze. It can be reached by a five-to-ten-minute dinghy run east along a narrow, fast running, and secluded creek, with low, overhanging mango growth. For me Kelly's has become a favorite for a change-of-pace breakfast.

A five-minute dinghy run in the opposite direction leads to another interesting place in the Soper's Hole area: The Jolly Roger restaurant. The restaurant's dinghy dock is literally at restaurant-side, and one steps from the dinghy directly to a table. As with all of the harbor restaurants frequented by sailors in the BVI, reservations for visiting sailors are made by VHF radio, and in many cases the dinner selections are worked out at the same time as the reservation is made. The restaurant's waterside signage is, appropriately, a Jolly Roger flag, flown from a mast next to the restaurant. The infamous black-and-white flag is one of the most efficient examples of outdoor advertising I have ever come across.

A Pirates' Place

In contrast to the feeling of fraternity with the fellow sailors who populate Soper's Hole, there have been quiet moments when I have thought of a different breed of seamen that populated the anchorage and surrounding area centuries ago: ruthless men and women whose trade was violent and threatening to all who approached.

Those prior occupants of Soper's Hole were in fact the first European settlers of the place. They were seventeenth century pirates, and the place was ideal for their purposes. The harbor was exceptionally well protected from the weather, and the pirate ships with their small, fast "fly-boats" could be anchored in the harbor so they were out of sight of ships coming and going in the area. On the other hand, a lookout at the top of the high hill that is Frenchman's Cay could see approaching ships from a considerable distance. Spanish treasure ships were prime targets, but no ship that could not adequately defend itself was safe.

The community of cutthroats that called Soper's Hole home in the sixteenth and seventeenth centuries lived off the booty taken from their hapless victims. And the availability of fresh water and even some wild animals on Tortola provided the day-to-day sustenance for the dangerous inhabitants of the place.

Sometimes, for a moment, I sense the spirits of those previous occupants of the site. It's generally when the strong winds that funnel between Tortola and Frenchman's Cay are compressed into dangerously fierce squalls that periodically roar through the place, roiling the water of the anchorage and hillsides of Tortola's West End and Frenchman's Cay. During some of those squalls, I have seen furniture from Pusser's harbor-side restaurant picked up and hurled for hundreds of yards. I wonder if those moments are messages from spirits who are saying "This is our place; get out!"

Nothing to It

There's a magical place off the eastern tip of the British Virgin Islands' Little Jost Van Dyke Island that fits the popular concept of a deserted island. It's a day anchorage called Sandy Spit, and it's well named. The stark white patch of sand, roughly two hundred yards long and a hundred yards wide, is surrounded by a collar of sparkling turquoise water set in a cobalt sea. A crown of impenetrable green scrub occupies the island's center, and two lonely palm trees, one at the center of the island and one at the very north end, stand out starkly. For time unmeasured, the sun, wind, and sea have purified this tiny spot in the Caribbean. Judged in the terms of most modern life, there's virtually nothing to Sandy Spit. And that's its beauty.

There are only three things to do on Sandy Spit. One is to walk around the perimeter of the island, along the water's edge. On the windward side of the island, it's rimmed by a shallow reef that runs up to the beach. Along this stretch there are usually shells, driftwood, and bits of coral that have been deposited there by the waves, which are endlessly driven on to the island by the prevailing onshore winds.

On one of my first visits to Sandy Spit, I was walking along the windward shore studiously looking for interesting shells, when I came across a young woman sitting on the beach sunning herself, without her bikini top. I saluted as I passed; she returned the salute. Since then every time I pass that spot, I smile.

The second option is to snorkel off the west side of the island, where a submerged rocky patch that begins about ten feet off the beach is home to a dazzling variety of tropical fish. The third thing to do involves just sitting on the beach and contemplating your place and time. And it's that third thing that marks Sandy Spit as a special place for me. Sitting on the beach and staring out over the scene is an opportunity to cleanse my mind and spirit with the tiny island's primal tropical beauty.

The view from the beach is south towards the north coastline and western end of Tortola, and just off Tortola's west end there are St. John and Great Thatch Islands, about three miles away. The panoramic view is almost always dotted with the white sails of boats slowly moving across the water's surface, completing the scene's mesmerizing, Zen-like effect.

I've been there scores of times, and have slowly come to realize that there's also a conflicting aspect of Sandy Spit, something that adds a negative factor to an otherwise perfect experience. The problem involves a special kind of fear that is rooted in a seaman's concern for the security of an anchored boat.

Anchoring in the shallow waters of the lee if the island, where there is a sandy bottom that is near perfect for digging in one's anchor, would seem to be a no-worry event. The problem is that at a clearly visible delineation between the shallow green and dark blue water, the depth of the water plummets quickly to fifty feet. Your anchor is on an increasingly steep slope, and if it drags even fifteen or twenty feet, the chances of it resetting itself begin to diminish rapidly; instead, your boat may drift away, leaving you stranded! And since the island is so low, there is always a lot of wind pressure on the boat, even in the anchorage on the island's lee side.

Because of the anchoring situation, I have two rules when stopping at Sandy Spit: first, after the anchor is set, back down really hard on the anchor to make sure it's really dug in and then second, dive on the anchor to make absolutely sure by visible observation that it is well dug in.

My sense of Sandy Spit is that it's a special metaphor for life in general, with the profound enjoyment of a the near-perfect, starkly simple natural beauty that is calming, contrasting with the anxiety of knowing that at a given moment, while I am on the island, my boat could be drifting towards a dangerous lee shore. The net takeaway of my time spent at Sandy Spit over the years is that there is nothing, not even experiencing nature in its most beautiful, unaltered state, that doesn't come without a price.

Paying Close Attention

Marina Cay is another very small island, and it's connected to a large reef that's located at the end of a deep and wide entrance from Sir Francis Drake Channel. Entering from seaward there is Beef Island Mountain to port, the long, hilly Scrub Island to starboard, and another hilly island, Great Camanoe, at the anchorage's back. There are generally significant waves and swells driven into the long harbor approach by the prevailing winds, but the seas are broken down by the Cay and the reef.

Ashore there's a fuel dock, a four-room mini-resort, and two small villas for vacationers who really want to get away from it all, plus a Pusser's Company Store and a Pusser's Restaurant. As with the Pusser's in Soper's Hole, there are members of the staff at the Marina Cay Store who welcome us back like returning family members.

For a reason I don't really understand, Marina Cay has always seemed to me to be a place for dreaming. There are anchorages that are smaller and there are anchorages that are quieter, but for me, sitting in the boat's cockpit alone at night in Marina Cay is a time when thoughts seem to travel more freely. Over the years I have come to the conclusion that there is an untold part of the place's history that has made it the way that it is, a way for those willing to sit quietly under the stars and pay close attention to what the surroundings are telling you.

Peter Island

During the years I have been sailing in the British Virgin Islands, I have changed my opinion about my favorite places. In recent years, for example, Peter Island, the location of the Peter Island Resort, has slowly crept to the top of my list.

In early nineteenth century an author who wrote a history of the area, Captain Thomas Southey, described his personal impression of Peter Island: "In May 1806 the author with a party visited Peter's Island...a kind of Robinson Caruso spot, where a man ought to be farmer, carpenter, doctor, fisherman, planter: everything himself."[17] At times some of that Robinson Caruso aspect can still be felt at Peter Island.

There are actually three separate anchorages at Peter Island. One is called Deadman's Bay, which has a tiny and attractive beach where during the day there are almost always four or five dinghy's from anchored boats pulled up on the shore. The Bay is centrally located in the Sir Frances Drake Channel and is an excellent lunch stop, but because of the swells that usually roll into the anchorage, I have found it a bit uncomfortable for an overnight.

Legend has it that the name of the Bay has to do with fifteen pirates who were marooned by Blackbeard with only a bottle of rum and a single cutlass. The men were abandoned on Dead Chest Cay, a small island, which when viewed from certain angles resembles a coffin. Thus the island became known during their time as a "dead man's chest."

As the story goes, some of the pirates died where they were marooned and the rest died trying to swim across the rough passage between Dead Chest Cay and Peter Island. The Bay into which the bodies would probably have drifted is named for the latter group. The legend lives on in the sea chantey, the first four lines of which are:

> Fifteen men on the Dead Man's Chest,
> Yo-ho-ho and a bottle of rum!
> Drink and the devil had done for the rest,
> Yo-ho-ho and a bottle of rum!

There also is a tiny anchorage at the west end of Peter Island called Little Harbor (not to be confused with Jost Van Dyke's Little Harbor), where the only sound from the shore comes from the twittering of hundreds of small birds that occupy the dense cover of low trees and shrubs running back from the edge of the harbor. Peter Island's Little Harbor is also known for its resident sea turtle that patrols the anchorage in slow sweeps, marked by periodic appearances of its head to survey its domain. It also had a resident barracuda for a number of years. Although we have overnighted there, Little Harbor at Peter Island is another venue that is more attractive as a lunch stop than an overnight stop.

In recent years we have zeroed in on Peter Island's third anchorage Sprat Bay, between Deadman's Bay and Little Harbor and at the center of the Peter Island Resort. It's a very small anchorage with only three or four permanent moorings, a small and exclusive marina, a tiny dinghy dock, and the central building of the upscale resort. The entrance to Sprat Bay is short and narrow and the small anchorage area is protected by steep hills on three sides. There's also a narrow strip of sand backing the anchorage.

Sprat Bay is very quiet, with gentle breezes and calm waters. Even during a squall, there simply isn't enough room for waves to build up. During the day, Resort ferries ease in and out with throttles on dead slow and a few private boats, often large yachts, come and go to the marina. For entertainment while sitting in the cockpit for an after-sail cup of tea, there are nose-diving pelicans feeding in the waters along the base of a small cliff on the western edge of the harbor.

Perhaps the most important reason for our attraction to Sprat Bay is that the Peter Island Resort area surrounding the anchorage is a stunning example of architectural gardening in a luxuriant out-of-the-ordinary environment. Brilliant tropical plants and a variety of palm trees line each pathway and the narrow concrete roadways that run through the resort. The grounds are meticulously maintained, and the flowers, trees, and plants accentuate the impact of the sea that is never really out of sight.

The buildings of the resort—many built of stone—blend into the landscape, unlike many tropical resorts that are built around a high-rise central building that rudely dominates its surroundings.

Just a few minutes walk from Sprat Bay, there is a scene that epitomizes the anchorage and Peter Island for me. It's marked by a large, canopy-like tree that forms the foreground as one looks towards the Sprat Bay harbor and across Sir Francis Drake Channel towards Tortola. During much of the year, the tree is covered with brilliant orange-colored blossoms, clusters of green berries, and dark, narrow two-foot long seed pods. One of Peter Island's gardeners identified it for me as a flamboyan tree.

As one approaches Sprat Bay along the narrow access road from the landward side of the Island, there is a point towards the top of a hill that overlooks the anchorage. The view is over the top of the flamboyan tree and then over Sprat Bay and ultimately across Sir Francis Drake Channel toward the south coast of Tortola in the distance. It's a singular perspective, a view that embraces the essence of the British Virgin Islands. At night, with the glittering pinpoint lights of Tortola in the distance, it's a softer version of the daytime panorama, and is perhaps even more evocative than the day view.

A Different Perspective

In July 2008, Sally and I decided to take a different approach to Peter Island. Instead of sailing there during a bareboat charter and anchoring overnight in Sprat Bay, we took a week and spent it as guests at the Peter Island Resort. It was an opportunity for a more leisurely visit and an opportunity for exploring a major part of the Island, snorkeling, and walking the beaches in the never-ending search for interesting seashells and coral bits. It also was an opportunity to visit with Jean Kelly, a member of the Resort staff, who has for many years welcomed us, our children, and our grandchildren as family during our stops there in the course of our sailing trips.

There are four beaches for swimming on Peter Island: Dead Man's Bay (used by the guests at the Resort), Little Deadman's Bay (used by those anchored in the Bay), Honeymoon Beach, and

White Bay. During a second trip in December of 2008, we decided to explore White Bay, since we had never been there. White Bay can only be reached by the Resort van and is limited to a specific number of people for the five palm-roofed huts spaced out along the beach.

White Bay also has a resident iguana that emerges promptly at lunch time each day. He always appears from the dense growth behind hut number three, with a determined expectation of joining the startled picnickers for their meal. During our visit to White Bay we were assigned to hut number three, without any warning about the iguana, I might add. I will vouch for the fact that eating a sandwich while being stared at by an unblinking, unmoving, cold-eyed, four-foot iguana that is approximately four feet away and that has ignored all efforts to be driven off is an unsettling experience.

Those two visits to Peter Island in 2008 were very, very different from the earlier, boat-based stays. One aspect of that difference was illustrated during our initial stay at Peter Island Resort, when I had an opportunity to watch a heavy squall sweep across Deadman's Bay, while we sat comfortably dry having lunch in the Resort's beach bar and grill.

The sky began to darken in the east, first slowly, and then rapidly and more ominously. Within ten minutes the wind was gusting and a few widely separated, large drops announced what was coming. Then it broke, with violence. Howling wind and sheets of rain blotted out everything beyond a hundred yards or so.

I could see the boats anchored off the beach tugging violently at their anchor lines. I knew that every one of the skippers was worrying about his or her boat dragging its anchor. And any boat skipper beyond view and under way in the storm would be getting a rough ride, with the accompanying problem of seriously limited visibility.

Then as rapidly as it started, the rain slackened and stopped. The wind dropped to more manageable levels, the sun came out, and the boats returned to their rhythmic and gentle tugging at their anchors. The squall had moved off to the west, and now it was someone else's issue. At first I had enjoyed being at the water's edge as a comfortable spectator during the squall. But then I began feeling that I had been cheated of the challenge of direct participation in one of nature's brief and challenging tantrums and the satisfaction of working through the challenge in a good boat with a good crew.

Emphasis on People

For me sailing has always been a people thing just as much as a place thing. In a boat acquaintances can become good friends, and conversely, long-time friendships can disintegrate in a few stressful moments. Family relationships can be extended or stunted. The intensity of the process of sailing and the close quarters of a boat are catalytic in that way. One of the special applications of that phenomenon has been the opportunity sailing has provided for me get to know my children as adults.

In June 1998 my oldest son Joe joined us for the first time on one of our BVI cruises. I had taught him as a child to sail in the Dyer Dinghy in Haverstraw Bay and we had sailed together in a 19-foot O'Day sloop during summer vacations in Wiscasset, Maine. In addition, he had competed for a number of years in the annual Fugawi Race series across Nantucket Sound. When I asked him about his recollections of that first experience sailing in the BVI, I was struck by how similar his sense of discovery was to my first visit there in 1976. This is what he said:

I remember leaving Road Town and those first several hours we spent beating up to Marina Cay in a strong breeze. There was the incredible tropical beauty of the surroundings, but what stands out in my mind are the sensations in the boat when we turned off the engine and set sail. The feeling of the wind on my face and the sound of the boat rushing through the water is hard to describe. It was overwhelming.

It was a hot day, but the heat wasn't oppressive; it just added to the intensity of everything. I also remember how fundamentally different everything was, including the food.

Cooking on the hibachi over the stern, the local seafood when we ate ashore, and even the beer sold locally all somehow seemed remarkable.

As our cruise rolled on it became obvious that this cluster of small islands was exploding with wildlife: domesticated chickens and goats, the high-diving pelicans, small land based birds, geckoes running wild everywhere, gulls and various other sea birds, and an unbelievable array of tropical reef fish.

One of the most striking things that occurred to me along the way was that sailing in the British Virgin Islands was a peak of life experience that began back on the dunes of Montauk Point and wound through Boy Scouts and high school in the Hudson Valley and then college in the Rocky Mountains. It had all taken me to the close quarters of that boat, with friends and family and where we relied on one another as part of a team.

But the one thing that really stands out above all else was the dinghy run in The Bight, when we were heading back to our boat in the pitch dark from the William Thornton restaurant and the white porpoise jumped right over our bow. That's an image and a moment I'll never, never forget.

Bridging the Double Generation Gap

Over the years, we have also found that sailing in the British Virgin Islands has been a great way to get to know the grandchildren and have them get to know me, and at one point we began taking them with us on our sailing vacations. One of our first tries at bridging the double generation gap occurred in 1996, when we invited Tomas, age thirteen, to join us.

The idea was to give one grandchild at a time an opportunity to break away for a while from siblings and parents, and to accomplish that while doing something interesting, exciting, and grown-up. In the last few years, however, we have begun to mix the grandchildren in with their siblings, parents, and other adults.

When we began to include the grandchildren, the idea also was that it would be an important learning experience for them, and indeed it has been that. They have learned the basics of sailing in fair weather and foul. But they also have learned that living in a boat, even if it's only for a week or ten days, requires a higher level of social agility than living at home. Small problems that would be glossed over at home can be incendiary in the close living of a boat, where there is neither the time nor the place for sulking.

There also have been lessons about responsibility. If one is to take the wheel of the boat or handle the dinghy, there are basic safety issues involved that rise above simply having fun. If one is responsible for getting the morning weather report, it's not a matter of comfort or if swimming will be on the day's agenda. It's a matter of the safety of the boat and its crew. The underlying lesson is that sailing is a profound pleasure, but it's by no means play.

Perhaps the most interesting aspect of sailing with our grandchildren is what they remind me of, and in the case of sailing, it's mostly the intense joy of the experience. It's not just a matter of exotic places; it also involves discovery of new capabilities. Perhaps one of the purest expressions of that latter kind of discovery was the look in the eyes of our grandson Tomas, who had just become a teenager, when he realized he was sailing— not just steering—a 47-foot boat in an 18-knot breeze.

Innocents' Humor

While in a boat, our grandchildren also have provided us with some special moments of family humor. Several have become family stories that are recounted with affection and laughter. Tomas was the source of one during his first cruise with us as a thirteen year old. As we walked along the waterfront in Soper's Hole one afternoon, an attractive young girl in a bikini—perhaps sixteen years old—passed in the opposite direction. Tomas' spontaneous and oh so casual comment was, "Ah, a woman in her prime."

David, who was probably ten years old at the time, contributed another memorable line as we sat around in the main cabin after dinner one evening. David's dad, R.J., pointed out at one point in the conversation that David frequently did not listen to what his father told him.

With a deeply sincere tone that was meant to please and appease, David responded, "Dad, when you say something, I'll listen." The roars of laughter bounced off the bulkheads as David, smiling slightly, realized he was off the hook, without grasping the double meaning of his response.

The sailing, swimming, snorkeling, and discovering notwithstanding, one of the most interesting features of our sailing trips with grandchildren are the conversations during dinners around the table in the main cabin. There are plenty of family reminiscences and talk of practical matters, such as the next day's destination and what time we should be getting under way. Most interesting however, are the things that leap across three generations. In one instance, for example, I was amazed to learn that our two grandsons from London, Henry and Ben, are interested in the music of such ancient—for them—artists as Neil Diamond and Linda Ronstadt.

To date we have sailed with eight of our twelve grandchildren: Emily, Tomas, Audra, Rima, David, Henry, Jordan, and Ben. Among my ambitions is to add Jake, Kelsey, Zoe, and Max to that roster.

CHAPTER SEVENTEEN
HM BARK ENDEAVOUR

The ship, a fragment detached from the earth,
went on lonely and swift like a small planet.

Joseph Conrad

In June 1998 I had a once-in-a-lifetime opportunity to sail in the full-scale recreation of HM Bark *Endeavour*. The three-masted square rigger in which I sailed is a very close duplication of the ship that Royal Navy Lieutenant James Cook took around the world, from August 1768 to July 1771. The *Endeavour* reproduction was built in a shipyard in Fremantle, Australia that specializes in the reproductions of famous ships from the Age of Sail, and at the time she was in the process of an around-the-world cruise to commemorate Cook's achievements as an explorer.

The opportunity involved an assignment for a magazine article about the ship and it was decided by the cruise organizers, the HM Bark *Endeavour* Foundation, that I would go aboard in Philadelphia and travel with the ship to New York. The transit would be a perfect opportunity to get background about the ship and photos for my article. But things don't always work out the way they are planned, and my experience turned out to be a lot more than a routine writing assignment about a famous exploration.

Because of a misunderstanding somewhere along the way, it turned out that I would not make the transit from Philadelphia the New York as a writer but as a working member of the crew. Although daunting, the inadvertent switch turned out to be fortuitous. And in the end, what I learned by the experience was considerably more significant than I anticipated.

The Ship's Background

The original *Endeavour* had a modest beginning. She was initially named *Earle of Pembroke* and launched in 1764 as a collier at Whitby on the Yorkshire coast of England. In 1768 she was purchased by the Royal Navy for Cook's scientific voyage westward into the Pacific Ocean and eventually around the world. Her sturdy, form-follows-function design was well suited for the three-year circumnavigation. And despite her very utilitarian design, she had a straightforward grace that grew from the designer's unyielding dedication to serviceability and the extraordinary skills of her builders.

With a length of 110 feet, a beam of 29 feet and a displacement of 550 tons, *Endeavour* was a typical example of the three-masted, square rigged barks that were sea-going workhorses of 18th-century ocean commerce.

The basic design features of Cook's *Endeavour* were reproduced faithfully in the 21st century version of the original ship, incorporating materials, techniques and tools that were similar to if not the same as those employed by the original builders. The rigging and sails were also created to follow the originals as closely as possible. For example, the sails were made of a synthetic canvass that handles much like the heavy canvass of the ship's original sails.

James Cook was an experienced 40-year-old Royal Navy lieutenant when he took command of *Endeavour*. In contrast, most of his crew of 90 officers and seamen were under the age of 30. Notwithstanding their relatively young ages, they were all veteran seamen. A 12-man Royal Marine contingent formed the ship's security force and had a dual purpose: assure good order and obedience to orders in the ship and protect the ship and her crew from external threats, particularly on the unfamiliar shores she would explore.

After the voyage Cook gave simple and appropriate credit to his crew, who underwent hardships during their journey that are almost incomprehensible today: "They have gone through the fatigue and dangers of the whole Voyage with that cheerfulness and Alertness that will always do honour to British seamen." [18]

Since Cook's circumnavigation was primarily a scientific mission, there were several scientists embarked in *Endeavour*. There were two botanists: Joseph Banks, a 24-year-old, and Daniel Solander, a 34-year-old. Two artists were also on board to record plant and animal specimens and landscapes. Charles Green, a 35- year old astronomer, was there as part of the global effort by the Royal Society of London to record the transit of Venus across the sun, as observed from the South Pacific.

A Strange Introduction

The crew that I joined in Philadelphia had a nucleus of 13 full-time professional seamen who were experienced in the complexities of sailing square-rigged ships. The nucleus crew was made up of mostly Australians, and they constituted the officers of the ship's company. In addition there was a voyage crew that averaged about 35 men and women, and the composition of this group changed with people being added and subtracted at each port-of-call along *Endeavour's* world-wide cruise. The voyage crew provided the watch standers, sail and line handlers and station cleaners. They were comparable, at least in status, to the working seamen of Cook's voyage.

When I walked across *Endeavour's* brow with my seabag over my shoulder, I was met with mass confusion—and nothing else. The ship was alongside one of Philadelphia's city docks and was attracting a lot of attention. There were groups of sightseers being conducted around the weather deck, fresh food and other supplies were being loaded across the gangway from the dock, and members of the crew were working on minor repairs to rigging and deck equipment. There seemed to be no one in charge.

Eventually I found a local volunteer from Philadelphia who was acting as liaison between the ship and groups from the Philadelphia area interested in the ship's visit. When I explained that I was a writer who would be riding the ship to New York, she seemed puzzled by the idea, but she volunteered to find someone who could help.

At this point it's worth explaining that in my experience writers with an assignment are usually welcomed enthusiastically and given an abundance of cooperation when they arrive at the site about which they are writing.

This situation was very different. Not only was there no enthusiasm for my arrival, the question of what to do with me seemed to be an annoyance to people who were much too busy to be concerned about my assignment. My reception could be described as aggressive indifference.

My initial reaction was to simply walk off the ship and move on. After all, I was doing them a favor, not the reverse. But something kept me standing there amid the bustle. Finally I was shown to a locker below deck and delivered to the new members of the voyage crew that had come aboard earlier in the day in Philadelphia. They were well along in their initial indoctrination when I was unceremoniously—pointedly unceremoniously—folded into the group.

It dawned on me at that point that it was assumed that I was a late-arriving member of the voyage crew for the transit to New York. There were advantages and disadvantages to the situation. The disadvantage was that I wouldn't be able to pick and choose what I was doing during the trip, including such obvious things as getting particular photographs, interviewing the captain, and delving into the backgrounds of the regular crew.

The advantage was that I was going to be seeing the ship, not as a guest, but to a small degree as the members of her crew had seen her. I would be seeing the ship from the inside out, rather than from the outside in. My ego was bruised, but my instincts as a writer told me I was on to something better than the conventional writer's trip, where you are shown only the best side of everything and everyone is making a special effort to make a good impression. My instincts were spot on.

As I joined what quickly evolved into a training session, I began to sort out my environment. The first thing that struck me was how crowded *Endeavour's* weather deck was, with three masts, numerous hatches, windlass, capstan, large tiller, ship's wheel, binnacle, countless cleats, bits, belaying pins, and rigging lines, plus four guns on wheeled carriages, just for a beginning. Then there were the people—usually moving at a brisk pace, and always between yourself and where you were going.

Below deck, in the living, eating, and working spaces, it was even more crowded. I was beginning to get a hint of what it was really like to work and live in that small world day-in-day-out, for months at time without setting foot off the decks of the ship. The final underscore for that feeling came when we were introduced to our "personal space," which was, in simple terms, where one slept. In specific terms the space amounted to about 100 cubic feet, about the size of a small clothes closet.

Because I had been a late arrival, my berthing area was set apart from the rest of the voyage crew. The area where I was to sling my canvass hammock—a basic 18th century model—was a small space located between the main crew quarters and the officers' quarters. In Cook's time, it was where the Marines were berthed. It occurred to me that there was some significance to the fact that the Marine's space was between the crew's living space and the ship's officers.

The headroom in my personal space was something under five feet, and there were beams that protruded down from the overhead. Setting up and taking down my canvass hammock, which was done each evening and each morning, and getting into and out of it, required moving about in a bent position. In fact after several bloody meetings between my head and the beams, I learned that the best way to carry out the twice-a-day hammock routine was to do everything from a kneeling or sitting position.

Next came our introduction to the ship's "main propulsion system," her sails and rigging. The introduction began with the opportunity to climb to the main top, which was a narrow platform surrounding the mainmast about halfway up from the deck, with a surface just wide enough to sit or stand on.

The main top was reached by climbing the ratlines from the main deck, which was an interesting first-time experience in itself. But the really interesting part came when the top was reached. The only way to accomplish the final distance to the top was to arch back from the ratlines and then reach up and pull your body out, up and over the edge of the top and onto its surface. The maneuver required a special combination of balance and sheer arm strength, all done while trying to ignore the fact that you were performing a gymnastic maneuver approximately four stories above the deck. Once safely onto the top, it occurred to me that the reverse process was going to be a different but equally interesting process.

After returning to the main deck we had no time to marvel at our accomplishments aloft. It was time for assignment to one of the three underway watch sections that would, for the next five days, be handling everything from setting and trimming sails (sometimes aloft), acting as lookouts (sometimes from the mizzen top and sometimes from the *forward* end of the bowsprit), acting as helmsman, and cleaning assigned workspaces (mostly on your hands and knees). Not surprisingly, the preferred assignment was on the helm.

Each of the three sections was supervised by a topman who was a member of the ship's regular crew. The three sections were identified as the foremast watch, the mainmast watch, and the mizzenmast watch. I was assignment to the mizzenmast watch, and our topman was a young Australian, Todd Vidgen, who knew his stuff and who turned out to be a good leader.

The days were organized navy-style, with every twenty-four hours divided into four-hour segments. The section on watch during a given period handled the assignments already mentioned. Off-duty periods were filled with briefings, training, eating, and sleeping. There wasn't much of the latter.

There was an interesting geographical breakdown among the mizzenmast watch: eight were from the Philadelphia area, two from England, one from Australia, and I was living in Kansas City at the time. None of us had sailed in a square rigger, and only a few of us had any sailing experience at all.

Underway

As the last line to the pier in Philadelphia was cast off and we started down the Delaware River for the long run to the open sea,

Endeavour fired a salute from one of her cannons. All the people strolling along the waterfront ducked and then looked up with a "What the hell was that!" look. For me, it provided new meaning to the term "parting shot."

It was a gray day, and as we eased away from the dock, there was a light drizzle falling. There was very little breeze, and we barely had steerage way. The mizzenmast duty section had the first underway watch and I was assigned to take the wheel. With my sailing experience I figured it would be easy; I was wrong.

The main problem was the vocabulary for communicating orders to the helm. It involved a completely different and more complicated approach than the one that had been drilled into me in the Navy. And because we were in a narrow channel with bare steerage way, there was an almost constant series of orders to the helm. In any event, things began to fall into place and when I reported to the pilot that I had been relieved as helmsman I was rewarded with a "well done." I was surprised at how much her brief acknowledgment meant to me.

The Real Meaning of the Word Shipmate

It's amazing what can be learned while draped over a yardarm. During one of my first underway watches, several of us were ordered aloft to set the mizzen topsail. We had worked our way out on the horses (footropes) under the mizzen topsail yard and loosed the lines that secured the sail, and on Todd's order, let the sail drop. His next order was "Okay, make up your gasket coils and get back down on deck." At that point I realized that I had missed the demonstration on making up gasket coils. My watchmate to my right recognized the problem, eased over to where I stood, reached down, took the line, and coiled it properly. His only comment was a quietly spoken "like this."

That simple act, and particularly the way that it was done, got me thinking about what makes someone a shipmate. And I was reminded that it's not matter of a mutual assignment to the same ship; it's a matter of mutual support.

It also became clear very quickly that the coming together of the mizzenmast watch did not extend only horizontally, it also extended upward to our topman. This was demonstrated as we went about one of the more menial tasks assigned to our watch section, cleaning the area for which we were responsible. I think it's fair to say that not one of us was accustomed to the scrubbing and polishing involved, yet that there was unanimous agreement among every member of the watch that the job must be done properly. The reason was simple: what we did reflected on Todd. During the first lieutenant's inspections of the ship, it was Todd who was held responsible for the condition of the spaces that were assigned to us for cleaning. It became clear very quickly among the mizzenmast watch—and without any discussion—that he was not to be embarrassed with his boss, the first lieutenant.

These were simple lessons that I had learned at sea long ago, and it had been a long time since I had seen them in practice from the most basic level of shipboard labor. I was being reminded that quality performance in a ship, or any organization for that matter, may start at the top, but if it doesn't permeate to the lowest level the performance of the organization suffers significantly.

Reward Enough

As I crossed the brow again with my seabag over my shoulder in New York, I realized that I had learned a lot about a famous ship. But I also realized that what I had learned was more about people than things. I had begun to experience, albeit for a very brief period, what it had been like for the seamen who kept their ship going all the way around the world. When I extended my experience to begin to comprehend what it must have been like for three years, more than 1,000 days, I could only marvel at what *Endeavour's* crew had accomplished.. It also occurred to be that in all of the narratives of Cook's voyage, there was virtually no recognition of what *Endeavour's* crew achieved.

In truth, the combination of skill and endurance of those unheralded sailors was the prime ingredient of the *Endeavour's* success. It was the sailors, simply doing their duty through the dangers and numbing fatigue that made one of history's great achievements at sea possible.

It has been said that the *Endeavour* replica captures the spirit of the Age of Discovery. So it does. But more important, it is a living monument to the ordinary sailors who, according to their captain, had with "cheerfulness and alertness," made one of history's great achievements at sea possible.

In December 1998, Naval History Magazine published an article I wrote about my experience in *Endeavour*. The article ended with the following thoughts:

> Two statements from my brief voyage stick in my mind. The first, spoken by our topman at the end of a particularly demanding watch, was a quiet, "A proper job, gang." The second, spoken by the first lieutenant Jeff Kerr, as I said good-bye in New York, was, "Joe, I'd sail again with you anytime." For me, those two lines were about doing one's duty to the best of your ability. They were reward enough for five days that turned out to be much harder—and much better—than expected.

Photos and Illustrations

USS SARASOTA   APA 204

Clawing to windward in the British Virgin Islands' Sir Francis Drake Channel, with 20 knots wind in your face.

Granddaughter Jordan and the author study the entrance buoys
marking the channel onto their next anchorage.

The weather was threatening off Australia's west coast, while heading for Rottnest Island in the Indian Ocean.

A social moment with the author, wife Sally, and Admiral Thomas Hayward. As Chief of Naval Operations, Admiral Hayward, along with then-Secretary of the Navy John Lehman, was an architect of the naval strategy that helped end the Cold War.

The author with grandson Tom, granddaughter Rima, and son
Joe, in Sopers Hole, Tortola, during a sailing trip.

Kat shares a special moment underway in the British Virgin
Islands with Dad.

After a midwatch in the full-size replica of James Cook's HMS Endeavour, even a canvass hammock slung in a cramped berthing space is welcoming.

Carmali rides quietly at anchor off the tiny island of Tintamarre in the Caribbean. Despite her good looks, she was tough enough to ride out Hurricane Frederick in Road Town, Tortola in '79

The author at a very early age, with his older sister, Toni, and
mother, at Miami Beach.

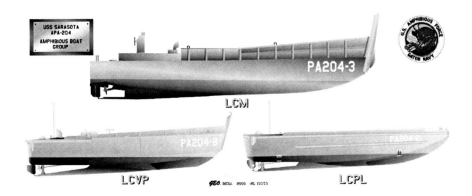

USS *Sarasota's* mini-fleet of 26 landing craft, consisting of three basic types of boats that measured from 36 to 60 feet in length. The boats were designed to deliver a battalion landing team of 1,500 U.S. Marines across hostile beaches. The author served for two years in *Sarasota*.

The author's parents, May (clearly "with child") and Joe Callo, Sr.,
possibly at the New Jersey shore. Their love of the sea was
transmitted to their son.

PART IV

SEA CONNECTIONS

WHAT I LEARNED FROM PLACES BY THE SEA

CHAPTER EIGHTEEN
HITHER HILLS

The sea belongs to us all, and every aspect of it...
is fraught with beauty.

Samuel Eliot Morison

In 1956, I moved to Croton-on-Hudson, about 35 miles up the Hudson River from New York City. It was a good place to raise kids, and it was a very manageable one-hour commute by train to my work in Manhattan. My family was expanding quickly. Joe had been born in '53 and Jim in '54. Mary Ellen arrived in '56, just in time to move in to the new house in Croton. Kathleen would be born in '58, and Patricia arrived in 1962.

With that household, finding an affordable vacation place was a challenge, and I found that camping was an excellent option. As a result, in the late 1950s and into the 1960s, Hither Hills campgrounds at Montauk, Long Island became the venue for our summer vacations. It was about a three hour drive from Croton, and its location at the very eastern tip of Long Island is a special place for anyone who is drawn to the sea.

Each summer on the day after school ended, the heavy canvass tent, Coleman stove and lantern, portable charcoal grill, and sleeping bags were lashed on top of and wedged into a station wagon, and the drive from Croton began. There was great anticipation among the group, punctuated only occasionally with a now legendary, "If I have to stop this car, you're going to be sorry."

The campsite at Hither Hills is located along two unbroken miles of Atlantic Ocean beach on Long Island's south shore. The landscape is stark: beach, dunes, dune grass, scrub and the endless stretch of ocean running to a wide horizon. The rhythmic sounds of the surf endlessly scrubbing the sandy shore permeate the place, sometimes murmuring, sometimes hissing, and sometimes pounding, and eternally repeating its cadence.

One of the things I remember about the beach is that there were very seldom any boats offshore. On occasion, merchant ships could be made out on the horizon, and there was an occasional fishing boat or pleasure boat going to or from Montauk Harbor; but most of the time there seemed to be an uninterrupted span of water stretching away from the beach. That circumstance, at least for me, seemed to continuously draw my attention toward the horizon and my mind to what was beyond that horizon.

One of the more off-trail bits of lore about the Hither Hills beach was that it was the drop-off site for saboteurs landed from German U-boats during World War II. That added a dash of mystery to the place, especially in the intense dark, where the only light came from the subdued glow of camp lanterns showing through the canvass of the tents ranged at intervals along the dune line.

Basic Living

The concrete platforms for tents were positioned roughly fifty yards from the water's edge. Our tent was a "two-room" model, made of heavy green canvass and with a footprint of roughly ten by fifteen feet. A canvass panel was strung between the tent walls, dividing the interior into two approximately equal sections. The back half was designated as the kid's sleeping area and was referred to as the bedroom. The front half was of course the living room. There were screened windows with roll-up flaps on the sides, so there was almost always an ocean breeze passing through the tent to keep it cool, even on the hottest days. Equally important, it was dry, even during heavy rain.

Cooking was done on a portable, propane-fired stove and a charcoal barbecue, and the meals were basic: cereal and fruit for breakfast, sandwiches for lunch, and hot dogs, hamburgers, chicken, tomatoes, corn, and cucumbers right out the fields of local farms and in various combinations for dinner. My Seven-Up pancakes on occasional mornings were a special attraction—and a reward for good behavior the previous day. [19]

The first cup of perked coffee in the morning was a transcending experience, usually enjoyed while sitting or standing in the sand, just above the beach's high-water line and facing the morning sun. After dinner there was a special concoction for the adults, something invented on a cold rainy evening during one of the first trips to Hither Hills: tea with a shot of vodka. For years, I have considered that combination to be one of nature's all-purpose antidotes for almost anything that ails you, physically or mentally.

Side Trips

Once or twice during each camping trip, there was a visit to the fishing piers at Montauk harbor. The anticipation that a recently caught shark might be on display there was always high. Bullheads and makos were the most common attractions, and they were studied in silent awe. Checking out the fishing boats as they eased along the jagged stone breakwater also was part of the routine during the excursions to Montauk harbor.

The fishing piers were the source of fresh lobsters, picked right out of the salt water tanks. The lobsters were brought back to the campsite and boiled in galvanized pails filled with sea water drawn directly from the ocean. No other version of lobster has ever come close to those we had at Hither Hills.

Rainy days in a tent with five kids were not good. In fact *ten minutes* on a rainy day in a tent with five kids were not good. Fortunately, there were alternatives. The two most common were the Coast Guard lighthouse at Montauk Point and the Whaling and Historical Museum in Sag Harbor. Each was within reasonable driving distance of the camp site.

The lighthouse, authorized by President George Washington in 1792 and completed in 1796, is the oldest in New York State and still is a working navigational aid. The octagon shaped tower stands at the top of a cliff, and facing east there's nothing but Atlantic Ocean between Montauk Point and the Azores. The Museum boasts artifacts from the 18th century.

If a stop for ice cream and some shopping between those two attractions was worked in, it could occupy the better part of a day. But the side visits were only accommodations of rainy days, necessary but brief interruptions that took you off the beach.

What Was It All About?

It was my sister Toni who first suggested camping at Hither Hills to me, and it turned out to be a stupendous idea. For one thing, the beach simply absorbed the kids during the day. I never really figured out specifically what they did all day, but I know I never heard those words all parents dread, "There's nothing to do"—not once in the ten years or so we camped at Hither Hills.

In fact the kids were never really *doing* much of anything, but they were totally absorbed from sunrise to sunset in the process. And between relentlessly not doing anything during the day and the sound of the surf lulling them to sleep at night, the average time it took for them to get to sleep in their sleeping bags was about ten seconds.

The Hither Hills camping trips were the kid's introduction to the ocean. As they roamed the dunes, collected seashells and driftwood, built sandcastles, body-surfed the waves, ran, and studied the horizon, they were beginning to think about the sea. They were doing the same thing I had been doing as a small child on the beach Provincetown. Watching my children as each began to explore the ocean's edge was eerily like seeing my own ghost at play, year after year.

When I asked my children what their memories of Hither Hills were, each responded with positive thoughts. My daughter Kat (I still think of her as Kathleen) provided an interesting summary, one that very pointedly goes to her and my relationships with the sea. This is what she wrote.

Our holidays at Montauk Point are amongst my sweetest childhood memories. Montauk Point was, for me, a kind of paradise—where time stopped and life was about play, play, play.

The smell of Coppertone suntan lotion and sea salt when we walked into the small shop at the campground always reminded me that we were back in this favourite magical place.

The waves were enormous, towering over my head and I loved it. It was funny to return to Montauk Point with Henry and Ben (Kat's sons) in 2002 and to see that the waves weren't six foot tall, as I had remembered.

I remember from our holidays at Montauk Point the sound of the ocean waves, when we were on the beach and when we were back at our campsite. The sound of the ocean waves is, for me, one of the most enjoyable, soul-enriching of sounds. It always calms me and reminds me how big the sea is, how powerful and profoundly beautiful nature is and how small are my perceived problems.

I loved the seagulls at Montauk Point. While others saw them as a nuisance, I loved the sound of their cry and the way they hovered in the air above our campsite when they thought that food was a possibility.

A favourite game for us kids was burying one another in the sand. One afternoon, it was my turn to get buried, up to the neck. Joe and Jim thought it was a lark to leave me there when Mum called us for dinner from over the dunes. It took me a long time to wriggle and eventually dig my way out.

The dunes—what made them so wonderful? They were the borderline between our timeless play on the beach and the more orderly family life back at our campsite. I loved to run down the dunes in my bare feet or to stand and let myself slowly sink down the slope.

Montauk Point, because it was a point of land, felt to me as a child like a wonderful place located at the end of the earth, far from every care. I always thought of that place as Montauk Point, rather than Hither Hills. I like the sound of Montauk, which reminded me of "tomahawk."

That's it for my daydreaming for now, Dad. I hope this helps. I'm off to the office.

Love,
Kat

My oldest daughter Mary Ellen also had pleasant recollections of our trips to Hither Hills.

My most outstanding and fondest memory of Hither Hills was simply going to sleep with the constant sound of the ocean, the murmur of pleasant adult conversation from the grown-ups collected outside the tent, the sound of the Coleman lantern being pumped then lit, and surprisingly, even the smell of the canvas tent. The quietness and peacefulness of that time each night is a treasured memory

A favourite time with the gaggle of kids that gathered each summer—the Callos, the Fontanas, the Wells [the Fontana kids were cousins from Westbury and the Wells were friends from Croton]—included sitting perfectly balanced on the see-saw for as long as my SugarDaddy caramel sucker would last.

Each sense was treated on the excursions to the general store —the squeak of the screen door swinging, the feel of the sand against the smooth concrete floor underfoot, the smell of the ocean, the warmth of the sun and wind and the taste of our favourite nickel candy.

When I look at the pictures I have from our trips, I can easily spot myself. I'm the kid with the big hat, long sleeves and zinc oxide on my face. I remember pouting about my prescribed wardrobe, but now I am forever grateful for my parent's insistence on my covering up. My dermatologist is quite surprised that I haven't had any problems. [Mary Ellen is a redhead.] It's one of my favourite stories to tell my kids about the difficulties of days gone bye. You know, back in the olden days before sun screen!

Hope this helps.

Love,
Mary Ellen

My daughter Trish was more expansive, talking of the broader implications of her remembrances:

Looking back at Hither Hills, I realize that the sea has always been a presence in my life, and in fact it has shaped not so much what I do, but how and where I do it.

Living near the ocean reminds me of the constant rhythm around me. Time is measured in the short cycles of sunrise and sunset, high tide and low tide, and also in the unending cycle that has been going on since the moon first rose over the earth and began its push-pull on the oceans.

Growing up on a coast, I was always aware of being on the edge of something, and beyond that edge there are others who are different. Growing up on a coast I was drawn to travel and explore those other places, and whenever I picked up a small piece of flotsam along the shore, I realized that someone far away may also have held that tiny bit of our world. That's a way that the sea symbolically connects us.

There also are the things learned in the sea: the dependence on others when swimming and the need for tightly coordinated effort when sailing. The sea also demands that we tune ourselves to changing conditions and to think quickly as those conditions often change unexpectedly. A good example of that is learning to react in a small sailboat that has capsized, something I learned at an early age.

Above all I've always appreciated the largesse and power of the sea. Those are constants that transcend.

Love,
Trish

My sons, Joe and Jim, focus on things like the sharks on display at the Montauk fishing piers, the opportunities for body-surfing to a point of exhaustion, endless exploring among the sand dunes, and watching the men surf-fishing as the sun came up. They also talk about the ice-cold showers that were part of the camp routine. During those daily showers, they were marvels of speed-washing, hopping, dancing, and twisting under the icy water. The upside was that the wood-walled area where one dried off had no roof, and the full strength of the sun would quickly drive off the chill of the ice-cold showers.

The days of living on the beach at Hither Hills were good days. Even bad weather played a positive role. We learned a lot about the moods of the sea in that place, and we learned them together. We also learned a great deal about what was best about one another.

Chapter Nineteen
Annapolis

The city lies along the Severn River at its mouth on Chesapeake Bay, 27 miles southeast of Baltimore. Settled in 1649 as Providence by Virginian Puritans, it was later known as Town of Proctor's, Town of the Severn, and Anne Arundel Town. In 1694 the provincial capital was moved there from St. Mary's City, and a year later it was renamed to honour Princess Anne, who as queen gave it a charter (1708).

The New Encyclopædia Britannica, Volume 1

I have seen two distinct versions of Annapolis over a period of more than fifty years. My initial recollections are of a grimy little backwater town with a very unattractive waterfront. In those early days of my visiting Annapolis, it was clear that it was an isolated town, a drive-by place off the New York-Baltimore-Washington corridor. No one really cared much about it, one way or another, despite its modern role as state capital of Maryland and its early, brief status as the U.S. capital from 1783-84.

A change in community attitude and a near-miraculous restoration program have created something very different. Today's Annapolis retains its ties with the past and the sea, and it lately has positioned its history in a most attractive context. Much of the city's Georgian architecture has been restored, and its predominantly old-red-brick look and tone are genuine, rather than replicated. It's different from the created restorations, such as Mystic and Williamsburg. People still live in the landmark houses and work in the landmark commercial and government office buildings.

The Heart of the Matter

Annapolis' waterfront is, for me, still its heart. In Colonial days, the harbor was populated by the speedy and flat bottomed "skipjacks" and the sturdy and hard working sloops, brigs and barks of the Age of Sail. Today those signs of a town that lived by the sea have been replaced by the masts and rigging of a scores upon scores of pleasure boats.

A long narrow inlet of the harbor points the way from the sea into the town and ends at a small plaza at the center of the waterfront. At times I have sat in that plaza with the first morning sun warming me and with a container of coffee and piece of pastry —just watching. From that vantage point the inlet's perspective is reversed: it points out to sea and the beyond.

Both sides of the narrow inlet are lined with sailboats and power boats, forming the City Dock. At the town end there is a small turning circle for boats and a dinghy dock for visiting sailors coming in from the harbor's outer anchorage. Boats occasionally come and go from the City Dock piers, and it's fascinating to watch the line handling and the maneuvering involved. It's an opportunity "to go to school" by studying the techniques, and levels, of seamanship involved. Well most of the time it is; sometimes it's just a few minutes of amusement.

Around the rim of the harbor there are restaurants, shops, galleries, a small museum, and a large boating supply and clothing store. At the center and opposite the small plaza is the Market House, a large enclosed shed with a great variety of food options that can be taken to the outside tables for a waterside breakfast or lunch. Naturally local seafood is much in evidence and many of the seafood variations involve crabcakes.

But the most striking thing about the harbor is the collection of restored eighteenth and nineteenth-century buildings that once housed taverns, coffee houses, a victualling warehouse, and chandleries and that now are occupied by twenty-first-century merchants and craftsmen.

When one enters Annapolis from the harbor today, the initial vista is much as it was during the Colonial days of the town. First there is the cluster of waterfront buildings ringing the harbor. Behind them and rising above the trees and buildings are church spires and the impressive dome of the Maryland State Capitol. It's seemingly unchanged waterfront is a vivid reminder of Annapolis' colonial history as a commercial seaport and shipbuilding center. With a change of the occupants' clothing, the Annapolis waterfront of today would be a duplicate image of Annapolis during its days as commercial center of the earliest United States of America.

The Beauty of Brick

The architectural mood in Annapolis is, as I said, set by brick. Among the surviving buildings of the eighteenth and nineteenth centuries, red brick dominates. Several signature buildings demonstrate the beauty of that ancient building material. One of the most interesting is the Maryland Inn, which occupies the site where the Drummer of the Town, the equivalent of the Town Crier, once dispensed the news. Each of the Inn's 40-plus rooms is different, and apart from the plumbing, resembles a room in a Colonial Inn. When I have stayed at the Maryland Inn it has been hard to not think about who could have stayed in the room I was occupying. Perhaps Jefferson, John Adams, or Washington had occupied the same four walls.

Close to the Maryland Inn is the State Circle, the geographical center of Annapolis. The impressive domed Capitol building at the center of the circle was begun in 1772 and it has been in continuous use since 1784. The pegged cypress dome is a tribute to the skill of the building's designers and construction workers. The Treaty of Paris formally ending the American Revolution was ratified by the Continental Congress here, and George Washington's resignation as commander-in-chief of the Continental Army was delivered in one of its chambers.

Paca House was among the first mansions of Annapolis. It was completed in 1765 for William Paca, a planter, a signer of the Declaration of Independence and three-time governor of Maryland. The building's exterior presents classic Georgian simplicity and proportion. The interior contains antique furniture, silver and art from its Colonial days. The street that it is on, Prince

George Street, is also representative of the days when the individual American Colonies were emerging as a unified nation. Unlike the vast majority of landmark buildings in Annapolis, this one has been turned into a museum.

Anchor's Aweigh

Although I didn't get my navy commission from the U.S. Naval Academy, I have always felt a connection with the place. Many of my friends are USNA graduates, and during my two years in USS *Sarasota,* my colleague Fay Lossing represented his alma mater well.

Part of the affinity that I feel for the Naval Academy obviously comes from its thoroughly nautical tone. With one edge of the campus on the Annapolis harbor and another on the Severn River, it's easy to sense the salt in the air. And it's a place where young men and women come and go while learning the skills and disciplines of warrior seamen. Their ubiquitous presence is the essence of their campus, and their looks combine the attitudes of honest seamen with those of committed patriots.

Traditions of Heroism and Victory

There is one very special place at the Naval Academy that I get to from time to time: the crypt of John Paul Jones. Centered under the impressive dome of the Naval Academy Chapel, one level beneath the main level of the church, it's the final resting place of a Continental Navy officer who had a lot to do with America's successful fight for independence. In a navy that began with eight converted merchant ships, Jones and his fellow captains of the Continental Navy challenged what was at the time the greatest navy of the world, the Royal Navy of Great Britain. And in Jones' case, he won implausible victories that represented maritime tipping points in America's War of Independence.

In 1782 Jones wrote to Robert Morris, then Minister of Marine in the Continental Congress, and pointed out the implausibility of the first Continental Navy squadron that deployed against Great Britain:

Was it a proof of madness in the first corps of sea officers, at so critical a period, to have launched out on the ocean with only two armed merchant ships, two armed brigantines, and one armed sloop, to make war against such a power as great Britain? [20]

Jones had gone to sea at the age of thirteen in the British merchant marine, where he became a successful captain at a young age. When he enlisted in the nascent Continental Navy as a lieutenant in 1775 he had no prior training as a military officer. He became, in effect, a seaman warrior, in contrast to his opposite numbers in the Royal Navy who were trained as warrior seamen. Against all odds, Jones achieved strategically and psychologically important victories that to this day are not adequately represented in our history books. And he captured the concept of political and personal liberty before he captured a single British ship.

Quiet time in Jones' crypt is a time for thinking about the incredible strength and sacrifices of those who took the American Colonies from political dependency on a mother country to independence and a form of governance that emphasized individual initiative and political liberty, rather than loyalty to a monarch. Jones' astonishing achievements at sea are also a reminder that there was a naval component to the American Revolution, an important reality that is often missed, even by a significant number of scholars and authors.

Jones' epitaph, which is set in the marble at the foot of his sarcophagus, sums up his achievements at sea in the plain language of a seaman: "He gave our Navy its earliest traditions of heroism and victory."

CHAPTER TWENTY

LONDON

Britannia needs no bulwarks,
No towers along the steep;
Her march is o'er the mountain waves,
Her home is on the deep.

Thomas Campbell

My first visit to London was in 1979, and I remember my reaction to walking along Piccadilly and Regent Street. I wasn't seeing shops and restaurants; I was remembering bomb craters and bombed out buildings. What was flooding my mind were the black and white newsreel images of crude, homemade signs reading "Open for Business" on the doors of shops with shattered windows and distorted door frames. And as I walked along side streets in Mayfair, I wasn't seeing elegant homes and chic business offices; I was remembering scenes of dazed people climbing over the rubble that used to be their homes, searching for loved ones and shattered remnants of their lives.

It was an unexpected and hard return to the childhood anxieties of World War II. Gradually those images receded, however, and I began to learn what a great city London is, and particularly, how deeply it's connected with the sea. In fact, although it isn't immediately apparent to most visitors—the Thames doesn't provide spectacular vistas—London is a city whose history is dominated by the sea, and that dominance has made its mark on the British in many subtle ways.

Shaped by Geography

No point in England is more than 70 miles from salt water. And her maritime past stretches back through millennia. There are theories that there were pre-Roman migrations to England in dugouts and crude boats, built with wicker and animal skins. The first English mariners could have poled and paddled through water channels in the marshes that are believed by some geologists to have once connected England with the main landmass of the European Continent. And those earliest migrations would have been followed by later migrations over open waters from the European Continent, initially from the area that is now Portugal.

The natural tendency of the early arrivals in England was to settle close the coasts. There was food to be caught in the offshore waters and the idea of moving into the unknown interior of the land had to be daunting. In their harsh world, there was at least relative security at the fringe of the sea.

The town that became London was established around 50 AD by Roman merchants. The area's location on the Thames was a key factor. There was a bridge there that had been built at the site by the Romans shortly after their invasion of England in 43 AD, and there was sufficient depth at that point in the river to handle the sea-going ships of the day. There also was the advantage of the site being far enough inland to make the place relatively safe from raiders from the sea. Legend has it that before the Romans arrived the area had been known as CaenLudein, and through the centuries, the Vikings, Saxons and Normans all left their mark on the port the Romans named Lundinium.

Then, as the Age of Discovery began, the English began to associate their well-being with probing farther and farther off shore. Eventually that impulse would drive men like Drake, Hawkins and the Cabots into the farthest reaches of the world's oceans.

The Trafalgar Monument

Since my first visited London thirty years ago, I probably have averaged two visits a year. Each trip has deepened my sense of that city's links to the sea. What started as a vague feeling three decades ago has become an engrossing interest, and there are a number of specific sites that stand out in my mind.

If Piccadilly is the traffic center of London, the Nelson Monument, just a short distance away at Trafalgar Square, is its spiritual center. There the scene is dominated by a 17-foot-foot sandstone statue of Admiral Lord Nelson atop a 185-foot granite column. The column and statue, designed by architect William Railton, were financed by public subscription and erected in 1841 to commemorate Nelson's history-changing victory over the combined French-Spanish Fleet at the Battle of Trafalgar in 1805.

The true-to-nature Nelson of the statue, executed by the sculptor Edward Baily, strikes a confident pose, with right foot and gaze extended towards the south and the English Channel. Nelson's left hand rests on the hilt of a sword, the tip of which is planted at his feet. The fact that his right arm is missing is evident, and his empty sleeve is pinned across his chest. Because of the height of the column, few people actually see the details of the statue, notwithstanding its 17-foot size. The Nelson of Trafalgar is confident, but the implied aggression he projects is disciplined. In that pose, Nelson represents some of the aspects of his own personality, as well as some of his countrymen.

Today the square that surrounds the Monument is known for special outdoor events and political rallies. Buses, taxis, trucks, and private cars endlessly swirl past the site. At any point in time during the day, scores of people are walking through the Square, and in warm weather it's a favored spot for an outdoor lunch or for just sitting and watching the passing scene. I've noticed something about the people walking past the

Nelson Monument, as well as those sitting there: it's extremely rare to see faces turned skyward and eyes focused on Nelson.

But for me, the determined and aggressive posture of the Nelson who Londoners seem to ignore is what the monument and the city are all about. It speaks clearly of the outward bound attitude that has characterized the British for so many centuries and the corollary of that attitude captured in the unrelenting tenacity of the Royal Navy. It also speaks of the qualities that imbued the American colonists who carved out new lives and shaped new ideas of government on a rich and rugged frontier.

The base of the column has its own special symbolisms related to Nelson, beginning with the lampposts at the four corners of the Square. The lights of the lampposts have a connection that, again, very few Londoners are aware of: the glass lamps are actually taken from Nelson's flagship at Trafalgar, HMS *Victory*.

Also at the base of the Nelson column are four bronze bas-reliefs, cast from captured French guns and representing Nelson's four major battles. Depicted are scenes from the Battle of Cape St. Vincent in 1791, where Nelson became a widely known hero in Britain, the Battle of the Nile fought in 1798, where Nelson frustrated Napoleon's ambitions in the Far East, the Battle of Copenhagen in 1801, where Nelson shattered the prospect of a pro-French alliance of maritime nations, and finally, the Battle Trafalgar in 1805, where Nelson defeated a combined French-Spanish Fleet and lost his life in the process.

In the longer term, Nelson's victory at Trafalgar also ended Napoleon's dreams of invading and conquering Great Britain. It was the beginning of a century of British dominance of the world's oceans that shaped the world as we know it today.

At each of those bloody battles and in different ways in each instance, Nelson shaped the course of history from the quarterdecks of his flagships. America's seapower theorist, Admiral A.T. Mahan, summed up Nelson's historic importance in the final paragraph of his 1895 biography, *The Life of Nelson*:

There were indeed consequences momentous and stupendous yet to flow from the decisive supremacy of Great Britain's sea-power...the establishment of which was Nelson's great achievement; but his part was done when Trafalgar was fought. [21]

Where World-Shaping Decisions were Made

Along Whitehall and within sight of the Trafalgar Monument is the Old Admiralty. The building, which was designed by Thomas Ripley, was completed in 1725 and has the authentic look of aged but unyielding granite. Until 1788, the First Lord of the Admiralty and other Lords of the Admiralty not only worked there, they also lived there. Today, it's not difficult to sense their spirits in its rooms and corridors. And within the Old Admiralty there is a very special room, The Admiralty Board Room, an inner sanctum that few are aware of and even fewer see today.

During its earliest history of The Board Room it was, in fact, part of the residence, office, and dining room of the First Lord and other members of the Admiralty. It was the place where, particularly during the Age of Sail, decisions that shaped our world were made, and thanks to special permission from the Royal Navy, I have had the experience of visiting and photographing the room on several occasions for writing projects.

In one instance, I was allowed to work alone in the room, and in a second instance, I was allowed to work in the room with Sally accompanying me. What I absorbed during those working sessions left imprints, ideas about the foresight and determination of our British "cousins."

During those quiet times in the Admiralty Board Room, I was able to sense things about it that could not have been absorbed in other circumstances. I began to think about the people who played roles that shaped the modern world during the Age of Sail as human beings, rather than one-dimensional images fixed on the pages of history books.

The central physical feature of the space, which is about the size of a large corporate board room, is the marble fireplace, which bears the seal of Charles II. The fireplace's surround is a priceless limewood carving by Grinling Gibbons. It is believed that this masterpiece of carving was created in 1695 and later transferred to the Admiralty Board Room. Among the many nautical items it depicts are navigational instruments of the 16th and 17th centuries, an Admiralty anchor, a crown, and laurel leaves.

In the center of the top portion of the implausibly intricate carving over the fireplace is "the Eye in Glory," which was used by the Stuart Kings to symbolize their divine right to rule. The design also is reminiscent of the ancient Egyptian udjat symbol. [22]

Directly over the fireplace is a piece of state-of the-art early eighteenth century technology, a dial with an indicator that is connected to a wind vane on the roof of the building and which indicates the direction of the wind at any moment. The wind dial, which dates from 1798, was used by the decision makers of the time to determine local wind conditions, a critical factor for the departure and arrival of ships and fleets powered by wind.

In addition to the wind vane on the roof of the Old Admiralty there is a large wood semaphore. The semaphore was used to initiate a series of signals along a system that ended in Portsmouth. Records indicate that a message started at the Board Room could be relayed station-to-station to Portsmouth in twelve minutes.

The Board Room Table was added to the room's furnishings in 1780 and it is distinguished by a sizable cut-away portion at one end. The resulting indentation in the table accommodated one First Lord of the Admiralty, whose weight exceeded three hundred pounds.

The modern history of the Board Room includes its World War II use by Winston Churchill and serious damage to its intricately painted ceiling by a World War II bomb blast. Following the war, the ceiling was restored to match the original.

The Board Room's oak paneling is believed to have come from an Admiralty building that predates the current structure. It radiates warmth, heightening the sense of important history that is palpable in the room. An animist would no doubt claim that the walls have become imbued with the spirits of those who deliberated and argued about world changing actions there. I must admit that while I was alone there, thoughts along those lines emerged.

During my sessions in the Admiralty Board Room, it was impossible not to think about the momentous discussions and decisions made within those oak paneled walls. In all probability, for example, the selection of Nelson to command the Mediterranean Fleet that prevailed at the Battle of Trafalgar on 21 October 1805 would have been conducted around the table—now perpetually ringed by empty (to the unknowing visitor) chairs.

Some of the Admiralty officials would have brought up Nelson's controversial affair with Lady Emma Hamilton, and others would have countered with his uniquely successful combat performance in the Battles of the Nile and Copenhagen, victories of great strategic importance in Britain's ongoing war with France. And at the end of the heated discussion, one can imagine Nelson's mentor, the Earl St. Vincent, guiding the decision to finally appoint Nelson to that historically momentous command. As they say, "the rest is history."

Mariners' Chapel at All Hallows

There's a church in central London with the unusual name of All Hallows, Barking. It's easy to miss but hard to forget by those who seek it out. What made it memorable to me are the Mariner's Chapel and its other unique, sea-related features.

The church, which is within feet of the Tower of London, is in fact more than 400 years older than that London landmark.

The original church was founded in 675 by the Abbey of Barking and an original arch from that church is still standing. Remnants of a paved Roman road also still exist on the site.

What makes All Hallows stand apart for me, however, is not its antiquity but the ancient links with the sea that permeate that antiquity. For example, it's impossible to miss the small ship models that are apparent everywhere. Some are skillfully crafted; some are crudely carved.

The individual models that form this mini-fleet are ubiquitous, hanging in arches and perched on ledges and shelves. They have been brought to the church over the years as thanksgiving for successful returns from the sea. They remind me how All Hallows once served a congregation involved on a daily basis with the sea.

Most of the models are of anonymous ships, but among those that are recognizable, one snatched my attention on my first visit. It depicted a relatively modern ship. It was a replica of the motor vessel *Royal Daffodil,* which was part of the armada of civilian ships and boats that accomplished the astonishing evacuation of more than 300,000 British troops trapped at Dunkirk in the early stages of World War II. During the end of May and the first week of June 1940, destroyers of the Royal Navy and an improvised fleet of fishing boats, civilian ferries, and private pleasure craft was organized in a unique effort, labeled Operation Dynamo, to get the trapped troops off the beaches at Dunkirk and back to Great Britain.

Royal Daffodil, which was a commercial ferry of slightly more than 300 feet in length, made seven roundtrips between Dunkirk and England, bringing a total of just under 10,000 troops to safety. At one point a bomb went completely through the ship and exploded under her. The hole was plugged with mattresses and *Royal Daffodil* continued on her transits.

The efforts of the ships and boats at the evacuation of Dunkirk were labeled "miraculous" by Winston Churchill, and that they may have been. But for me, what *Royal Daffodil* did under the most difficult of circumstances and in the darkest early stages of World War II was the result of something very earthbound. It was made possible by the skill and determination of seamen, who acted out traditions of the sea that had evolved over many centuries.

The National Maritime Museum

The National Maritime Museum at Greenwich, which is one of the outer sections of London, has a well-deserved reputation as the site of one of the world's premier maritime museums. Greenwich is also the area of the City where King Henry VIII and his daughter Queen Elizabeth were born.

The Museum is a fifteen minute ride by train from central London, or a bit longer but an infinitely more interesting boat ride down the Thames to the Greenwich Dock. From the Dock or from the Greenwich train station, it's a short walk to the Museum, along streets marked by restaurants and small shops that I have come to know since my first visit to Britain.

Among the shops along that way is Anthony Simmonds book shop, appropriately situated on Nelson Road. And it was there that I located a first edition copy of Robert Southey's *The Life of Nelson,* the book that was my initial introduction to Admiral Lord Nelson.

Naval historians credit the National Maritime Museum with the most comprehensive collection of maritime artifacts in the world. This amazing collection is housed in one of a series of interconnected buildings designed by Christopher Wren. A major redesign of the building's interior was recently completed, and ships' figureheads, models, paintings, documents, navigation instruments, and interactive displays come together there to relate the long maritime accomplishments that eventually made Great Britain dominant at sea during the nineteenth century.

The largest exhibit and one of the Museum's signature attractions is an actual steam tugboat launched in 1907, a hardworking vessel that operated on the Manchester Ship Canal.

The exhibits that have had the greatest impact on me are those devoted to Nelson. During the Bicentennial of the Battle of Trafalgar in 2005, the Museum's ongoing Nelson exhibit was redone and expanded in scope. One of the central themes of the exhibit focused on Nelson's ability to thwart Napoleon Bonaparte's global ambition.

Details of the Battle of Trafalgar are demonstrated in the Museum in an audio-visual presentation that illuminates such things as relative fleet strength, tactics and casualties. The relation of Nelson and Napoleon and the impact of that relationship on history adds important new appreciation to the global significance of Nelson's victory at Cape Trafalgar in the early nineteenth century.

The Trafalgar Bicentennial exhibit also included many of Nelson's personal effccts which were gathered after the Battle. Among those effects was a ring that had been given to him by Lady Emma Hamilton just before he left England to fight the Battle of Trafalgar.

Clearly the most poignant of the exhibit items, however, was the uniform jacket worn by Nelson at his last and greatest battle. The jacket is in nearly perfect condition. The exception is the small musket ball hole in the garment's shoulder, where the fatal bullet struck Nelson at the height of the action at Trafalgar.

The uniform jacket with the tiny musket ball hole evoked imaginings about the three hours that followed Nelson's fatal wound on the afternoon of 21 October 1805. During those hours Nelson lay in *Victory's* orlop, surrounding by the other wounded men of the battle. It's a scene of abject suffering as the combat swirls in and around *Victory*. It's a scene that demolishes glorified visions of combat in war.

Notwithstanding his personal suffering, Nelson's thoughts were not about himself. He was instead concerned about the future wellbeing of his lover and their daughter Horatia, and he worried constantly about how the battle was going. Finally, as he realized that his end had come, he focused on his life and its

---

meaning with a typical sailor's economy of words: "Thank God I have done my duty."

That scene, with its contradictory violence and humane concerns, has for me, come to be the final punctuation on Nelson's life, notwithstanding the incredible state funeral in London that followed his death or the many other tributes to the hero of Trafalgar that have followed over the years.

The Mystery Ships of Pall Mall

An observant visitor driving along Pall Mall in London might notice something unusual about the lamp posts. Each is topped with a model of a small square-rigged warship. The miniature vessels are cast in metal and fixed permanently at the very top of each light.

The ships were pointed out to me by a taxi driver on one of my first visits to London. He said they represent Nelson's victorious fleet at the Battle of Trafalgar. In my own mind I added that also there's a connection between the ships of Pall Mall and the Trafalgar Monument a short distance away, where Nelson faces south from atop his column and overlooks this fleet of tiny ships, now impervious to wind, rain or enemy action.

Those miniature Royal Navy ships pointing towards the sea along Pall Mall are, however, more than an obscure factoid about London with which I can amuse friends. They are evidence of how thoroughly the maritime history of London's occupants is woven into the fabric of their city.

CHAPTER TWENTY-ONE

PORTSMOUTH

*The royal navy of England has ever been its greatest
defence and ornament, it is its ancient and natural
strength, the floating bulwark of our island.*

Sir William Blackstone 1723-1780

My initial visit to Portsmouth took place during one of my
first visits to London in 1979-80. Only two-plus hours from
London by train, it was an obvious side trip. And as I had
discovered previously in London, I found a city with a fascinating
maritime history stretching far into the past, a place that enlarges
the narrative of how the British and their cultural descendants are
bound to the sea.

Portsmouth was founded early in the twelfth century by a
merchant who owned land on Portsea Island, and it is Great
Britain's only island city. In 1194, King Richard the Lionhearted
gave the city its first charter, and by the beginning of the
thirteenth century it was a thriving port. In the fourteenth century,
when Portsmouth was still a town of wood buildings with thatched
roofs, it was burned down four times. It was also a time of
constant warfare between England and France, a condition that
would last on and off for five centuries.

In 1380, after the fourth attack, crude fortifications were built
to protect the town. In 1494 Henry VII built a second stone tower
to protect the harbor, and a year later, he built the harbor's first

dockyard. That was the beginning of the port as a naval base, a role that has been maintained to the present, and for centuries Portsmouth has been the primary base for the Royal Navy.

The original section of the Southsea Castle was built in the mid-1500s, during Henry VIII's reign, and I've stood on the battlements of that Castle, with my face to the sea breeze, just as Henry surely did. In 1522 a massive chain that could be raised and lowered also was extended across the entrance to the harbor to further protect the growing port.

Wooden Walls

By the early nineteenth century, at the peak of the Age of Sail, Portsmouth was a main operations base for the "wooden walls" of the Royal Navy that were maintaining Great Britain as the dominant maritime power of the world. Fleets from Portsmouth went forth to every corner of the globe, and it was said that those fleets extended Britain's national power to the six fathom curve off every shoreline of the world.

A particularly poignant scene from that era was captured by Robert Southey, once-Poet Laureate of Great Britain and arguably the first modern biographer of Admiral Lord Nelson. In his biography of Nelson, Southey wrote of the harbor-side scene as England's most famous fighting admiral left Portsmouth on 14 September 1805 to board HMS *Victory*. He was heading for his command in the Mediterranean and the place in history he would establish off Cape Trafalgar. Nelson had just come from Merton and his paramour Lady Emma Hamilton, and it would be the last time he would sail from the shores of England. Southey puts us with Nelson in the waterfront scene:

> [H]e reached Portsmouth; and, having dispatched his business on shore, endeavoured to elude the populace by taking a byway to the beach; but a crowd collected in his train, pressing forward to obtain a sight of his face;—many were in tears, and many knelt down before him, and blessed him as he passed. England has had many heroes, but never one who so entirely possessed the love of his fellow country-

men as Nelson. All men knew that his heart was as humane as it was fearless...he served his country with all his soul, and with all his strength; and, therefore, they loved him as truly and as fervently as he loved England. [23]

As Southey goes on, he shows how Nelson understood the relationship that linked him with the English public. As he pulled away from the shore, Nelson turned to his flag captain Thomas Hardy, and with penetrating insight he remarked, "I had their huzzas before—I have their hearts now!"[24] The comment demonstrated that Nelson was considerably ahead of his time in recognizing the importance of public opinion to the career of a senior military leader. Understanding the basis of that relationship has been an ongoing study, a continuing search for the essentials of real leadership.

Around almost every corner in Portsmouth, I have found evocative signs of Nelson and much more: echoes of things that played importantly in the history of the Royal Navy and this seaport with a history that spans nine centuries. Tall masts, inns with hinged signs that creak rhythmically over their entrances in the breeze and then more assertively as the wind rises, monuments to seamen claimed by their workplace, and many visual images have transported me to other times and history-shaping events.

Those different pieces of Portsmouth's landscape combine to create a special perspective of people and events that have a prominent place in our own history and also our present lives.

The Historic Dockyard

The first place I was drawn to in Portsmouth is the area known as the Historic Dockyard, which dates to 1194, when the first dock was built along the harbor shore. At the Dockyard, an ancient wall built in 1212 by the order of King John, square-rigged ships, uneven cobblestone streets, and the Dockyard's massive wood gate—added in 1711—all tell me of historic times, times when the Royal Navy carried British policies and way of thinking across the world's oceans and delivered them with permanence in places like the American Colonies.

The Historic Dockyard is a unique and proximate link with today's Royal Navy, since it's contained within the active Portsmouth navy base, where there is ongoing activity involving ships and sailors of today's Royal Navy in constant view.

Within the Dockyard walls, there endures a palpable feeling of hard work. And it's been impossible for me, as I've walked along the Dockyard's main street, to not think about the scores of generations of ship riggers, carpenters, sail makers, and their fellow workers who strode over the ancient cobblestones on which I was stepping. And it's not hard for me to believe that a lot of their "just get on with the job" spirit continues to go to sea in the ships that currently are based or repaired there.

HMS *Victory*

The dramatic centerpiece of Britain's naval history, as well as Portsmouth's Historic Dockyard, is HMS *Victory*. She is dry-moored at one end of the Dockyard, in what used to be a working dry dock. She is still in commission in the Royal Navy, and is recognized as the oldest commissioned naval vessel in the world. She is the flagship of the Second Sea Lord.

HMS *Victory* was launched in 1765 and ended her active service in 1812. Once separated from the Royal Navy's operational activities, she was anchored in Portsmouth Harbor, where she remained until 1922. In 1922 *Victory* was moved to the dry dock where she is maintained for those who want to learn about, and from, the sea.

The ship is massive. Her hull is pierced with three long rows of gun ports that run virtually the full length of the ship. Her one hundred-plus guns made her a floating artillery platform of awesome power, in the terms of measurement of her day, a "first-rate" ship. But when you get close to her and look up, she takes on a slightly more benign aspect. Her masts and rigging seem to be touching the clouds. Those who worked in her rigging were more of the sky than of the earth.

Victory is motionless now, but when her sails were set and driving her through the seas, she exuded immense energy. When she fired a broadside, the potential for death and destruction was shocking. *Victory* was typical of the capital ships of her day, but her crews were not. Their proficiency was special, a force multiplier that was recognized by all who met *Victory* in combat. And her crews were the enablers for Nelson and those who served under him to shape the course of history.

When standing on *Victory's* quarterdeck it is impossible for me not to think of Nelson, especially when standing next to the brass plate that reads "Here Nelson Fell—21st Oct 1805." Once below, however, where hammocks were slung and most of the guns were manned, my attention is elsewhere. There my thoughts turn to the seamen, the skilled, durable, and motivated sailors who were the indispensible, but mostly unseen and unrecognized catalyst of history. They slept, ate, and fought in the dim light that is symbolic of the degree of attention accorded to *their* achievements.

In September of 2007, Sally and I had an opportunity to meet the then-commanding officer of this amazing example of the Age of Sail, Lieutenant Commander John Scivier. And while there is an appropriate focus on Nelson throughout the ship, Lieutenant Commander Scivier added a sometimes neglected aspect of *Victory's* dramatic history. He emphasized the incredible courage and discipline of the more than 800 enlisted seamen and Royal Marines who fought their ship successfully through one of the bloodiest and most historically significant naval battles in history.

Over the years, I have managed to see much of *Victory,* including Nelson's great cabin—where a poignant portrait of Lady Emma Hamilton looks forever for the return of her lover, and where one can almost see the admiral hunched over his small desk and writing to his beloved Emma. I also have walked the three gun decks, where men ate and slept in the seemingly endless ship's routine and then, in hellish combat, fought their guns in hope of seeing another day.

On *Victory's* quarterdeck, I've paused to stand at the exact spot where Nelson was felled by a musket ball fired from the

French ship *Redoubtable* during the Battle of Trafalgar. His words to his flag captain at the moment were a simple statement of fact: "They have done for me at last, Hardy." [25]

But the most moving place in the ship for me is the orlop, deep below the ship's main deck. There, in a dimly lit small space, the ships' surgeon dealt with those wounded in battle, using instruments and techniques that were developed for speed and efficiency. Mitigating pain was not a major concern.

It was to *Victory's* orlop that Nelson was carried when he was fatally wounded at Trafalgar. It also was there, among the wounded and the dying that he breathed his last words: "Thank God I have done my duty."[26] Nelson's choice of words in his last moments led me to some serious thinking about the definition of and the relevance of the concept of "duty."

The Mary Rose

The *Mary Rose* was one of Henry VIII's favorite ships, and she too has found a resting place at Portsmouth's Royal Naval Dockyard. In 1545, during an engagement with a French invasion fleet, she sank. The disaster took place within sight of Southsea Castle. There are differing reasons advanced for her sinking. One is that the lower gun ports (*Mary Rose* was one of the first ships with pierced gun ports for firing broadsides) were left open, causing the ship to flood and sink. Another hypothesis was that the ship, with a high center of gravity, was simply mishandled and capsized as a result of that mishandling.

During the excavation and raising of the remnants of the ship in 1986, it was discovered that her ballast had shifted to the starboard side. This also could have been the cause of the sinking, or the shift in the ballast simply could have been a result of the capsizing. In any event, no accounts attribute the sinking to the French.

For more than 400 years, the silt of Portsmouth harbor held *Mary Rose* and most of her crew of between 400 and 700 in a common tomb. Then in 1982, a team using sophisticated salvage methods succeeded in raising her. Today a major section of the remarkably preserved hull is on display in an environmentally controlled building in the Historic Dockyard, not far from HMS *Victory*.

In a nearby building, a wealth of artifacts, such as stone cannon balls, longbows, pewter tableware, bosun's pipes and other items from shipboard life in Tudor times are on display. These common articles add to the human dimension of *Mary Rose's* sudden sinking. But the experience I found most moving was walking within a few feet the preserved section of her hull and imaging the chaos and terror of her crew's last moments. It was a very different experience from what I felt exploring *Victory*. It was the difference between a sense of life and a feeling of death.

The Royal Naval Museum

The Royal Naval Museum is the intellectual center of the Historic Dockyard. The Museum was established in 1911 and it occupies three distinct galleries. Two of the buildings are former Dockyard storehouse, constructed between 1760 and 1790.

The Museum is an incredible collection of ship's figureheads, artwork, artifacts and special exhibits. I can still remember walking into the main display area for the first time, looking up and seeing a funeral barge suspended overhead. It was the barge that carried Nelson's body along the Thames River from Greenwich to the steps of Whitehall, where the state funeral procession to St. Paul's Cathedral for Nelson's interment began. From the surrounding gallery, I was able to inspect the barge in detail.

The Battle of Trafalgar gets special attention at the Museum with "The Trafalgar Experience," a vivid recreation of the action on one of *Victory's* gundecks during that violent event. This unusual exhibit was created in anticipation of the Bicentennial of the Battle of Trafalgar in 2005. The exhibit's sounds and scenes are arresting, to say the least, and it made a special point for me: there's a big difference between reading about the incredible level of noise during combat in a ship like *Victory* and actually experiencing it.

When the exhibit was under construction, then museum director and good friend Dr. Colin White conducted Sally and me through a preview of the experience. The accompanying commentary of Dr. White, who died on Christmas Day in 2007, transported us and we were made to experience those moments, not through the eyes those above-deck, but through the eyes of those who fought for their lives and country in the dark, cramped, and smoke-filled gun deck.

Nelson also is featured at the Museum in a special collection of items donated by American Nelson enthusiast Lily Lambert McCarthy. As a young girl, Lily McCarthy became fascinated by Nelson and his astonishing career; and then over the years, she contributed hundreds of items that she collected to the Royal Naval Museum. Today, Lily McCarthy's family continues their support of the Museum. These rare items range from ceramics, to paintings, medals, sculptures, letters, and more. [27]

Spinnaker Tower

One of the most recent additions to the Portsmouth harbor scene is a dramatic, five hundred-plus-foot tower, erected at the harbor's edge in 2005. The tower's abstract design appropriately suggests a tall mast with billowing sails. Spinnaker Tower's ultra modern architecture may not mesh with ancient history of Portsmouth, but I found that its nautical impressionism does. In the tourist literature it's referred to as Britain's "new national icon."

Visitors who ascend the tower get a feel of those who entered and left Portsmouth harbor in the rigging of tall ships. There are even "Time Telescopes" at View Deck 2 of the Tower, where tourists can see simulations of HMS *Victory* and *Mary Rose* sailing past. And if you are willing to venture to the Towers "crow's nest," you can, as those able seamen who worked handling sail far above deck in the square riggers of the past, become part of the sky, separated for a time from the earth's surface.

And Beyond

Spinnaker Tower, Southsea Castle, HMS *Victory, Mary Rose,* and the Royal Naval Museum are the starting points for anyone who wants to probe the truths of the sea embedded below the surface of Portsmouth's evocative sights. I have explored the first iron-hulled warship, HMS *Warrior,* several small maritime museums, shops stocked with nautical items, figureheads taken from the cutwaters of ships that sail no more, anchors that once gripped the bottom of harbors in the farthest corners of the earth, and random nautical artifacts. Each item has stories to tell to those of us willing to stop and listen.

After just a few visits, I came to realize that throughout the sea stories one hears at Portsmouth there is an over-arching theme: the near-mystical relationship between ships and those who go to sea in them.

Ships are not inanimate; they have a life, an essence. And many who spend time at sea will claim that ships have distinctive personalities. I am among those. The skilled men and women who build and repair ships often claim the same thing. The characteristics of a ship's personality emerge over time, and particularly in times of stress or danger.

It is those times of danger that not only draw out the character of a ship but also bond her seamen with her, forever. At sea and in danger, you and your ship survive or meet disaster together. It's a relationship that's not easy to define, and sailors are generally reluctant, perhaps even embarrassed, to talk about it.

The eighteenth century minister, lecturer and writer Thomas Gibbons did, however, manage to distill the true essence of the relationship into a very few words: "There is but a plank between a sailor and eternity." [28]

CHAPTER TWENTY-TWO

BERMUDA

[I]t is not the land, a meager total of approximately 20 square miles in all, that rivets the traveler's attention, but the sea itself, of an incredible cerulean and aquamarine shot with purple above the underlying reefs, that dazzles and astounds. Bermuda is indeed the Land of Water.

Terry Tucker

Bermuda was a relatively late addition to my travels to places with close connections with the sea. I had been there very briefly in 1983 but only for an overnight, and it wasn't until September of 1993 that Sally and I made a spontaneous decision and headed off to Bermuda for a brief break from the daily grind. During the four days we were there, I discovered it was that it was worth the wait.

Formerly a Place to Avoid

Bermuda began its recorded history as a strange and a dangerous hazard for mariners. Many early charts of the Atlantic did not include it at all, and because of its small land area and low profile, even those who passed as close as fifteen miles or so simply missed seeing it, especially in foul weather or at night.

For those who did come across it, the submerged reefs that guard its shorelines were a deadly barrier to getting ashore. Uncounted shipwrecks lying on Bermuda's reefs are testament to that danger. In fact, during the sixteenth century, Bermuda was considered a navigation hazard to avoid, and captains who passed it safely often celebrated the event with a special toast.

Most historians agree that the first European discoverer of this special island was a Spaniard, Juan Bermudez, who passed it in his ship *La Garza* in 1503, and a French map of the world showing "La Bermuda" was published in 1543. A rock on the south shore of Bermuda, now known as "Spanish Rock," has that date, a cross, and several undecipherable markings cut into its surface. It's presumed that the markings were made by a castaway. The anonymous shipwreck victim of 1543, most probably a Portuguese, was followed by other shipwrecked sailors. Some of these later castaways managed to build small ships, in which they escaped from what early seamen called "the Uninhabited Islands."

The First to Stay

In 1609 seven ships left England to relieve the settlers in Jamestown in Britain's Virginia Colony. The leader of the project was Admiral Sir George Somers, who was embarked in *Sea Venture,* along with 150 men, women and children. During the voyage, Somers and *Sea Venture* became separated from the other ships and subsequently ran into a violent storm. For days they fought the storm, and finally, at the point of sinking, Somers and his companions sighted Bermuda.

Somers and his crew managed to run their ship aground deliberately, and as the storm subsided, the 150 men, women, and children in *Sea Venture* were ferried ashore. Unwittingly, Somers and his fellow countrymen became the first, albeit unintended, wave of settlers in Bermuda. From the day Sir George and his companions stepped ashore, the island of Bermuda was no longer "the Uninhabited Islands."

Eventually the *Sea Venture* survivors were able to build two new ships, *Deliverance* and *Patience,* with the intention of completing their voyage to Jamestown. And despite a series of rebellions among the small society that had been established ashore, the ships were completed and the Somers' group, minus several mutineers who were left behind, sailed on to Jamestown. In all probability, the accounts of the Somers' group that found their way back to England were the basis of Shakespeare's play *The Tempest,* which appeared around 1623.

In 1610 Somers sailed back to Bermuda to gather food that was desperately needed at Jamestown. He died while there, and for many years following his death, the islands were known as the Somers Islands. Eventually, in May 1612, the Virginia Company sent a small ship named *Plough* back to Bermuda, with 60 permanent settlers. Bermuda became, at that point, a colony and part of the populated world.

A Very Brief First Visit

My first visit to Bermuda was in 1983, and it had an unusual purpose. I was part of a small group of civilian guests invited for the transit of the U.S. Coast Guard training bark *Eagle* to Newport, Rhode Island.

The final approach to the airport and the short taxi ride from the airport to *Eagle* revealed the astonishing colors of the sea that surrounds Bermuda. I saw shades of blue and green that I had never experienced. The profusion of flowers that grew almost everywhere competed with the intensity of the surrounding sea.

After my flight landed, I went straight to the ship, which was alongside a pier in St. George's, reported aboard and stowed my gear. I had a few hours to spend ashore, just enough time to walk around St. George's and have dinner.

Within a few blocks, I came across St. Paul's Church. The exceptionally wide but steep and high brick steps led to a double-door entrance that was inviting, and as I stepped through the doors the odor of cedar swept over me. The interior was softly lit. I sat for a while and prayed. It definitely was the thing to do in that environment.

Subsequently I learned that the original church on the site was built in 1612 with Bermuda cedar and a palm-thatched roof. It is considered the oldest continually used Anglican Church in the Western Hemisphere. The present structure was built in 1713, and the original altar and the font that were brought with the first English settlers were incorporated into the present building.

By the time I left St. Peter's it was time for dinner, which I had in a nearby restaurant. It was a good, honest meal, more memorable for its mood than for the cuisine. There was one specific feature of the meal, however, that I do remember. I ordered a bottle of ale, which turned out to be Watney's. It really hit the spot. Later I learned that Watney's is not considered a premium brand of ale, but because of the special association, there will never be another that will be more enjoyable.

The following morning *Eagle* eased away from the pier, and we moved out slowly through St. George's Channel and into the Atlantic on the engine. Then the ship's sails were set smartly and the wind grabbed her. The sense of power that was palpable in those few seconds as *Eagle* gathered speed was astounding. She was no ordinary bark. She had been built originally for speed and not only to handle but to *use* almost anything the sea could deliver.

Eagle's 295-foot steel hull and 1,800 tons of weight drove through the Atlantic's waters with monstrous force, powered by more than 21,000 square feet of sail area bent onto rigging that, at its highest point, reached fifteen stories into the sky. In the first moment of that initial surge, everyone on the ship fell quiet. Even those working aloft were doing so with a bare minimum of talking. It was as if everyone in the ship understood the power they were dealing with and their silence was a sign of respect for its potential.

Return Trip

It wasn't until 1993 that I returned to Bermuda, and that second trip set the tone for each visit that has followed. Sally was with me, and we stayed in a small resort hotel on Bermuda's South Shore, called White Sands. The hotel hung on a hillside overlooking the ocean at Grape Bay.

The place had an English tone, with a serious afternoon tea and roast beef featured on the dinner menu. And in the evening, a jacket was expected in the dining room. Otherwise it was low-key, putting the emphasis on the intense beauty of its surroundings.

The walk to the beach from the hotel took about a minute. As I remember the walk, it was along a narrow path between thick foliage and wildflowers, and it emerged abruptly and spectacularly on the soft sand of the beach.

The beach was small but with never more than a few people on it, and with water that was refreshing but never chilling. Sitting in the sand, feeling the ocean breeze on my face and the sun on my back, I slowly changed from a visitor to part of the scene. It was a time for studying the horizon and thinking about important things.

It also was time to begin appreciating one of Bermuda's special qualities: her subtle moods. Those moods are an aspect of the place that provides an intriguing vista with its vivid natural, weather-blessed surroundings of pink beaches, stark white cottages, ubiquitous flowers, and luminescent waters.

Best of all on Grape Bay Beach were the sunrises. The slow-motion pyrotechnics in the east each morning were profoundly moving, suggesting something much more than the beginning of a day. There was a message from the primordial in them, and standing at the water's edge or sitting in the cool sand and absorbing the process as the dark dissolved, I realized that there was much more to Bermuda than surface beauty, no matter how spectacular that might be. There was an essence, a unique compound of nature and history, people, and things, something simultaneously elusive and evocative.

It's those moods beyond Bermuda's unique natural assets that give the place a personality, something that has to do with past and present occupants and something that is constantly changing. Those Bermuda moods were something I had to wait and watch for, but as I discovered them over time, each would be matchless. And the unpredictability of the process added to its fascination.

Wheels

One of the main components of Bermuda's special tone is its limit on cars. Tourists can't rent them, and even Bermudians are permitted only one car per family. That limits the visitors' options for getting around to taxis, bicycles, scooters and mopeds. Taxis are limiting and expensive. Bicycles are good exercise but they really are for people who are visiting for weeks, rather than days. We opted for the scooter, and that meant flying in the face of friends and our children, who ominously and continuously warned of their dangers.

A compensating factor was that Bermudians, in general, are polite drivers. They accept bikes, scooters, and mopeds as a necessary part of the traffic, and act accordingly. Bermuda's drivers also generally lack the road aggressiveness that exists in so many other places today. In fact, they have a way of greeting friends with a series of short beeps of their horns as they pass on the narrow roads. At first I wondered what the constant beeping was about. It seemed out of character with the general behavior of the drivers. But I eventually figured out it was a matter of friends saying "Hi" as they passed one another. And among the small population of Bermuda, there seemed to be a lot of friends.

So, on our rented wheels we set off to begin an exploration of Bermuda, which is actually a tight collection of islands and which has the approximate shape of a giant fishhook. St. George's is at the ring end and Ireland Islands are at the sharp end. There are several substantial interior bodies of water: Castle Harbor and Harrington Sound in the northeast and Great Sound, around which the land forms the giant hook. There are two major harbors: St. George's at the northeast end and Hamilton on the Great Sound.

The long axis of the land runs southwest from St. George's and then curves north and northeast to form the hook. At both ends, the land breaks into a series of small islands, which are linked by narrow bridges. Bermuda is mostly flat; there are hills, but there are no mountains.

The distance from one end of Bermuda to the other is approximately 22 miles. At the White Sands we were at roughly the middle of the land and on its South Shore. On our first day, we decided to head along South Road toward Ireland Islands and land's end to the southwest.

One of the important things about Bermuda that began to sink in as we drove was that, on the road in Bermuda, I was almost never out of sight of the sea. Past almost every cluster of buildings or stretch of road walled with foliage, there was a nautical vista. It might be a small inlet, or it might be a sweeping ocean view.

Along South Road the panoramic view of the ocean was a constant. And always there was the astonishing variation of blue and green water, sometimes subtly blending, sometimes distinct, but always with implausible depth and luminosity. There could be nothing bluer and nothing greener.

As we rolled along South Road, it also occurred to me that there is a sharp contrast between the dangers and suffering of the first inhabitants of Bermuda and the profoundly pleasant effect of the unique combination of land and sea that is home to today's Bermudians.

Beaches

The famous Bermuda beaches are strung out along South Road. There are more than twenty, and each is a relatively brief interruption along the rugged coastline. No two are alike. A few are dominated by resort hotels; many are accessible to the public. Over the years we have never found one that was crowded. The sand is fine bordering on powdery, and it's either very white or it sometimes has a slightly pink cast.

Many of the beaches are simply small, sandy coves, flanked by dark and jagged rocks that stand out against the striking beaches they enclose. And it's the smaller beaches, where the sea meets one personally, that I found the most interesting. Their intimacy is conducive to thought, even when the weather is not benign.

In fact, I have sat on one of the South Road beaches on a windy and gray day, looking seaward as a major storm passed beyond the empty horizon. There wasn't anything to separate me from my thoughts of other times and other people who had come over that horizon and towards a mysterious place marked on their charts as "the uninhabited island."

Let there be Light

As we traveled for about four miles along South Road, we came upon the Gibbs Hill Light. It would have been hard to miss. It's a stark, white, looming presence, just a short way uphill from South Road. It contrasts with Bermuda's horizontalness. Instead of looking *out,* the Gibbs Hill Light required me to look *up.*

The 245-foot high structure is cast iron and its brilliant white surface reveals little texture. Even on an overcast day, with the lighthouse standing in relief against a grey sky, its whiteness is intense, almost seeming to vibrate. Its hardness and its whiteness also contrasted with its immediate surroundings: a lush green lawn accented with prolific, vibrant flowers.

Although the Lighthouse is hard to miss, the Lighthouse Tea Room, nestled at the base of the structure, is unobtrusive. In earlier times and before automation, it was the home of the lighthouse keeper. It's plain and functional décor was in keeping with the building's original purpose. At the time Sally and I first visited, the warm hospitality of the proprietors, Bermudian Kevin Burke and his daughter Janice, was in keeping with the friendly national personalities of Bermuda and Ireland, the latter being Burke's original homeland.

We sat for a while enjoying our tea and the hilltop breeze that entered through the open windows, literally air conditioning the small room. There was a modest welcoming booklet on each table. The key line described the Gibbs Hill Lighthouse Tea Room as "providing the warmest of hospitality and a sampling of traditional English light dining served in a relaxing historic setting." There was truth in that advertising.

The menu also provided a gentle admonition: "One must know how to take time to relax, how to leave daily cares behind, and appreciate the simple pleasures of the moment." Perhaps it was the circumstances, but that bit of philosophical nourishment taken from the Gibbs Hill Lighthouse Tea Room menu has stayed with me.

To the Far End

From Gibbs Hill we continued on our scooter along South Road, first slightly northwest and then, as South Road merges into Middle Road, in a long arc that eventually winds up heading northeast at the end. Crossroads along the way, like Whale Bay Road and Wreck Road, told something about each neighborhood's history. Three small bridges kept reminding me just how omnipresent the ocean was, and the final bridge put us on Ireland Island North, a neck of land jutting into the Atlantic. We were at Bermuda's Royal Naval Dockyard.

At one time, the dockyard was an important part of the geographically strategic role played by Bermuda in the British Empire; and ships of the Royal Navy often rode to their anchors there. Between 1848 and 1851, the Dockyard was commanded by Vice Admiral Sir Thomas Cochrane, among the most daring and controversial, and without doubt among the most famous, of Britain's naval heroes during the Age of Sail.

The dockyard also was the construction site for the famous Bermuda-built, cedar sloops of the same era. Today it's a major tourist attraction, with a marina, boutiques, restaurants, and craft shops.

There is, however, one very significant link with the sea that remains at the dockyard: The Bermuda Maritime Museum. The Museum is spread out among eight of the original Dockyard structures. Those original buildings were all part of the fort that guarded the dockyard and they include a former gunpowder magazine and an ordinance storage building. These purpose-built structures add to the sense of history communicated by less ominous representatives.

One of the most interesting exhibits I found in the Museum was devoted to Bermuda's harbor pilots, a group of professional seamen whose activities are woven into the history of the island where they still ply their trade. A good part of the exhibit told of a pilot named James Darrell, who guided the 74-gun HMS *Resolution* into a safe anchorage in St. George's Harbour in the late eighteenth century. For his skill, Darrell, who was a slave, was declared a free man. His was the first recorded ownership of a home by a black Bermudian, and his descendants still occupy the home at 5 Aunt Peggy's Lane today.

The most impressive of the Dockyard buildings was the Commissioner's House, constructed in the late 1820's. One of the more interesting features of the house, which is perched on a bluff overlooking the Atlantic and surrounding dockyard facilities, is that it's built around a cast iron frame. The frame was fabricated in England and shipped to Bermuda in sections, where it was assembled and a Bermuda limestone exterior added.

Since my first visit with Sally, the Commissioner's House has been restored to a degree of its early elegance and in the process, illuminating the craftsmanship of its nineteenth-century builders. The Commissioner's House is now the site of a number of the Museum's major exhibits, including archival items and indigenous art.

At the Heart of Hamilton

The day after the South Road and Royal Naval Dockyard excursions, we went "downtown." In Bermuda that's Hamilton. The principal street, Front Street, runs along the main section of the harbor for about a mile. We strolled along, with giant ocean liners looming one side and an array of interesting shops and a small department store or two on the landward side of the street.

At the western end of Front Street is Abouy's Point, a small park where we sat for a while and watched the activity in the mini-sea that is the Great Sound at the western end of Bermuda.

The Great Sound and its numerous small ferries form one of the basic transportation systems of Bermuda. Virtually one half of Bermuda's communities can be reached efficiently from Hamilton with the system, and the regularly scheduled ferries carry a mix of Bermudians going to and fro and sightseeing tourists.

Watching from Abouy's Point eventually reveals a unique visual music being played on the Great Sound. The ferries are the beat and the ubiquitous sailboats are the melody. The gulls and other sea birds add special chords. It's both constant and ever changing.

Abouy's Point also is the location of the historic Royal Bermuda Yacht Club, which was established in 1844. The Club is the Bermuda terminus of the famous—some sailors who have competed call it infamous—Newport to Bermuda yacht race. The Club's dark-rose-colored, two-story clubhouse is a Hamilton landmark, as are its graceful yachts tugging at their moorings just offshore from the Club.

Two blocks off Front Street we found a special place where some of Bermuda's more interesting moods can be felt: Holy Trinity Cathedral. There were no soaring spires there. Instead we found a relatively low, sturdy stone building, a structure that would survive hurricanes screaming across the relatively high point of land it occupies and also a cool environment under the summer's hammering sun.

The Cathedral's scale is appropriate to the land its serves. Its exterior created angles that, in turn, created shadows that contrasted sharply with the sunlit portions of the exterior. In a country of pastel buildings, turquoise and cobalt water and vivid flowers, the Cathedral was a black-and-white-and-grey anomaly and a visual relief of sorts.

The Cathedral's stone walls created a special feeling inside, where subtle light and hushed phrases communicated restraint. The tiny Warriors Chapel to one side summed up a lot about the Cathedral and its place. The Chapel is dedicated to the Bermudians who lost their lives in World Wars I and II. Flags added splashes of color and regimental plaques added specificity to those honored. Overhead the flags of Bermuda and Great Britain hung side by side. With them was the "white ensign" of the Royal Navy, uncharacteristically but fittingly motionless.

Framed stanzas from a poem "For the Fallen" by English literary figure Laurence Binyon hung on the cast iron work that separated the Chapel from the rest of the church. The poem, written in 1914, is often read during World War I and World War II memorial ceremonies in the British Commonwealth on 11 November, Britain's Remembrance Day. Two brief stanzas speak with simplicity and particular eloquence of the Bermudians who lost their lives in war. It also speaks of the Bermudians who loved those lost in those wars:

> They went with songs to the battle, they were young,
> Straight of limb, true of eye, steady and aglow.
> They were staunch to the end against odds uncounted:
> They fell with their faces to the foe.

> They shall not grow old, as we that are left to grow old:
> Age shall not weary them, nor the years condemn.
> At the going down of the sun and in the morning
> We will remember them.

What's in a Bermuda Name?

One of the most fascinating things about Bermuda is its place and street names. Some are interesting because they suggest things about the islands' historical roots and ties with the sea, such as Admiralty Walk, Ballast Point Road, One Gun Alley, Mizzentop, Naval Tanks Hill, Pieces of Eight Lane, and Wreck Road.

The most interesting street names, however, are the ones that reveal a lot about the spirit and humor of the people who have made Bermuda the special place that it is. They make us wonder at the stories behind the names, and they invite us to indulge in gentle humor at the expense of our hosts.

One wonders, for example, if the women who live on Hesitation Lane have to move at a certain age to Old Maid's Lane. Do the people from Fractious Lane and Controversy Lane ever get together with the folks from Friendly Lane and Happy Talk Lane? What the hell happened at Devil's Hole Hill and Brimstone Hill that earned them their labels? What has the right of way on Ten Pin Crescent, a car or a bowling ball?

Does anyone know who lives on Secret Lane? Does Sunset Pass lead to Featherbed Alley? Is it true that the movie *The Informer* was written on Point Finger Road? Does Hightime Drive end at Convict Lane? Finally, would someone from Bermuda please explain Sofar Close to me?

CHAPTER TWENTY-THREE
SAGRES

The ever-changing cape, where the starry light fades, rises lofty and is Europe's last outpost, losing itself in the salty waters of the monster-filled ocean.

Avienus, 350 AD

I had never been to Portugal. Then, in 1994 I had an opportunity for a writer's trip that was too good to turn down. There were several reasons. First the trip involved traveling on my own, rather than with a group of writers. Second, Portugal has rich maritime history that doesn't get much attention. Third, I had never been to Portugal. The trip turned out to be even more enlightening than I anticipated.

A Starting Point

As a bonus Sally was able to accompany me, and during the first few days of the visit, which were spent in the Lisbon region, we were joined by friends, Rear Admiral Bob Ravitz and his wife Micki. We stayed in Cascais, a coastal resort town about 17 miles west of Lisbon. The original settlement that became the town was established in the Twelfth century, and like so many cities and towns, its strategic location near the estuary of the Tagus River was a primary reason for its growth.

In addition to being a resort area, Cascais still functions as a working fishing center, and it was the signs of that ancient enterprise that stood out in a number of ways for me.

While in Cascais we initially stayed at a modest resort complex called Estalagen Senhora da Guia. I learned that "estalagen" was the term for a small, privately owned hotel, and it became clear immediately that Senhora da Guias' hotel had a down-to-earth staff with a straightforward attitude. They lacked affectation and took things (and people) at face value, two qualities that I have come to associate with people whose livelihoods are connected with the sea.

From the front patio of the Estalagen, we overlooked a bay filled with a fleet of traditionally designed and colorful Portuguese fishing boats, each with the exaggerated, upswept bow and stern and bright, individualized paintwork that mark the sturdy boats that have remained an essential part of Portugal's fishing industry. Notwithstanding the chic tone of the area, the colorful fishing fleet didn't seem at all incongruous. In fact it added a note of genuineness that is so often lacking in today's high-rise, casino-dominated ocean resorts, where the fresh-water pool attracts more of the guests than the adjacent sea.

Along the coastal stretch between Lisbon and Cascais, we explored the evocative tower of Belém, approximately 100 feet high and positioned in the edge of the Tagus River. Constructed in the early 1500s and still serving as a navigation mark at the mouth of the River, the Tower's seemingly incongruous combination of heavy Gothic design and intricate Moorish decoration triggered images of the struggle between Christian and Muslim zeal that was fought out on the Iberian Peninsula centuries ago. In an anomaly that would seem strange in another country, the Tower's most elaborate decorations face seaward, a possible indication of how the lives of the region's earlier inhabitants were focused on the sea.

Not far from the Balém Tower, I also explored the Museu de Marinha, with its constant reminders of Purtugal's past maritime dominance and the nearby Mosteiro dos Jerónimos. The latter is the architecturally striking 16th century monastery where Vasco da Gama prayed for divine blessing before departing on his history-making voyage around the Cape of Good Hope and into a hitherto unknown region of the Indian Ocean.

It wasn't taking long to absorb the historic sea connections that permeate Portugal's national psyche and which include successive waves of Phoenicians, Carthaginians, Greeks, Romans, and Moors that sailed to and from its many natural harbors.

Castle in the Air

From Cascais and Lisbon, and now on our own, Sally and I drove across the Vasco da Gama Bridge, which spans the Tagus River. Once over the river, we headed for the major industrial city of Setúbal. At the edge of that city, we drove up a winding road to Castelo da São Filipe, a 17th century fortress whose hilltop ramparts dominate the entire area. The Castle was built by Philip II of Spain, who was also Filipe I of Portugal.

Like a significant number of Portuguese landmark sites, Castelo da São Filipe is a government-run Pousada.[29] There are more than 40 state-owned Pousadas in Portugal, and they include former castles, manor houses, monasteries and convents that have been converted into inns and small hotels. The architecture and settings reflect the regions in which these unique facilities are located. With 15 rooms and one suite, Castelo da São Filipe's facilities are completely integrated into the basic structure, and there never was a sense of being anyplace other than in an ancient castle. In fact it occurred to me quickly, not only were we occupying the Castle, its mood was occupying us.

In the late afternoon light, we walked the ramparts of the castle, just as the pike-bearing guards of centuries ago did. Our view alternated among the modern Setúbal shipyard, with its sky-reaching cranes in one direction, the Tagus River with its commercial life blood flowing to and from Lisbon in another direction, and peaceful, rolling hills in a third direction.

Within the castle's massive walls, we discovered a tiny chapel with walls and ceiling elaborately decorated with "azulejos," blue tiles for which Portugal is famous. The colorful tiles blend with simple architecture to create an unusual aura of serenity that contrasts with the massive walls, stone surfaces, and sharp angles of the rest of the Castle.

As darkness fell it was impossible to avoid imagining the dramas, some violent and some tender, that surely had played out in Castelo da São Filipe. We stayed the night, and then drove on towards Portugal's southwestern tip. The best was yet to come.

A Far Corner

The following day we drove almost directly south down the lower third of Portugal to a strange, isolated town called Sagres. It's a stark, barren place you feel in your bones, a place where the storms that sweep in from the Atlantic, the on-shore wind, and an unrelenting sun work endlessly at cleansing the landscape. What little natural growth manages to survives the elements never manages to stand very tall, and the sun bleaches the landscape to a purity that challenges man's intrusion. Once again, we stayed in a Pousada. In this case it was a relatively modern building that clings to the top of a cliff that drops precipitously into the sea.

Set on a small plateau on the most southwesterly point of Europe, Sagres' long arc of towering cliffs looks towards a horizon that was once considered to be the gateway to the edge of the earth, and even in calm weather, Sagres and the sea meet violently at the base of the area's massive cliffs.

At times, distant storms create huge swells that curl and pound the cliffs with the kind of hostility only nature in its extreme moments can compose. And storms that sweep ashore from the sea hurl salt spray over the tops of the hundred-foot-high bulwarks against the Atlantic.

It was the Romans who, during their occupation, named the site "Promontorium Sacrum," the term which evolved to Sagres, meaning "sacred" or "awesome." That ancient Roman name says a lot about the sense of the place that I was discovering in 1994.

Launching an Era

The area's history reaches back beyond recorded times, and like the rest of Portugal, Sagres' history is inexorably linked to the sea. It was, for example, the location of Prince Henry the Navigator's school in the middle of the fifteenth century. In Sagres, Henry, son of Portugal's King John I, was a rare combination: scholar, teacher, warrior, prince, and religious aesthetic. But Henry's most important skill was his ability to gather the early mathematicians, cartographers, shipbuilders, astronomers, knights, and priests who helped conquer fear with a growing knowledge of geography, navigation, and ship design.

At Prince Henry's time, the dreaded cape at Bojador on the West Coast of Africa, with its violent waters, mists, and dangerous shallows, represented an impenetrable psychological barrier to anyone who ventured southward at sea. It was Gil Eanes from Lagos, only a few miles from Sagres, who penetrated that barrier and then returned safely to Lagos in 1434.

With the fearsome mental barrier at Cape Bojador pierced, it was the fifteenth-century scholars assembled by Henry who were the enablers for the navigators like Bartolomeu Diaz, Vasco da Gama, and Pedro Alvares Cabral who sailed over the horizon to find, not boiling seas, monsters, or the edge of the earth but exotic new lands, and the ocean pathways that linked them. It was Diaz, for example, who, in 1488, was the first European to round the Cape of Good Hope. It was Da Gama who sailed on past the Cape to establish the sea link with India in 1498. And it was Cabral who was the first European to sail west to reach the coast of Brazil in 1500.

Sagres' special aura—with its combination of the fearfulness of the sea's often dangerous powers and the profound pull towards whatever might be over the horizon—provided an appropriate backdrop for Prince Henry. A local history of the area alludes to that aura: "And here, until his death in 1460, he was able to develop a mystical awareness cultivated throughout an austere and devout life." [30]

One of the major and relatively unknown technological achievements during Henry's time at Sagres was the design and construction of the fore-and-aft, lateen rigged caravel. That technological breakthrough combined the sturdiness of the square-rigged cargo ships that had plied the European coasts for uncounted years with the ability of Arab dhows to sail closer to the wind with their fore-and-aft-rigged lateen sails.

These early caravels, with their more adaptable rigs, became the basic vehicles for the earliest stages of the Age of Discovery. They carried the early navigators around the Cape of Good Hope, into the Indian Ocean, and back to Portugal. They also carried explorers westward to the Americas. They were, in fact, the technological means of converting the world's oceans from barriers to bridges, and they were designed and built in Sagres and nearby Lagos.

A Violent Side of History

Perhaps it's a product of the imagination, but sometimes there seems to be the faintest whiff of the smoke of cannon fire in Sagres' air. For centuries both pirate attacks and major sea battles took place off the shore of this special generator of maritime history.

In 1474, for example, when Christopher Columbus was 24 years old, he was a victim of a pirate attack within sight of Sagres' cliffs. The convoy in which he was sailing was transiting from Genoa to England, and the ship in which Columbus was embarked was sunk. He survived by swimming six miles to one of the small inlets that punctuate the cliffs of the area.

More than a century later, in 1587, the English sea-dog Sir Frances Drake came ashore and razed the area. As a result of that raid, a fort was built at Sagres Point and vestiges of it remain today. In 1693 British fortunes were reversed at Cape St. Vincent when a French fleet, commanded by the Compte de Tourville, overcame a British force led by Admiral Sir George Rooke. In 1790, the gods of war again reversed British fortunes, and Admiral Sir George Rodney defeated a Spanish fleet led by Admiral Don Juan de Langara.

Arguably the most noteworthy sea battle fought off the cliffs of Sagres was the Battle of Cape St. Vincent in 1797. The action involved a fleet commanded by British admiral Sir John Jervis pitted against a Spanish fleet led by Admiral Don José de Cordoba. During the action then-captain Horatio Nelson, acting on his own initiative, pulled out of the British line-ahead formation and cut off the escape of the Spanish fleet. As a direct result of Nelson's action, the Spanish attempt to reach the safety of Cadiz was thwarted, and the British achieved a naval victory that was unusually decisive for the time, as well as strategically important.

During the ensuing combat, Nelson also captured two of the Spanish ships with unusually aggressive tactics. Nelson brought his seriously damaged 74-gun HMS *Captain* alongside the Spanish 114-gun *San Josef,* and boarded and captured her. He then used *San Joseph* to cross over and board the Spanish 80-gun *San Nicolas,* completing the capture of two ships, each of which was more powerfully gunned than *Captain.*

With some active letter-writing on Nelson's part, his unusual combat tactic became known as "Nelson's patent bridge for boarding First Rates." In an unabashed effort to advance his reputation and coincidentally his naval career, Nelson prepared a summary of his actions at the Battle of Cape St. Vincent, captioned "A FEW REMARKS RELATIVE TO MYSELF IN THE CAPTAIN, IN WHICH MY PENDENT WAS FLYING ON THE GLORIOUS VALENTINE'S DAY, 1797."

The document was distributed liberally, and its circulation included His Royal Highness the Duke of Clarence, the future King William. In his Remarks, Nelson described the key moment when he exhibited the kind of initiative that became the hallmark of his successes in battle:

> [T]he Admiral made the signal to 'tack in succession;' but I, perceiving the Spanish Ships all to bear up before the wind, or nearly so, evidently with the intention of forming their line going large, joining their separated Division, at that time engaged with some of our centre Ships, or flying from us—to prevent either of their schemes from taking effect, I ordered the ship to be wore, and passing between the Diadem and Excellent, at a quarter past one o'clock, was engaged with the headmost, and of course with the leeward most of the Spanish Division. [31]

With his audacious action, Nelson achieved the initial public and official attention that would grow and carry him on to his famous victories at the Battles of the Nile in 1798, Copenhagen in 1801 and Trafalgar in 1805. The Battle of Cape St. Vincent earned an earldom for Jervis, who, after Nelson's death at the Battle of Trafalgar, wrote: "There is but one Nelson." Nelson's actions at Cape Saint Vincent were also a significant step towards displacing the conservative combat doctrine that had been the hallmark of combat at sea up to Nelson's day. That shift in combat doctrine changed the role of sea power for all time.

In the course of his career, both before and after the Battle of Cape St. Vincent, Nelson passed off the cliffs of Sagres many times. The next to last time was in July 1805, when he was deployed from England in HMS *Victory*. The final time was three months later, when his remains were returned home to England, after his victory over the French-Spanish Combined Fleet at the Battle of Trafalgar.

Augmenting the Intangibles

The tangible evidence of Sagres' early history includes the chapel of Our Lady of Grace, mentioned in correspondence between Prince Henry and Pope Pius II in 1459. Close by is a square cistern tower that is also believed to go back to Prince Henry's time.

The most intriguing link to the Age of Discovery is, however, an enigmatic circle of small stones laid out on the ground, not far from the Chapel and cistern. The circle is roughly 140 feet in diameter and is divided into 48 pie-shaped sections. There is no known record of how the circle, discovered in the 18th century, was used, and it is generally referred to as a "wind rose." Standing at the edge of the stone-delineated circle, I could visualize the knowledge-seeking scholars of Prince Henry's school.

The area containing the "wind rose," cistern, and chapel is surrounded by the walls of Sagres Fortaleza, which was begun in Prince Henry's time. The Fort provided the surrounding area with protection against shore parties of pirates, who found the sandy inlets along the coast inviting, as well as French and British naval forces that also took advantage of the natural accesses along the rugged coastline. The original structure was enhanced and rebuilt at several points during the 17th and 18th centuries.

Not far from the Fortaleza is the Cape St. Vincent Lighthouse, known as "the light at the end of the world." It is still a working lighthouse that serves as an aide to navigation for local fishermen and ships passing along the coast.

Following my trip to Portugal, in an article for the National Maritime Historical Society's *Sea History* magazine, I wrote:

> Sagres is one of those rare places where history is palpable. Standing on the Sagres Point promontory, one can hear the booming of cannons as Nelson fought his way to fame—or is it just the surf below? One can feel the call, as explorers like Da Gama and Cabral must have, to learn what lies beyond the horizon—or is it just the wind climbing over the cliff's jagged face? With all of its mystery, one thing about Sagres is sure; it will leave its mark on anyone who knows the sea.

CHAPTER TWENTY-FOUR
THE CANARY ISLANDS

Where men live peacefully...enjoying perennially cool air,
a product of breezes from the ocean to give men freshness.

Homer

In 1996, I went to the Canary Islands on another solo writing assignment. I knew almost nothing about the small and relatively isolated archipelago in the eastern Atlantic. What I did know, however, was that it was a place of the sea.

The eastern-most island in the group is less than 100 miles from the coast of Morocco. The earliest inhabitants, the cave-dwelling Guanche, probably came from North Africa's Berber Region, possibly around 1,000 BC. Vestiges of the names of some of the Guanche kings remain in the family names of some of today's Canary Islanders, and ancient cave drawings give hints of a culture that predates the Cartheginian, Greek, and Roman cultures that developed in the Mediterranean.

Such a sea voyage was a considerable achievement for its time, and represented a great deal of courage and a certain level of seamanship on the part of those who risked all to push off a North African beach and sail for an unknown land beyond the horizon. The Roman author Pliny wrote of an expedition to the Canary Islands around 50 BC that discovered the ruins of magnificent buildings, the remnants of a culture that existed in almost complete isolation for countless years.

Geologically, the islands are part of the mostly-submerged, volcanic mountain range that also includes the Azores, Madeira, Cape Verde, and the Savage Islands. Four of the seven main islands of the Canary Islands have the basic profile of a mountain peak. The entire chain of islands, from the Azores to the northwest to the Canary Islands off Africa's coast, was formed eons ago by massive geological forces pushing portions of the earth's crust up into a series of mountain peaks.

But the violence of the Canary Islands' geological beginnings is belied by the Islands' climate, which is softly spring-like through the year. And this is the first of several contradictions that I found in the land that earliest historians labeled "The Favored Islands."

A Shrouded Past

The Canary Islands' earliest inhabitants have mystical origins. Around 50 BC the Roman scholar Pliny gave their home its name, based on the large, ferocious dogs (Latin "canes") that roamed the islands during Roman times. The story of the Islands' mysterious earliest occupants reaches back far past the Roman Empire, however, and even further back than the Phoenician and Carthaginian sailors that also are believed to have visited there.

The way life of the Guanche is recorded sketchily in rare archeological fragments and rock carvings that provide only tantalizing glimpses of their culture. And because there was no written record of the islands' pre-European inhabitants, legend and mythology dominate accounts of their distant past. Some accounts even suggest that the Canary Islands were the fabled kingdom of Atlantis.

At the beginning of the fifteenth century, the Spanish began their conquest of the Canaries. It wasn't easy. The aboriginal Guanche were tough, and it took nearly 100 years for the Spanish to conquer them. In the process, many were killed, but also many were assimilated into the Spanish colonial culture that took over the Islands.

Today the Canary Islands remain a part of Spain, but there clearly is in the place a sense of detachment from that nation—and for that matter from just about any other place. Perhaps it's the

Guanche blood that still flows among the inhabitants, perhaps it's something else, but that psychological disconnect with other places and people is something that I felt as soon as I arrived.

Gran Canaria

My flight of slightly more than a thousand miles from Madrid to Gran Canaria, the third largest of the Canary Islands, was uneventful. There was nothing along the way to prepare me for the unusual corner of the world I was about to enter.

Gran Canaria has somewhat more of the outsider about it than its sister islands, two of which I would have an opportunity to visit briefly during my trip. But I also quickly found that it has a wide variety of vistas: sandy, desert-like areas, rugged mountains, resort beaches, misty tropical forests, and craggy moon-like panoramas. And the transitions from those starkly different environments are abrupt. I was stunned by the beautiful otherworldliness I had entered.

During the first day after I arrived, I had a whirlwind tour by car that covered La Cumbre, which is the highest peak of the Island; the sun-soaked and tourist-packed beach area called Playa del Inglés on Gran Canaria's south coast; and the Island's capital city, Las Palmas. The latter was founded in 1478 by the invading Castillian army.

Las Palmas was the most cosmopolitan of the cities and towns I visited during my trip, and merchants from Africa, Asia, China, and Europe can be found along its streets. The large harbor was a trading hub between Europe and the New World during the era of colonization and the Age of Sail. Today, it's a nexus for global shipping and the ubiquitous container ships that ply the ocean lanes that connect the centers of today's global economy.

After a day and two evenings exploring Gran Canaria, I began a series of island-hopping flights between two of the other Islands, Tenerife and La Palma. One of the things that emerged from the aerial views that punctuated those flights was the volcanic character of the Islands.

Tenerife

Tenerife is the largest of the Canary Islands. Its port city of Santa Cruz de Tenerife is backed by mountains. The largest, El Teide, is the first bit of land that appears on the horizon for mariners—and in my case an air traveler—approaching the Canary Islands, and it serves as a huge, white-topped navigation aide for mariners. Its snow capped peak rises 12,100 feet above sea level and it's the tallest Spanish mountain. As recently as 1909, El Teide had a significant volcanic eruption.

Santa Cruz, like many other places of the Canary Islands, is quintessential Spanish Colonial in look and feel, with wide boulevards, pleasant squares, and streets lined with tropical flowers. I took the time to walk the street, gradually absorbing the more subtle feelings of the place.

Naval History

Because of its strategic location along major sea lanes of commerce, Santa Cruz has been the site of many historic naval actions. One of the earliest occurred in 1585, when Sir Francis Drake destroyed the harbor fort. In 1656, British admiral Robert Blake executed an audacious amphibious attack on the port and destroyed a Spanish silver fleet of 16 ships.

The result was different, however, when Britain's John Jennings attacked Tenerife 50 years later during the War of the Spanish Succession and was driven off by the local inhabitants. During those attacks and those by pirates without formal government connections, the Spanish treasure ships on their way to Spain from the New World were the targets.

The city's signature naval event was, however, the resounding defeat of a British fleet led by arguably the world's most famous naval officer, Admiral Lord Nelson. In July 1797, Nelson, who was aware of Blake's dramatic success a century earlier, attempted to reprise it with another amphibious assault on Santa Cruz. Nelson attacked with a powerful squadron that included three ships-of-the line and three frigates. His main objective was the capture of a Spanish treasure ship believed to be there at the time.

In April 1797, Nelson wrote to his commander-in-chief:

> I do not reckon myself equal to Blake; but if I recollect right, he was more obliged to the wind coming off the land, than any exertions of his own: fortune favored the gallant attempt, and may do so again. [32]

Further on, after outlining his plan, Nelson revealed the hubris that would be his downfall at Santa Cruz: "In short, the business could not miscarry."

The Battle of Santa Cruz

After Nelson's participation several months earlier in the British victory over a Spanish fleet at the Battle of Cape St. Vincent, his career was gathering momentum, and his confidence was high—too high. His basic plan was overly optimistic and he seriously underestimated the abilities of Castillian general, Antonio Gutiérrez, who led the defense of Santa Cruz. He also misjudged the weather that had favored Blake. Nelson not only was resoundingly defeated, he lost his right arm in the battle and nearly his career in its aftermath.

Nelson counted on surprise but the seaman's best friend (or worst enemy) the weather, betrayed him. That and the skill and determination of General Gutiérrez were too much for Nelson and the British force to overcome. Events went from bad to worse as the first British attempt to take the town, led by Captain Thomas Troubridge, was hurled back in a bloody action.

Nelson regrouped and tried again, but the second effort also failed, and his right elbow was shattered as he was about to step ashore from a boat. At that point, Nelson's life was saved by the quick action of his stepson Josiah, and he was rowed back to his flagship, HMS *Theseus,* where his arm was amputated above the elbow. Later Nelson would complain about the coldness of the surgeon's blades as they severed his arm a short distance from his shoulder. Finally, after suffering heavy casualties, and a failed bluff to torch the city, the British were forced to surrender.

During a visit to The Museo Militar in Santa Cruz, I found many artifacts from Nelson's historic defeat, including captured British battle flags, the cannon named "El Tigre" that the Spanish claim shattered Nelson's arm with a volley of grapeshot, a tabletop diorama of the battle, models of the British ships involved in the assault, and the table upon which the truce that ended the struggle between the British and Spanish was signed.

On the waterfront of Santa Cruz, I also found a monument to the defenders of the city, located near the site where Nelson was wounded. And there is a palm-lined, main street near the Museo Militar, named to mark the Spanish victory. It is not, as one might expect, named for the victor, General Gutiérrez. In a surprising twist and a gallant salute to a defeated but honorable enemy, the street is named "Avenida Horacio Nelson." The boulevard in a quirky reminder of the code of honor that existed in eighteenth century combat and that guided both victor and vanquished after the combat ended.

During the aftermath of the struggle, which involved an ongoing series of bloody actions, exceptional humaneness towards the British was evidenced by Gutiérrez and the local population. The British wounded were provided with medical treatment by the victors, who also supplied provisioning for the ships of Nelson's squadron before they withdrew.

A Spanish account of the aftermath described what transpired: "[T]he generosity of the islanders under the direction of their commander overflowed. The Santa Cruz hospitals were opened for all the wounded, the soldiers from both factions fraternized, food, and wine generously distributed and the Spanish ships returned the freed Englishmen to their fleet." Nelson reciprocated the Spanish humanity with a token gift of cheese and beer and a note of thanks to General Gutiérrez, which said in part:

> I cannot take my departure from this Island without returning your Excellency my sincere thanks for your attention towards me, by your humanity in favor of our wounded men in your

power...and for your generosity towards all our people who were disembarked, which I shall not fail to represent to my Sovereign, hoping also, at a proper time, to assure your Excellency how truly I am, Sir, your most obedient , humble servant, Horatio Nelson. [33]

A Career is Saved

Following this event, the badly wounded, chastened, and despondent Nelson wrote to his commander-in-chief, the Earl St. Vincent: "I am become a burthen to my friends, and useless to my Country...I go hence, and am no more seen." [34]

The Earl St. Vincent, who was a mentor to Nelson and recognized his exceptional courage and future potential, replied: "Mortals cannot command success; you and your Companions have certainly deserved it, by the greatest degree of heroism and perseverance that ever was exhibited." [35]

Nelson went on to achieve strategically important victories for his country at the Battles of the Nile, Copenhagen, and Trafalgar, but it was at Santa Cruz de Tenerife, during several violent days in July 1797, that his career, indeed his life, came very close to ending. And that victory of Spanish arms against Briton's most famous admiral continues as a significant part of the folklore of Tenerife's port of Santa Cruz.

La Palma

The mountain under the island of La Palma, one of the smallest of the seven main Canary Islands, actually rises more than 21,000 feet from the ocean floor. The mountain top that is La Palma rises almost 8,000 feet above the ocean's surface, and the black rocks and black sand that are omnipresent give away the island's clearly volcanic genesis.

The main town is the port of Santa Cruz de la Palma. As elsewhere in the Canary Islands, I found that a Spanish colonial atmosphere still dominates there. Flower-draped balconies line the streets, and a quiet elegance dominates the general tone. Perhaps the quintessential example of the town's colonial history that I found is the City Hall, with four nicely proportioned stone arches that face onto a small square and that are topped by the crest of the House of Asturias.

The colonial San Francisco Church and Convent face the square on its opposite side. One of the unusual beauties of the scene is the native pine used in much of the construction. Unlike most pine, it has a reddish tone, and in the sunlight, the wood takes on a glow that adds a special character to the square.

As I walked the narrow streets, I realized that there were unusual bulges on the upper floors of many of the town's buildings, projections that extended out and over the street below. I eventually learned that the bulges, which are about the size of a kitchen stove, relate to a time when pirate attacks were common in the Canary Islands. The most infamous of those pirates was a Frenchman, Jambe de Bois (Peg-leg), who looted and destroyed Santa Cruz de la Palma in 1553.

Since there was no indigenous military force to fend off the corsairs, it was up to the local populace to defend their own homes. The bulges, I was told, are ovens designed to allow the local citizens to drop burning coals on the pirates in the narrow streets below.

The violent images called up by the overhead ovens contrasted vividly with the soft charm of Santa Cruz de la Palma that I had felt initially. And those violent images also got me thinking that, in their special way, the colonial inhabitants of the Canary Islands had a degree of courage that matched that of the aboriginal Guanche inhabitants of the Islands. Clearly, the colonial townspeople of Santa Cruz de la Palma were no pushover for the attacking corsairs.

Above the Clouds

The mountainous interior of La Palma is lush, and its vistas are amazing. The price for entering this spectacular world was a heart-stopping drive up a long, climbing road of seemingly never-ending switchbacks that's definitely not for the faint of heart.

On the way up the mountain, I stopped at the village of Las Nieves. There the 16th century Renaissance church of Nuestro Señora de las Nieves features a spectacular main altar completely covered with silver mined in the Americas and brought to Las Palmas in the 1600s. The Church also is the repository of a statue of La Palma's patron saint, Our Lady of the Snows.

The Palmeros believe that their devotion to the Virgin has protected their ships from the tragedies that are visited on so many who take to the sea for their livelihoods. The statue and its history were an additional reminder of the profound connection between the inhabitants of the Canary Islands and the sea.

My ultimate destination was the Parque Nacional de la Caldera de Taburiente, 6,000 feet above sea level, and the signal that a different world had been entered was the realization that I had actually emerged above the clouds. As I gazed over the astonishing scene, the connection with "Caldera" (Spanish for "kettle") was apparent. I was looking out over an immense geological cavity, initially created by volcanic activity and subsequently sculpted by eons of erosion.

For the present Caldera de Taburiente is filled with lush— in places impenetrable—vegetation. But there have been seven recorded volcanic eruptions on La Palma since its Spanish occupation, and looking out over Caldera de Taburiente it was impossible for me not to realize that the ground on which I stood would, at some future point, almost surely disappear in almost unimaginable volcanic violence.

After the equally attention-getting, reverse ride down from La Caldera, Bodegón Tamanco, an inexpensive restaurant in a mountain cave, was an appropriate end of my visit to the Canary Islands. That homely meal of ham, bread, cheese, and an honest red wine in a mountain restaurant created in a cave linked somehow with the mystical natural beauty of the Canary Islands.

Most significant, however, was my sense in the cave of the spirits of the place's ancient and isolated inhabitants, people who found the courage to sail somehow from the African shore to place now known as the Canary Islands, there to begin a new life and an isolated culture that lasted for uncounted years, before being overcome by determined Spanish Conquistadores.

CHAPTER TWENTY-FIVE

SYDNEY AND FREMANTLE

Australia is full of surprises and adventures and incongruities and incredibilities: but they are all true, they all happened.

Mark Twain

The island continent of Australia has almost 23,000 miles of coastline. Its shores are washed by two oceans and four seas: the Timor and Arafura Seas to its north and the Coral Sea, Pacific Ocean and Tasman Sea to the east. To the south and west, the Indian Ocean defines the edge of the continent. In the opinion of most geographers, there has never been a land bridge connecting Australia to another land mass and the continent's earliest inhabitants are believed to have come to Australia by sea. Australia's rugged and largely barren interior has further accentuated the country's nautical focus and historic connections to the sea.

I had always wanted to get to Australia, mostly because of my impression of the people. Like so many impressions, my images of Australia (big, uninviting, and far away) and Australians (tough but friendly) were to a large extent created during World War II. In 1997 I wrote an article for *Canadian Yachting* about charter bareboat cruising in the Sidney area. In the article I described how I thought there was a pervasive Australian attitude that pulled all of the different physical features of the locale together:

Stitching it all together is the special Australian attitude that somehow blends unpretentiousness with a relaxed outlook. It is an attitude reflected in their use of the short form, 'Oz' for Australia, or...a smile hooked to 'G'day.

In 1997 I had my chance with a writer's trip that took me to two cities on opposite coasts of the continent "down under," two cities that spoke differently about Australia. My first stop was Sydney.

Landing on "The Rocks"

The "modern" history of Australia begins with a sea story that ended at the port of Sydney, at about 34 degrees south latitude along the continent's east coast. There, after 250 days at sea, a small fleet from England anchored in 1788. The eleven battered square-rigged sailing ships had a cargo of convicted prisoners, among them petty thieves, gamblers, prostitutes, and rebels. The prisoners' first assignment ashore was to build their own prison. Although it surely wasn't thought of in those terms, the prisoners were also taking the first steps towards building a nation. That small cove where the penal colony started became known as The Rocks, because of its prominent outcroppings of sandstone. It was obviously a hard place.

Over more than two centuries, that initial settlement evolved into one of Sidney's most popular areas—for both 'Sidney siders' and visitors from around the world alike. And the restored eighteenth and nineteenth century neighborhood is still full of tangible reminders of its tough history, one founded on the forced labor of convicted criminals who were sent, not to jail, but to an incarceration based on not just social isolation but on extraordinary geographical isolation as well.

Standing at the very place where the prisoners were brought ashore and imagining the feelings of total abandonment combined with the faintest flickerings of hope for a second life was the beginning of my understanding of the country and its people. As they placed stone upon stone, they were someplace that was, at least for them, *new*.

292

It took a few moments to break loose from thoughts of the far past and return to my present reality, but soon I set out to see what today's Sydney would tell me about Australia and Australians and especially about their links with the sea.

Now known as "Sydney's First Place," I found The Rocks to be a lively cosmopolitan centre of culture and entertainment, and a special attraction in the Pacific Rim city that grew up around it. I enjoyed the spectacular views of the easily recognized and world-famous Sydney Opera House, located at the harbor's edge, the signature single arch of the city's Harbour Bridge, the city's dynamic skyline, and the never-ending crisscrossing harbor traffic.

As I continued to explore, I kept reaching for a firmer grip on the people who had brought such a positive result from such a negative beginning. Who and what were the people who created the beginnings of such things as the globally-recognized architecture of the Sydney Opera House? And beyond such tangibles, who were the people whose love of competition has made Australia a consistent contender—and winner in 1983—in the America's Cup sailing competition?

A Blend of Old and New

My exploration expanded through The Rocks' closely laid out streets, with a variety of shops, outdoor cafes, restaurants, tea rooms and galleries. The galleries are a particularly good source of contemporary Australian arts and crafts, as well as Australia's unique Aboriginal art, with the latter recognizing in art those who made the place their home before the Europeans arrived.

There were cobblestone and tree-lined streets, graceful terraces, secluded courtyards, and restored landmark buildings that transported me back in time. And there was Cadman's Cottage, the oldest building in the neighborhood. The Cottage was built by convicts in 1816 and was originally the home of a pardoned convict who became Sydney's superintendent of the governor's boats and an early symbol of Australia's transition from a hard-labor camp to a nation.

Close by was Dawes Point Battery, which also was constructed by the first convict settlers, and which now gave me the best overall view of Sydney Harbour, with its never ending parade of commercial and pleasure sites. Right in the middle of it all was Sydney's Harbour Bridge, formerly the largest single-arch bridge in the world and still a famous Sydney landmark.

Another site of special interest was the landmark building known as Campbell's Storehouse, which dates to the mid-1800s. Located on Circular Quay West, this building was part of Sydney's working waterfront, and now it houses a number of attractive restaurants. And a reminder of the place's maritime roots couldn't be missed as I looked out on the full-scale recreation of HMS *Bounty* that was secured alongside the pier.

Next in my walking tour of the earliest beginnings of Sydney was The Rocks Market, a unique, rain-or-shine street market covered by a canopy that appropriately resembles a series of sails. At The Market, there were more than 100 stalls selling a huge variety of wares, ranging from antiques, to crafts, toys, homewares—and much, much more. What I was discovering was a trendy throwback to the days when major portions of a ship's cargo was sold in the open on the pier where the ships landed.

In The Rocks Market, there also are places to relax from the sightseeing and shopping, like espresso bars, pubs, cafes, and restaurants. The oldest pub, The Hero of Waterloo, was built in 1809. The pub's name, like so many names of Australian places, harks back to the country and culture that drove the first settlers to a place that was, for them, half way around the world.

Sydney's newest museum, the Museum of Contemporary Art, is located in a small park at the southeast corner of The Rocks. There are more than 5,000 items in its permanent collection, which includes works by modern art notables such as Andy Warhol and Roy Lichtenstein. The Museum's ongoing series of themed exhibitions is varied and evocative. A sampling of offerings included *Indigenous Australian Artists*, focusing on five major Australian artistic traditions; *Aboriginal Art*, with thematic selections from a comprehensive collection of bark paintings; *Revisiting Minimalism*, focusing on key minimalist works of the '60s and *Pictura Britannica*, featuring 48 newly emerging British artists.

The Australian National Maritime Museum

Not surprisingly, Sydney is the home of a world class maritime museum. The relatively new building is located at the city's Darling Harbor, an inlet from the main harbor and a waterfront recreational area. This purpose-built structure, with soaring arches and glass paneling that mirrors its waterside location, visually echoes the stunning architectural boldness of the nearby Sydney Opera.

The Museum's exhibits reflect the sweep of Australia's unusual maritime past. The displays that stood out for me included a video tracing the story of the maritime aspects of the Yanuwa Aborigines, a single cannon jettisoned from Captain James Cook's Bark *Endeavour*— which reached Australia in 1770 —and the fully rigged *Australia II* that brought the America's Cup to Australia from the United States in 1983. [36]

I also was struck by an exhibit that traced the story of Australia's friendship with the United States in a special gallery. The exhibit was presented to the Museum by the U.S. government on the occasion of the 1988 bicentennial of the European settlement of Australia. A special feature of this display records the naval cooperation between the two countries, extending through World War II, the Korean War, the Vietnam War, Operation Desert Storm, and then-current military operations in the Pacific and the Middle East. This sobering exhibit highlights the violent chapters of history that demonstrate that the relationship between the United States and Australia is by no means a "fair-weather friendship."

Relatively modern naval history is represented in the Museum's waterfront "fleet," which includes the retired Royal Australian Navy destroyer *Vampire,* a former USSR submarine; and the sharply contrasting *Sekar Aman,* a wooden fishing vessel typical of the Indonesian fishing boats that have plied the waters of Australia's northern reefs for centuries. The inclusion of a relatively modern, former Soviet ship and the timeless Indonesian fishing boat was a reminder of the diversity of Austalia's maritime history.

An All-encompassing Maritime Perspective

The highlight of my visit to Sydney was a circumnavigation of the harbor in an open, eighteen-foot day-sailer from an operation called Sydney by the Sea. My young Australian guide was gracious enough to let me do the sailing, which gave me a real fringe benefit while seeing Sydney from a maritime perspective.

Sydney Harbour is actually a mini-sea in its own right, and because of the many bays and river estuaries in the harbor, its shoreline measures approximately 180 miles. Strung along that long shoreline there are scores of mini-harbors that form unique "nautical neighborhoods" within the land-side city. The axis of the harbor is approximately ten miles long, and the width varies from a half mile to a mile. The waters are generally fairly calm, with winds from six to sixteen knots—ideal for small-boat sailing. On the day I was circumnavigating the harbor, there were several dinghy races spotted at various points.

The harbor is not always idyllic, however. The entrance from the Tasman Sea is turbulent and there are periodic weather systems from the open seas to the south, referred to by local sailors as "southern busters," with sustained winds of thirty-plus knots. According to the local sailors to whom I spoke, "the southern busters" are a significant challenge to even the larger boats in the harbor.

As I sailed along the harbor's edge, I enjoyed the special perspective of a place that one gets viewing it from the sea. Each small bay revealed something different, ranging from an urban marina, to beaches filled with bathers, to quiet anchorages backed by wooded areas. And during that personal circumnavigation of Sydney Harbour I was able to add to my sense of the special maritime quality of the city and of the Australian's ongoing association with the sea.

Beyond Expectations

The two thousand-plus mile cross-continent flight from Sydney to Fremantle revealed a stark and seemingly never ending Outback landscape, separating, in extreme geological contrasts, the east and west coasts of Australia. Even at 35,000 feet, the Outback projected an unmistakable message: "Enter at your own risk."

I must admit as the hours and miles went by, I was not overly enthusiastic about leaving Sydney and going to Fremantle. First, there was much more for me to explore in and around Sydney. Second, my general expectation of Fremantle was that it is not much more than a gritty commercial seaport on the Indian Ocean. The only thing I had right was that it's on the Indian Ocean.

I was greeted at the Perth airport, and I was then hustled from the airport to a pier on the Fremantle waterfront. At that point I was launched, luggage and all, on another exploration in a small boat. This one was only slightly larger than the boat I had sailed in Sydney Harbour.

The Fremantle tourist people had learned that I was interested in sailing and had arranged for me to do exactly that, directly from my transcontinental flight. A local Australian was to be my crew and guide, and, reprising my circumnavigation of Sydney Harbour, I had the extra enjoyment of skippering the boat.

An easy sail of about three hours took us almost due west into the Indian Ocean and to Rottnest Island, which is a small natural preserve favored by whale watching enthusiasts and other nature-focused tourists. The odd name derives from the first known European visitor, a Dutch captain named Willem de Vlamingh, who reached the island and the Swan River estuary in 1697. When Vlamingh observed the small marsupials that populated the Island, now called quokkas by Australians, he mistook them for large rats and named the Island accordingly.

The twenty-foot boat was a lively day-sailer and her small cutty provided just enough cover for a sleeping area forward. The accommodations consisted of a sleeping bag and nothing more for an overnight at Rottnest Island. It had been a while since I had slept in my clothes, but after the flight from the States to Sydney, the transcontinental flight to Fremantle, and three hours of sailing, sleep was not elusive. Rain would have been a disaster, but the weather was kind.

I went to sleep that night practically wrapped around the base of the boat's bowsprit, which projected about three feet back into the bow of the boat and under the cutty. And as I went to sleep, I thought (for about ten seconds) of the durability of the common sailors of the Age of Sail who often spent years at sea, under what could be described generously as minimal living conditions, before returning to their home ports and families. And of course, many of them died at sea.

By noon the following day, we had sailed back to Fremantle Harbor, and I was checked into my room at the Esplanade Hotel, with its unique, rambling Australian colonial architecture that had the exterior appearance—but fortunately far superior amenities— of a frontier hotel in America's Wild West.

After getting cleaned up and downing cup of strong coffee, I was ready to begin learning just how wrong my opinion of Fremantle was. Instead of a gritty port city, I began discovering a laid-back, charming seacoast town that had been transformed from a place that had been in fact pretty close to my preconceived view into something completely unanticipated.

The catalyst for the change had been Australia's first America's Cup series, which took place outside Fremantle Harbour in 1987. That event and the people and activities associated with it had triggered the transition that created the exotic Indian Ocean seacoast town I was discovering.

A Maritime Mood

Fremantle grew around not one but three small, adjacent harbors. The southernmost is Success Harbour, home of the famous Fremantle Sailing Club and a major yachting center. At the center is Fishing Boat Harbour, location of the Fremantle's working fishing fleet and ringed with restaurants, cafes and bars. At the northern end is Challenger Harbour. Visiting America's Cup teams were accommodated there in 1987, during Australia's defense of the most famous of sailing trophies.

I realized quickly that there was, at least for me, something different about the sense of the sea in Fremantle. At one point, when I found time to sit quietly and study the horizon, I realized what it was: As I looked west from Fremantle I was looking towards the southern tip of South Africa. In between there was only the huge expanse of the southern Indian Ocean. It was an exotic orientation.

As I moved my attention from the waterfront to Fremantle itself, the sense of the sea was blended with a special Western Australian laid-back attitude. It was palpable in the shops, restaurants, and cafes concentrated along "Cappuccino Strip," just off the waterfront. And it was all nicely blended into the term the locals used to label their unique place: "Freo."

Among the small sea-themed shops, several still stand out in my memory. One specialized in charts. There, in addition to standard nautical charts, I found an illuminated map of Western Australia that delineated its topography and identified its counties. The names of the counties were a reminder of British history before the continent-country of Australia joined the mapmaker's vocabulary. York, Wellington, Nelson (Fremantle is named after one of Nelson's most aggressive captains, Thomas Fremantle), Victoria, Carnarvon, Minto, and Peel are representative among the place names.

Another memorable shop was the small but elegant establishment that featured Australia's Broome Pearls, farmed in the waters off the northwest coast of Australia and world renowned for their luster.

Putting Western Australia's Maritime History in its Place

As one might expect, there is a Western Australian Maritime Museum, where the pervasive sense of the sea is intertwined with the special culture of Western Australia. Not surprisingly, the Museum was at that time housed in a mostly convict-built commissary that has a history of its own. Construction of the initial buildings was begun in 1851, with the intention of providing storage for the food, clothing, and tools used by the prisoners and their overseers. Before the roof was on, the structure was filled.

The flat but textured limestone block exterior and box-like architecture of the two initial structures speak clearly of the time when functionality and the natural elements were the overriding architectural issues in Fremantle. Space and simplicity are the leading qualities of the structure, and its rugged survivability reflects the basic stonemason craftsmanship of its builders. In 1856 an adjacent "new store" was constructed with a similar look but lower profile.

In 1868 the transportation of prisoners to Australia was stopped, and the commissariat was turned over to the colonial government for use as a customs house. The Museum took over the site in 1979. [37]

For me the Museum's signature exhibit was the former Dutch East Indiaman *Batavia,* which was wrecked on a reef off Australia's west coast in 1629. A major portion of the ship's hull and items from her cargo were discovered in 1963, during a marine archeology project. Among the items recovered from the ship were a coin dated 1542, construction materials, and silverware. Perhaps the most unusual recovery was a disassembled stone portico destined for a castle in Jakarta, which was known as Batavia in the seventeenth century. The portico has been reassembled and is displayed in the same area of the Museum that houses the remnants of *Batavia's* hull.

A companion exhibit at the Museum traced the almost one-hundred-year span between the arrival of the first European explorer to reach the west coast of Australia, Dirk Hartog, in the Dutch ship *Eendracht* in 1616, and the exploration of the Rottnest Island-Swan River estuary in 1697 by Dutch Captain Willem de Vlamingh. This exhibit included original charts and ship's logs and other artifacts associated with the spice trade of the time.

When I was visiting the Western Australian Maritime Museum, I discovered an area adjacent to the Museum building, where a reconstruction of another Dutch East Indiaman, *Duyfken,* was taking shape. This specialized mini-shipyard employs materials and building methods that are matched to the originals as closely as possible. The original *Duyfken* sailed from the Indonesian island of Banda in 1606 in search of trading opportunities and gold.

When the ship reached the northern coast of Australia, it marked the first known European contact with the continent that would become known as Australia. The charts made by the captain, Willem Janszoom, were the beginning of Australia's recorded history. The recreation of *Duyfken* is now exhibited in Fishing Boat Harbour.

The small shipyard adjacent to the Fremantle Maritime Museum also had a special connection for me personally. It was where the full-scale recreation of Captain Cook's bark *Endeavour* had been constructed, but at the time I was in Fremantle, I had no idea that before long I would be serving in the crew of that ship!

Fremantle was a discovery. I flew across a continent expecting to find an uninteresting commercial port. What I found was an exotic sense of the sea blended with a pioneering spirit, plus a welcoming tradition. There were clear signs of prosperity in the pleasure yachts contrasting with the hard labor represented by the commercial fishing fleet. There were geographical names that called up images of the rolling green hills of England combined with hard evidence of tough Dutch seamen who conquered fear and lack of knowledge to simply get to the places beyond.

What I had found in Fremantle was a dual view to the east, towards the major cosmopolitan cities of Sydney and Melbourne, that constantly tugged against a view towards the western horizon that whispered of places like Madagascar and the Seychelles.

And it was all combined in a fascinating state of mind labeled "Freo."

Illumination

My trip to Sydney and Fremantle illuminate two things: First, my very early impressions of Australians as tough, friendly, and self-reliant people turned out to be correct. Second, during the ongoing process of learning about the sea, I had simultaneously been learning things, important things, not just about a special place but about its people as well. And it all seemed to come together during what was a lot of hard traveling in the compressed span of a week.

PART V

LEADERSHIP IN STRESS
WHAT I LEARNED FROM HORATIO NELSON AND JOHN PAUL JONES

CHAPTER TWENTY-SIX

VICE ADMIRAL LORD NELSON

He was Superman with Everyman's weaknesses.

Tom Pocock

It was sometime around 1993. I was getting ready to leave London for New York City the next day, and I stopped by Hatchards on Piccadilly to pick up a book for the flight back home. As I began scanning the shelves in the military history section, my eyes went to a rather small book high up on the shelves, titled simply *The Life of Nelson*. It was the Everyman's Library edition of Robert Southey's classic biography. I knew very little about the British admiral, other than a few details of his dramatic victory over a combined French-Spanish Fleet at Trafalgar and his romance with Lady Emma Hamilton.

"The Man Who Befits the Hour"

The dust jacket copy was enough to suggest that the time had come to learn more. It was direct:

> Southey's life of the hero who saved the nation appeared eight years after the death of Nelson. It has all the fevered urgency of the times when the 'tyrant' (Napoleon) troubled men's minds and hearts with his growing power on land and sea, and the possible ultimate invasion of Britain...Nelson emerges memorably as the man who befits the hour.

The words "all the fevered urgency of the times when the 'tyrant' troubled men's minds" triggered a flashback to some of the feelings I experienced while growing up during World War II. The fact that I was standing in an old-line book shop on Picadilly, at the epicenter of the London Blitz of 1940 and 1941, intensified those feelings. My mind was clicking through black-and-white childhood visions of London, as the city and its people were blasted unmercifully from the sky for 57 straight days and nights.

The book's introduction by Carola Oman, the author of a later biography of Nelson, led me on with a comment about Southey: "He brought greatness to his great task: and of this the reader becomes aware the moment he opens Southey's *Nelson.*"

Despite the fact that Southey lacked the naval background to write in detail about sea battles and the Royal Navy, and notwithstanding his laudatory approach to his subject, his account of Nelson's life has become a literary classic. Its graceful style and "modern" format have made it a must-read for students of naval history who want to get beyond one-dimensional characters. It's also a natural for those who are fascinated by the sea and those whose lives are connected with it.

By the time I landed at John F. Kennedy Airport in New York, I had concluded that there was still more to know more about Vice Admiral Lord Nelson—much more. And today Southey's smallish book has been joined on my own bookshelves by approximately 200 more volumes related to the man who shaped the course of history from the quarterdecks of his ships.

The contents of those books—day-by-day, page-by-page—have revealed not only the complex and at times implausible character of Horatio Nelson but they have added an important historical dimension to what I have learned from the sea. In addition, those pages have provided clues to the how and why of leadership under stress.

Over time, probably around the one-hundredth book, I transitioned from simply absorbing facts about the man and began getting "inside his character." It became a matter of not only seeing his actions, but of also beginning to understand what was behind those actions. I had begun to know him as a person, rather than an historical figure frozen in images on the pages of a book.

At times I find myself asking "What would Nelson have done in this situation?" The answer is often somewhat different from my own inclination and frequently a help for thinking things through before taking action. It's not a matter of trying to emulate Nelson, but of using the knowledge of his life, and particularly his leadership, to test and temper my own thought processes.

The Beginnings

Nelson was the son of a parson. He was born in 1758, and at the age of twelve he went to sea as a midshipman in Great Britain's Royal Navy. The Royal Navy was a common career for someone who was neither titled nor landed gentry, but who was above the peasant class. As the son of a parson, Nelson could be considered part of the nascent middle class that was beginning to develop in Britain in the latter part of the eighteenth century, and the navy was an acceptable path to status and financial security. It could sometimes lead to great wealth.

In Nelson's case, he did achieve a small degree of financial security, but throughout his life he worried about money. And he never achieved the wealth of some of his Royal Navy contemporaries, men who amassed large fortunes through the prize system of the time. [38]

Like most midshipmen in the Royal Navy of his time, Nelson gained his appointment through the influence of a relative. In his case it was an uncle, Captain Maurice Suckling, who set his nephew's navy career in motion by appointing him, at the age of twelve, a midshipman in his 64-gun ship-of-the line HMS *Raisonable.*

At the time, Suckling focused on his nephew's less than powerful physique and showed little optimism for his potential in the Royal Navy. When asked to take young Horatio aboard *Raisonable,* he responded, "What has poor Horatio done, who is so weak, that he, above all the rest, should be sent to rough it out at sea?" Responding to his own question, Suckling added: "But let him come and the first time we go into action a cannon-ball may knock off his head, and provide for him at once." [39]

Little did Suckling know how that boy "who is so weak" would become a giant in his country's service, a man feared by his enemies for his courage and intellect and revered by his own nation for the crucial victories he won over those who threatened their way of life.

During his early career, Nelson demonstrated both a seaman's skill and a warrior's audacity, and by his early twenties he had reached the rank of captain and was in command of his own ship. During that early period, he commanded HMS *Boreas* in the West Indies. That tour of duty was the subject of my third book about Nelson: *Nelson in the Caribbean—the Hero Emerges, 1784-1787.*[40]

Going Public

Then in 1797, while in command of the 74-gun ship-of-the line HMS *Captain,* Nelson's career took on a significantly expanded dimension. In February of that year, he fought in the Battle of Cape St. Vincent off the southwest tip of Portugal. The Cape was the site of a number of previous sea battles of the Age of Sail and close to the town of Sagres, where Prince Henry the Navigator gathered the maritime talents of his time and became a driving force during the Age of Exploration in the fifteenth century.

In the course of the action at Cape St. Vincent, fought against a Spanish fleet, Nelson turned *Captain* out of formation without a direct order from the fleet's Commander-in-Chief Admiral Sir John Jervis. As a result of his aggressive, tactically brilliant, and clearly risky action, the withdrawal of the Spanish fleet was cut off. In the ensuing action, Nelson implausibly boarded and captured *two* Spanish ships, boarding the first Spanish ship from his own, and then using the captured ship to board and capture his second victim. With his actions, a significant British victory was assured, the phrase "Nelson's Patent Bridge for Crossing First-rates" (capital ships) was immortalized, and an astonishing military narrative entered the public domain.

One of his fellow captains complained to Jervis that Nelson had actually acted contrary to his commander-in-chief's orders by taking his ship out formation. Jervis's response went beyond the technical rationale for Nelson's maneuver in validating Nelson's action: "It certainly was so, and if you ever commit such a breach of orders I will forgive you also."[41] That was the beginning of a relationship that was important to Nelson for the rest of his career.

Nelson's actions at Cape St. Vincent catapulted him into the public eye. It must be noted that Nelson's own writing skill, in the form of letters to friends and relatives, which included his dramatic accounts of his performance and which clearly were intended to be shared with the media of the time, had a lot to do with that emergence as a national hero. In any event, he was no longer just one among many highly regarded captains in the Royal Navy. He became a national figure of significant dimensions, and in Jervis he gained an invaluable mentor and an "anchor to windward" for the rest of Nelson's increasingly stormy career.

Beyond his newfound fame, there were several additional results of the Battle of Cape St. Vincent that had long-term influence on Nelson's unique career. The first was the reinforcement of his aggressive inclinations in combat by Jervis's approbation. And as Nelson's career developed, we see that strong inclination towards seizing the initiative frequently repeated, often with great risk to both his life and his career. In fact, for Nelson, seizing the initiative became more than a tactic; it became part of a combat doctrine, the overarching attitude that guided him in the chaos of combat and in the similarly dangerous political crosscurrents at the Admiralty and Whitehall.

A second result of the victory over the Spanish in February 1797 was that Jervis was raised to earldom. As the Earl St. Vincent, he would play an important role in Nelson's career as a mentor and protector in the Admiralty and at Court, right up to the dramatic climax of Nelson's life.

The third result of the Battle of Cape St. Vincent was that it demonstrated to Nelson his ability to generate favorable public awareness about himself. Over the course of his career he went on to demonstrate that he understood and relied on that relationship to sustain him during the ups and downs that were to come. And there were extremes of both in the offing, which would include strategically important victories at the Battles of the Nile in 1798, Copenhagen in 1801, and Trafalgar in 1805, as well as his resounding defeat at the Battle of Santa Cruz in 1797.

The Defining Day

It would be impossible to deny that the Battle of Trafalgar on 21 October 1805 was anything but the zenith of Nelson's career. During that day's events, he wrote his name large in world history.

The day that would crown Nelson's career began quietly. At sunrise there was an overcast sky and a whisper of a breeze out of the west-northwest. A growing swell from the west rolled under the ships, introducing an almost hypnotic motion as the crews went about their duties with accelerating intensity. Those few relatively peaceful moments at sunrise soon would be shattered, however, by almost unimaginable violence as the day matured.

In the first light, two large fleets were in sight of one another. Nelson had twenty-seven ships-of-the-line in his fleet. The combined French-Spanish force, led by French Vice Admiral Pierre Villeneuve, had 33. Nelson's flag flew from the 100-gun HMS *Victory*. Villeneuve's flagship was the 80-gun *Bucentaure*. Cumulatively the Combined Fleet mounted 2,632 guns and the British 2,148. The largest ship in the action was the massive 130-gun Spanish ship-of-the-line *Santisima Trinidad*. But if the Combined Fleet seemed to have an advantage in terms of the order of battle, it would be heavily outweighed by the combat doctrine Nelson brought to the engagement. If ever there was a force multiplier, it was the combination of Nelson's dominant pursuit of the initiative and unyielding determination.

Nelson had been trying for months to lure the French and Spanish into battle, and on 21 October 1805, that confrontation was finally realized. As the two fleets came together, the Combined Fleet was roughly formed into a shallow arc sailing towards the north, with the concave side of the arc facing the British.

Nelson's fleet was divided into two very roughly formed lines sailing eastward, approaching their enemy at approximately right angles. The British took heavy broadsides from the Combined Fleet during their final approach, but at that stage of the Battle, they were unable to bring their own broadsides to bear against their enemy.

As the battle was joined, Nelson sent his final signal to his captains: "Engage the enemy more closely." It was the last signal hoisted from *Victory* during the action. It was a measure of Nelson's leadership style that he flew no more signals during the day. As it turned out, none were needed. There were two important lessons from that circumstance. First Nelson had briefed his subordinates so thoroughly that each of his "Band of Brothers" knew exactly what he was to do. Second, Nelson had absolute confidence that his captains had both the determination and skill to carry out his wishes, and he had overtly demonstrated that confidence consistently during his career. In the final analysis, once the fleets were engaged, there was little more for Nelson to do than to demonstrate that he would expose himself to the same risks faced by those who served under him. That last element of leadership that he employed at Trafalgar cost him his life.

Around noon, the British line, which was led by Vice Admiral Cuthbert Collingwood in the 100-gun HMS *Royal Sovereign*, smashed into the Combined Fleet. They struck about two-thirds from the van of the French-Spanish line. Approximately thirty minutes later Nelson did the same at about the middle of the enemy force.

The initial devastation was shocking. The 100-gun *Royal Sovereign* unleashed a double-shotted raking broadside into the stern of the 120-gun Spanish *Santa Ana*. The 100 cannon balls flew along the length of the gun decks and down the axis of the ship, killing or wounding approximately 400 men.

Nelson in *Victory* matched Collingwood's first blow. As he crossed under the stern of *Bucentaure,* he fired a 68-pound carronade loaded with round shot and a keg of 500 musket balls into his enemy's stern. The carronade shot was followed by a raking broadside from *Victory* as her guns came to bear on the French flagship. Again, the devastation was horrific. Nelson had returned payment, with exorbitant interest, for the pounding his ships had taken as they approached the Combined Fleet.

What followed as more and more of the British ships engaged the enemy was a frenzied series of separate actions among the ships of the two fleets. And although the French and Spanish fought with courage, the greater rate of fire and aggressive tactics of the Royal Navy carried the day.

When the battle ended at about five in the afternoon, the results added up to a decisive victory for the Royal Navy. Eighteen ships of the Combined Fleet had been sunk or captured. No British ships had been sunk or captured. The toll in human suffering was equally unbalanced. The British suffered 449 killed and 1,214 wounded, while the Combined Fleet had more than 4,400 killed and more than 2,500 wounded.

Before the battle, Nelson had written from *Victory* to an influential friend George Rose: "It is, as Mr. Pitt knows, annihilation that the Country wants."[42] Nelson's use of the term "the Country," in addition to his reference to the British prime minister, is interesting. It indicates a sense of the importance of public opinion that was rare for a military officer of the time.

In any event Nelson had delivered what his government and his country wanted: a strategically decisive victory in Britain's ongoing struggle against Napoleon. But he paid for the victory with his life, when a lethal musket ball found its mark as Nelson walked his quarterdeck during the early stages of the battle.

Death and Legacy

When Nelson was felled by the musket ball, which entered his shoulder and lodged in his spine, he was carried below to *Victory's* orlop, a small space—usually at the lowest deck of a warship—far below *Victory's* main deck. In battle the orlop was where the wounded were treated. There was no point in treating Nelson, however, since it was agreed by all, including Nelson, that he was dying. The only efforts made during the three hours-plus that he suffered were to comfort him.

Despite his wound, Nelson stayed mentally involved in the battle. He worried continuously about its progress, and on several occasions, his flag captain Thomas Hardy came below to assure Nelson that it was going well for the British. He also worried about the future welfare of his paramour Lady Emma Hamilton and their daughter Horatia. He seemed to fear instinctively that they would be treated indifferently by society after he was gone. He was right.

While Nelson lay in the orlop, he also repeatedly ordered that *Victory* and the other British ships anchor immediately after the battle. His seaman's experience told him the heavy swells from the west they had been experiencing were a portent of an approaching, extremely violent storm. Again he was right.

He knew he would be dead soon and he focused from time to time on issues beyond the Battle. He declared at one point, "I have not been a great sinner." It was Nelson's final statement, however, that was the best measure of the man. It created an epitaph for his career and was uttered just before he died: "Thank God I have done my duty."

Nelson's victory at Trafalgar established British maritime dominance for the next century, plus. And it was only a matter of ten years before Great Britain finally triumphed over Emperor Napoleon's army at Waterloo in June 1815, accelerating the growth of the colonial empire that lasted until World War II.

Life Lessons

Many of the most important lessons I have taken from Nelson's life have to do with leadership. He not only was successful in terms of the victories he achieved on behalf of his country and countrymen, he was loved, yes loved, by most of his officers, crews, and the British public.

Nelson certainly wasn't saintly, and he could be a tough, even brutal, disciplinarian. Similarly, at times he dealt very harshly, even savagely, with his enemies. Some of his fellow officers resented his aggressive style, and his very visible success with it. He *hated* the French, blaming his feelings on his mother's negative attitude toward them. His treatment of his wife Fanny, who remained loyal to him throughout his very public relationship with Lady Hamilton and until her own death, was shabby. In plain language, he made mistakes. As British author and acknowledged

Nelson expert, Tom Pocock, had expressed it, he indeed had plenty of Everyman's weaknesses. [43]

Obviously much of his popularity was due to the fact that he was a winner in combat. At a time when an invasion by France was imminent and his countrymen feared for their personal safety and their futures, he won psychologically and strategically decisive victories at sea against the French. But at this point in my study of Nelson, I am convinced that the single most important factor in generating the affection of so many of those with whom he came in contact was that he genuinely cared about them. And somehow he was able to communicate that.

To his officers and crews and the public he was indeed a hero, but they also saw him as one of *them,* perhaps because of his clearly visible shortcomings, some of which came close to ending his career prematurely. His manner and his instincts communicated something special to the ordinary people of his country. It was a connection that was understood by the general public and it's clear that he was not above using that popularity to support his career during what he described as "scrapes" with the Admiralty.

Nelson's sense of this relationship with the public was illuminated in a brief moment as he was leaving Portsmouth for the final time to fight his country's battles. Crowds gathered around him wherever he went in England and this day was no exception. To avoid the worst of the crush, he was picked up by a ship's boat along a beach, rather than at a dock.

With the crowds along the waterfront cheering him as his boat pulled away, Nelson remarked to his flag captain Thomas Hardy that the support that he was seeing came from the hearts of the people.

Nelson in His Own Words

One of the most amazing things about Nelson was his own writing ability. He wrote prodigiously, and fortunately a lot of his writing has survived. It continues to be a rich source for drawing lessons from his life, and the source continues to grow. For example, in 2005 then-Director of the Royal Naval Museum and leading Nelson expert Colin White created a five-hundred-page-plus volume: *Nelson—The New Letters.*[44] The book includes more than 1,300 previously unpublished letters and documents written by Nelson.

And it's not just the factual content of Nelson's words that is important. The ideas communicated between the lines, as well as the overall tone of what he wrote and said, speak volumes about the man and his times. White gives us a clue about why Nelson's own words are so revealing with a brief and insightful comment at the very beginning of his book: "Nelson loved telling his own story."[45] Nelson himself described his writing as "the inward monitor of my heart." [46]

Between 1844 and1846, Sir Nicholas Harris Nicolas edited a seven-volume work of Nelson's Letters titled *The Dispatches and Letters of Vice Admiral Lord Viscount Nelson.* To this day, "the Nicolas" remains the foundation of Nelson's story. And that work remains a good beginning point for the study of Nelson's life, despite the fact the Nicolas did some gratuitous editing of his subject's original words. Nicolas did his "improving" with the intention of protecting Nelson's character and advancing his public image. Although well meaning, Nicolas' efforts could not have been more irrelevant. When a paperback version of the Nicolas appeared in 1997, I reread all seven volumes, copiously marking up the contents as I progressed. In the process of reading "The Nicolas," it became increasingly clear that on occasion Nelson was writing for an audience beyond the addressee.

In 2001 I tried my own hand at capitalizing on Nelson's writing abilities and wrote a book, *Nelson Speaks,* my second book about "the Hero of Trafalgar." My book cited especially interesting quotes from Nelson, with my own brief commentary with each quote for perspective and context.

The thirteen categories of Nelson's words that became chapters in the book covered: Duty, Toughness, Combat, Nelson's Navy, Politics, Armies, Foreigners, Sea Power, A Good Heart, Fanny and Emma, Reputation, Life and Death, and Himself. Among my favorites are the following, all of which appear in the seven volumes of *The Dispatches and Letters of Vice Admiral Lord Viscount Nelson*:

❖Nelson wrote to his future wife Frances (Fanny) Nisbet in 1786 in an attempt to help her to understand the priorities of his career— *Duty is the great business of a Sea-officer. All private considerations must give way to it.* Vol. I, 167

❖Soaring ambition was a powerful factor in Nelson's career. In 1795 he wrote to Fanny from HMS *Agamemnon* about his frustration with inaction—*I am...at this moment in the horrors, fearing from idling here, that the active Enemy may send out two or three Sail of the Line, and some Frigates to intercept our Convoy...in short, I wish to be an Admiral, and in the command of the English Fleet; I should very soon either do much, or be ruined.* Vol. II, 26

❖Six years later, in the run-up to the Battle of Copenhagen, a letter to his paramour Lady Emma Hamilton revealed a powerful motivation rooted in eighteenth and nineteenth century ideas of women: *It is your sex that make us go forth; and seem to tell us—"None but the brave deserve the fair!" and, if we fall, we still live in the hearts of those females, who are dear to us...You know how to reward virtue, honour, and courage.* Vol. IV, 284

❖Some weeks after his letter to Lady Hamilton, the focus was on the forthcoming battle and convincing his commander-in-chief to take aggressive action—*The boldest measures are the safest.* Vol. IV, 297

❖In 1801Nelson wrote a long memo to the forces he commanded to meet an imminent invasion of England by Napoleon. At one point he added brilliantly concise admonition— *Never fear the event.* Vol. IV, 428

❖At times Nelson could be philosophical. In 1804 he wrote to an Italian Count— *In Sea affairs, nothing is impossible, and nothing improbable.* Vol. VI, *133*

❖It's important to note that Nelson was not universally loved by his fellow officers. In 1796, before he reached the pinnacle of fame, he complained to his wife Fanny about the criticism of a fellow officer—*[O]ne Captain told me, 'You did just as you pleased in Lord Hood's time, the same in Admiral Hotham's, and now again with Sir John Jervis; it makes no difference to you who is Commander-in-Chief.' I returned a pretty strong answer to his speech."* Vol. II, 126

❖ Part of Nelson's brilliance as a leader was that he knew that being constructive was more important than being critical. In a meeting with his captains shortly after he took command of Britain's Mediterranean fleet and just before the Battle of Trafalgar in 1805, he wrote— *I am not come forth to find difficulties, but to remove them.* Vol. VII 55. Then a few weeks later he established his combat doctrine towards the end of a memo the same group—*But in case Signals can neither be seen or perfectly understood, no Captain can do very wrong if he places his Ship alongside that of an Enemy.* Vol. VII, 91

❖ As he made final personal preparations for the Battle of Trafalgar, Nelson wrote a prayer that reveals much about his personality. The first paragraph reveals that he was concerned with much more than the Battle for its own sake—*May the great God, whom I worship, grant to my country and for the benefit of Europe in general, a great and glorious victory: and may no misconduct, in any one, tarnish it: and may humanity after victory be the predominant feature in the British fleet.* Vol. VII, 139

Immortality

When news of the hugely important victory at Trafalgar and the accompanying death of Nelson arrived in Great Britain in November 1805, it initially precipitated a celebration from a nation that understood that it finally was free from the threat of invasion by France. Then in January, it became the reason for something very different, a funeral that has never been matched in Britain.

Nelson's funeral procession began at Greenwich, whence the body was transported by barge up the Thames to the steps at Whitehall. From Whitehall the funeral procession progressed to St. Paul's Cathedral, where Nelson's remains were interred directly under the Cathedral's dome. When Nelson's body was placed in its final resting place, he had achieved an unparalleled esteem in the hearts of his countrymen and global respect as a professional warfighter.

American navalist Admiral A.T. Mahan summed up Nelson's legacy in his biography, *The Life of Nelson*:

> The words "I have done my duty," sealed the closed book of Nelson's story with a truth broader and deeper than he himself could suspect....Other men have died in the hour of victory, but for no other has the hour of victory so singular and so signal graced the fulfillment and ending of a great life's work....The coincidence of his death with the moment of completed success has impressed upon that superb battle [The Battle of Trafalgar] a stamp of finality and immortality of fame, which even its own grandeur scarcely could have insured. He needed and he left no successor. [47]

Nelson, with all of his writing skill and instincts for self-promotion, could not have written a more appropriate summation of his life.

CHAPTER TWENTY-SEVEN
COMMODORE JOHN PAUL JONES

Was it a proof of madness in the first corps of sea officers to have, at so critical a period, launched out on the ocean...to make war against such a power as Great Britain?

John Paul Jones

Between 2002 and 2004 I worked as the co-editor/writer for a book titled *Who's Who in Naval History—From 1550 to the Present*.[48] The project had been initiated and led by a friend, retired Royal Navy Commander Alastair Wilson. In addition to coming up with the idea, Alastair edited and wrote the major portion of the book, which covered the noteworthy naval persons from all nations other than the United States, and I was responsible for selecting and writing the two hundred-plus entries for the U.S. Navy.

Towards the middle of the project the idea that the time was right for a new biography of John Paul Jones began to emerge in the back of my mind. It had been fifty years since the last major biography of Jones, the definitive *John Paul Jones—A Sailor's Biography* by Samuel Eliot Morison. And the view of him from the beginning of the twenty-first century would, I believed, be significantly different from that of the 1950s.

I started putting aside notes and articles that related to the subject. Then, when *Who's Who in Naval History* was completed, I made a quick transition to the book that would be published in

2006 by the United States Naval Institute Press, *John Paul Jones: America's First Sea Warrior*. [49]

A Controversial Character

Besides the timing, there was another factor that urged me on: Jones has always been an enigmatic figure, a unique challenge for a biographer. He was a hero to many and a rogue to others. He was glorified for his victories and then shunted aside after the American Revolution by the new nation he helped establish. He was raised to fame at the beginning of the twentieth century largely for the purposes of then-president Theodore Roosevelt and then forgotten again. It seemed to me that the beginning of the 21st century was a good time to examine Jones' relevance to our own lives and times.

Jones had been despised and denigrated as a traitor and pirate in Great Britain, but he was celebrated as a hero in Paris and other European capitals. His civilian leaders in America recognized his importance as a combat commander, but as the U.S. armed forces' civilian leadership often does with aggressive and politically risky military leaders, he was kept at arm's length by them. As a man infused with patriotism and a vision of naval strategy that was ahead of its time, he was inevitably destined for a contentious career.

At times he was clearly ill-used by the Continental Congress and his principal contacts there, but somehow he managed to maneuver his way into a number of strategically important missions. Notwithstanding his dramatic successes, however, he never achieved much recognition during his life from the countrymen for whom he fought.

Then at the beginning of the twentieth century there was significant change. His career began receiving considerable public attention in the United States. Much of that attention was the direct result of President Theodore Roosevelt's commitment to making the United States a global naval power, with its first truly blue-water navy.

Jones' biographers have differed widely in their views of his life. In the years immediately following the American War of

Independence he was lauded with emotional fervor that carried over from his implausible military achievements and the equally implausible national independence achieved by the United States of America in 1783. He was praised by writers with such labels as a "knight of the seas" and "a genius prone to adventure."

In yet another reversal of fortunes for Jones, contemporary historians have frequently dismissed him as a cantankerous, ego-driven naval officer, someone who was only a minor figure in the American Revolution. One recent biographer even characterized him as a "violent tempered, self dramatizing paranoiac" who was "too suspicious and self-defeating to be a gifted leader." Such characterizations are as wide of the mark as the preceding efforts to establish Jones as hero of mythological proportions.

An additional challenge to a Jones biography was the unfortunate fact that some highly respected contemporary historians even miss the reality that there was such a thing as a naval component of the American Revolution. And to others the maritime aspects of the War of Independence are simply irrelevant.

Getting to the Heart of the Matter

The challenge then was to find the real person behind such contrasting and shifting views and determine what relevance, especially to our own lives, could be found in the narrative that emerged.

Against that complicated background, seeking the real John Paul Jones became a personal challenge, and I found a degree of guidance in something written by Admiral Lord Nelson in 1801. He was writing to a friend about creating a monument for a fellow captain, Ralph Willett Miller, who had been killed in an accidental explosion aboard HMS *Theseus*. Nelson's words were, as usual, to the point and instructive: "[W]e must take care not to say too much, or too little. The language must be plain, as if flowing from the heart of one of us Sailors who have fought with him." [50]

If, as Nelson recommended, avoiding hyperbole was one objective, emphasizing what was most important about Jones was another. Here I found a simple but profound guide in a line from retired U.S. Army General Robert Scales, spoken during a panel discussion at the United States Naval War College. Scales was quoting his platoon sergeant in Vietnam, an experienced Army man and a combat veteran. The sergeant realized that Scales, at the time a brand new second lieutenant who had just arrived to take over a platoon in Vietnam, was more than a little worried about his assignment. The sergeant's no-nonsense advice to Scales was startlingly uncomplicated: "The main thing is to keep the main thing the main thing."

Rather than concentrating excessively on Jones' abrasive—at times violent—personality and his serial—mostly shallow—love affairs, which were the things friends told me was the stuff of a popular biography, my focus would be on the main thing: his nature as a warfighter. To that end, I set out to illuminate what he did to advance the cause of a new nation struggling for independence against very long odds and what the qualities were that led to his achievements for his country.

As I had found with my books written about Admiral Lord Nelson, I learned a lot of important things in the process of writing about John Paul Jones and developing insights on his career.

The Early Years

Jones' early years were more important in shaping his character than many historians realize. A clearer understanding of those years go a long way towards illuminating the essence of the man who did so much at sea to advance the cause of American independence.

Jones was born John Paul in 1747 in a cottage on the estate of William Craik, a local squire and member of the British Parliament, in the Dumphries and Galloway Region of southern Scotland. His father was an architectural gardener on the estate, a respected position at that time. His mother worked in the manor house. The cottage he grew up in was no mere hovel, as some have depicted it. [51]

One of the important factors connected with the Craik Estate was its location on the northern shore of Solway Firth. John Paul was born close to the sea, and the first breath he drew was laced with salt air swept in from the Firth. Later as a young boy he watched ships coming from and going to the Irish Sea and even places beyond those waters, places where he would achieve immortal fame in a history-making struggle for political liberty.

In addition, during young John Paul's early years in the Galloway area, he inevitably would have been influenced by legends of early Scottish mariners, such as the Leith Sea Dogs, and warriors such as William Wallace. Of more than passing interest, many of those legends were about those who fought against the rule of governments in London. There was a pattern in those legends of rebellious warriors that would eventually carry over to the time when Jones found himself in America, during the run-up to the War of Independence.

Perhaps the most important factor in John Paul's early years is something that generally isn't recognized even in passing by historians: the influence on young John Paul of the Scottish Enlightenment. It was a time of great intellectual energy in Scotland. Political liberty, architecture, city planning, new economic theories, literature, and art were in the forefront of Scottish life at the time.

In his book *How the Scots Invented the Modern World,* historian Arthur Herman wrote that it was a time when "Scots created the basic idea of modernity."[52] This part of Jones' background directly contradicts the frequently advanced characterization that Jones came from what one recent biographer called a "threadbare" beginning. Economically, he came from the closest thing to a middle class that existed at the time. Intellectually he came from an environment that arguably was more advanced than that in other areas of Great Britain and Continental Europe. He was a person for whom ideas were important, and thus his seizing on America's cause of liberty was a major motivation for his actions in the Continental Navy.

Young John Paul would have been exposed to considerable political stirring in his classrooms and in daily life as he approached his teen years. And that stirring inevitably would have influenced his decision later in life to join in the American

Revolution. In a very real sense, the man who later became known as John Paul Jones captured the idea of liberty before he ever captured a single Royal Navy ship.

As a child, John Paul surely stood on the shore of Solway Firth and looked across the water towards England and the port of Whitehaven in the distance. It was not surprising then that he was apprenticed at age thirteen to a British merchantman out of that port.

Paul did well in his apprenticeship. He had an aptitude for the sea, and he quickly became a good seaman. His potential as a leader also became apparent, and based on his capabilities, which were demonstrated dramatically when he took command of a ship after her captain and first mate both died at sea, he became a merchant ship captain at age twenty-one. Jones' unexpected accession to command was a classic example of how leadership is, in sudden and unanticipated circumstances, thrust upon those who pursue a career at sea.

By that point, the general shape of his future was established. As I wrote in my biography of Jones:

> It was at sea where the young man proved himself, and it was there that he was hardened physically and tempered mentally. It was at sea where he developed the self confidence that would enable him to achieve his history-changing combat victories. It was the sea that became Jones' life-long mistress, and combat would become their ultimate intimacy. [53]

Fate Intervenes

In all likelihood, Captain Paul would have continued to succeed in the British merchant marine, and it's not unreasonable to assume that he could have accumulated a personal fortune if he had continued on that course. In October 1773, however, his course was radically altered.

Captain Paul had never been anything but a tough captain. He was demanding and he had a temper. Those qualities came to the fore, in the extreme, during a port call in Tobago, where there was a disagreement over wages with a member of his crew. The disagreement escalated into a physical altercation, and according to the available accounts, which are meager, Jones ended the confrontation by running his attacker through with his sword.

Under most circumstances, the incident would have been investigated by an Admiralty court, and in such a court, the odds were very strong that Captain Paul's actions would have been deemed justified, and that would have been that. The circumstances in Tobago were different, however. There was no British admiralty court there, and the slain man was from that island. In all likelihood, it would have been a local court that Captain Paul faced, one that might well have been influenced by the dead man's family. That was a risky prospect, and John Paul fled.

The details of Captain Paul's flight from Tobago are vague, but he wound up in Virginia, where he had a brother. And as records of his presence there began to emerge, it was evident that after his arrival in Virginia he assumed the name John Paul Jones. During those early months in America, another thing became clear: the man who had become known as John Paul Jones might have been a fugitive, but he was not a fugitive in hiding. For one thing he quickly became involved in the local scene as a Mason. And that special source of influential connections would help Jones at critical points throughout his lifetime, in both America and in Europe.

Among his new friends, for example, were men who went on to play major roles in the revolution that was developing. They included fellow Virginian and American Founding Father Thomas Jefferson, who would be a positive influence throughout Jones' career. They also included the successful merchant and influential member of the Continental Congress Joseph Hewes, who held important positions that dealt with naval matters in that legislature. Men like Jefferson and Hewes turned out to be powerful supporters as Jones navigated the frequently dangerous political crosscurrents running through his career. And Jones, as a recent emigrant without long-standing contacts and influence in America, needed all the political help he could get.

It's also important to point out that public opinion in the American Colonies was almost equally divided between those committed to independence and those committed to continued negotiations with Parliament and the King. Jones, as an early volunteer for the Continental Navy, would not have been popular with all of his neighbors in Virginia, making his position similar to that of those serving in the military during the Vietnam War and other politically divisive wars in our history.

Jones Commits to the Cause

When Jones arrived in America, political turbulence was mounting. In fact, revolution was in the air. In December 1773, the Boston Tea Party enraged many of the politicians in London, along with the merchants whose tea was destroyed. The result was that the Royal Navy closed the port of Boston, inflicting severe economic distress on the local inhabitants. The American Colonies were splitting along an increasingly unstable fault line, dividing those who were becoming more and more inclined to separate from Great Britain from those who were loyal to the King and wanted to continue to negotiate their grievances with London.

Then, in April 1775, the arguing escalated to armed combat between the regulars of the British Army and Continental militias. When the first shots were fired at Lexington, the American militiamen got the worst of the action. But as the British troops marched back towards Boston, the militiamen, firing from behind trees and stone walls, inflicted heavy casualties on the British professionals. When the actions at Lexington and Concord were over, Great Britain and her American Colonies were at war.

As Jones had entered this rapidly escalating political storm, his antipathy towards the government in London and his ideas of political liberty planted during the Scottish Enlightenment were brought to the fore. Among the catalysts was the volatile combination of increasing military pressure by Britain and an increasingly aroused public opinion fanned by advocates of American independence.

Thomas Paine was a leader among those advocates, and in February 1776 he articulated the rising mood of rebellion that was sweeping the American Colonies. He was reaching beyond economic issues, such as "taxation without representation." He was addressing ethical and moral issues that exponentially increased the depth of feelings sweeping through the Colonies. In the Introduction of his booklet *Common Sense* he wrote:

> The cause of America is in a great measure the cause of all mankind. Many circumstances hath, and will arise, which are not local, but universal, and through which the principles of all Lovers of Mankind are affected, and in the Event of which, their Affections are interested. The laying a country desolate with Fire and Sword, declaring War against the natural rights of all Mankind, and extirpating the Defenders thereof from the Face of the Earth, is the concern of every Man to whom Nature hath given the power of feeling; of which Class, regardless of Party Censure, is the *author*. [54]

To that emotionally loaded mood, add the circumstances of Jones' flight from Tobago, and you have everything you need to precipitate Jones' voluntary enlistment in the Continental Navy, and so he did. In 1775 he joined the naval force being cobbled together by Congress. It's important to note, however, that Jones brought no military experience to his new career. It was, in his case, a matter of on-the-job training.

Among the original eight ships commissioned in the Continental Navy, not a single one was a purpose-built warship. And the two largest ships of America's new navy, with twenty and twenty-four guns respectively, were at the small end of "rated" warships during the Age of Sail. [55]

To top matters off, Jones enlisted as a lieutenant, which was a significant comedown from being a captain of his own ship. If Jones had more political influence in the Continental Congress, his chances of commanding his own ship would have been much greater, and that lack sufficient political influence came back repeatedly to haunt him during his naval career. The result was bitterness with the way the Continental Congress managed—or mismanaged—that career.

At the end of the American Revolution, Jones addressed a long letter to Robert Morris, Head of the Marine Committee of Congress reflecting his bitterness. In the letter, he catalogued his grievances with Congress, ranging from a complaint about captains who had achieved less than Jones being placed ahead of him on the navy's seniority list, to fleet operations, and even to prize monies still owed to him and the crews of his ships. [56]

In any event, Jones was assigned to take charge of the fitting out of the 24-gun Continental Navy Ship *Alfred*, named for the Saxon king who generally is considered to be the founder of the English Navy. In her previous life, *Alfred* was the merchant vessel *Black Prince*. Her conversion into a warship would have been a challenge to Jones' skills a as a seaman and a leader.

When *Alfred* was officially commissioned in December 1775, it was Jones who raised the national ensign, making him the first to hoist an American national ensign in an American ship.

It must be reemphasized that Jones had no initial training as a naval officer. In most cases his contemporaries in the Royal Navy would have begun their careers as midshipmen. There was no naval tradition or naval culture to support his career in the Continental Navy. For that reason, in my biography of Jones, I refer to him as a *seaman warrior,* rather than a *warrior seaman.* And the fact that Jones was a self-taught naval officer in an improvised navy could account for the edginess that was an integral part of his personality.

Jones and *Alfred* saw action quickly in the early spring of 1776, when *Alfred* was designated the flagship for a small American squadron that attacked New Providence (now Nassau) in the Bahamas. The attack had limited military impact, but it was a very forward-leaning mission for the nascent Continental Navy, and its audacity established an aggressive naval posture for some but not all in the Continental Navy. Jones, however, would later apply the inclination towards offensive rather than defensive action to an astonishing degree.

In May, Jones advanced to captain and command of the 12-gun sloop of war *Providence,* and he demonstrated his preference for offensive tactics as a successful raider who disrupted British commerce in attacks against British merchant ships and fishing ports along the Canadian coast. Then in November 1776 Jones was placed in command of *Alfred,* and he continued his successful raiding along the Canadian coast.

Jones' deployments in *Providence* and *Alfred* were not only demonstrations of his aggressive inclinations; they were also early indications that he had a strategic vision of naval warfare that went beyond that of his contemporaries in the Continental Navy. He saw the Continental Navy as a means of projecting military power outward against the British, and he did so while almost all of his fellow captains and civilian leadership saw the Continental Navy in a limited, defensive role. In time he would pursue that vision in attacks against the British homeland.

In 2008, I wrote a magazine article devoted to Jones's strategic naval vision.[57] The article pointed out that, in terms of his understanding of the concept of naval power projection, Jones was considerably ahead of his time. These were ideas that would fully mature in the twentieth century and that remain elements of military strategy today. Soon Jones would gain the opportunity to put his farsighted vision of naval power into action.

Deployment in *Ranger*

Following his successes in *Providence* and *Alfred,* Jones was placed in command of the 18-gun sloop of war *Ranger.* He had been aggressive in seeking a bigger ship, but as it turned out, *Ranger* was big enough for his purpose, which was to project the naval power of the American Colonies against the British Isles, notwithstanding its size limitations.

It was a bold mission and it took considerable convincing of his civilian leaders before he was allowed to depart for Europe, but eventually Jones' lobbying of the Continental Congress succeeded. *Ranger's* transit was difficult, partly because of overpromising when recruiting the crew and partly because Jones was an outsider with a crew recruited almost exclusively from the Portsmouth, New Hampshire region. In fact, the transit to France was marked by near mutiny among her crew. If Jones had been a professionally trained naval officer, those problems and many that followed might have been avoided.

Jones arrived in France in late December 1777, and he immediately began lobbying his civilian leaders in Paris—primarily Benjamin Franklin—and the French for a larger ship. When it was clear that he was not going to get a more powerful ship, however, Jones departed in *Ranger* for the Irish Sea in April 1778. He had a three-part plan. First, he would attack British maritime commerce at every opportunity. Attacking Britain's ocean commerce had been a part of the American naval strategy from the beginning of the Revolution. And as the Revolution developed, that part of America's maritime strategy was accomplished with considerable success, mostly by privateers, many of whom became rich in the process.

Second, he would attack an English port. Attacking the homeland of one of the world's leading powers by sea was, in this instance, a bold example of using a navy force for power projection. Although describing *Ranger* as a "force" could be considered a stretch.

Finally, Jones intended to capture a British nobleman, someone who could be exchanged for American seamen being held in British prisons. Trading prisoners was common among warring nations of the eighteenth century, and the captured members of the Continental Navy faced particularly harsh captivity. They were considered by the British to be renegades, traitors, and pirates, rather than military prisoners of war.

Before even reaching the Irish Sea, Jones began his successful attacks on British merchant ships. Then, once in the Irish Sea, he headed for Whitehaven on the south shore of Solway Firth. It was the homeport of the ship in which he began his apprenticeship in the British merchant marine, and the fact that he knew the approaches to the harbor and its layout well would have contributed to Jones' decision to make that port the target of his attack.

Notwithstanding the reluctance of his officers and crew to mount the assault and the loss of the advantage of surprise, Jones got ashore with a small landing party. There he set fire to a collier at its pier, spiked the guns protecting the harbor, and escaped without a single casualty. The action was far from a textbook example of expeditionary warfare, but it had been successfully executed, and there were no casualties.

The psychological impact of the Whitehaven raid was enlarged by the fact that it was the first time in a century that an enemy had mounted a successful naval attack against an English port. As a result, it attracted considerable attention among the British public and the political leaders in London. In modern strategic terms, Jones was getting inside the enemy's decision cycle. He was forcing them to react to an American military initiative, and that was very different from what had been going on up to that point in the naval part of the American Revolution.

From a strictly tactical point of view, the Whitehaven raid was not significant. From a psychological and strategic point of view, however, it was huge. It came at a time when there was increasing concern within the British government about the cost of pursuing the American Revolution. It was a circumstance that has been reprised during my lifetime, with the difference that America has been on the opposite side of the equation.

Immediately following the Whitehaven raid, there was another event that reinforced the British concerns about the American War of Independence. While still in the Irish Sea, Jones precipitated a single ship action between *Ranger* and the 20-gun sloop of war HMS *Drake*, a ship of approximately the same size and power as *Ranger*. In that one-on-one battle, Jones defeated and captured *Drake* and her crew. Jones' victory over *Drake* stood out among a string of defeats of the Continental Navy by the Royal Navy, and it showed the America's improvised navy could, on occasion, take on the Royal Navy and win. It was another disquieting piece of news at Whitehall and the Admiralty, and another lesson in how far audacity married to skill and courage can overcome a military imbalance in an asymmetrical war.

The negative part of Jones' deployment in the Irish Sea was his attempt to kidnap Lord Selkirk in order to exchange him for Continental Navy prisoners held by the British. Jones and a landing party managed to get ashore at St. Mary's Island, the home of Lord Selkirk. Unfortunately, Selkirk was in London at the time and the effort took on near-comic-opera dimensions, when Jones allowed the landing party to loot the Selkirk home of its household silver.

The incident at St. Mary's Island was a blot on Jones' record as a leader, and it was clear from correspondence that Jones was embarrassed by the event. The silver eventually was returned to Lord and Lady Selkirk by Jones, but the return had absolutely no impact on the low opinion of Jones held by the British.

Pressing On

Despite Jones' unlikely accomplishments in *Ranger,* he was greeted on his return to France by silence from the American Commissioners in Paris, except for a letter from Commissioners Arthur Lee that at the very least was insulting. Lee's letter not only didn't acknowledge Jones' achievements, it didn't contain a single mention of Jones' skill and determination and the importance of his accomplishments in the Irish Sea. The letter focused on administrative matters, lectured Jones on the cost of his deployment, and expressed displeasure with Jones for the way he handled a perceived disobedience to his orders by his first lieutenant. Jones had placed the officer under arrest when he returned from their deployment into the Irish Sea.

Jones' reaction to Lee's letter and the lack of recognition from Franklin was a significant milestone in his career and coincidentally in the developing American concept of civilian control of the military. Despite the deeply discouraging response from his civilian leaders, Jones pressed on, and his reaction to ill treatment by his civilian leaders stands in thought-provoking contrast to the reaction of Benedict Arnold to similar circumstances in the Continental Army.

Following his deployment in *Ranger,* Jones resumed his lobbying for a larger ship and another forward-leaning assignment. It was during those efforts that he wrote a letter to the French minister of marine with the often quoted lines: "I wish to have no connection with any ship that does not sail *fast,* for I intend to go in harm's way."

Jones eventually succeeded in getting a frigate provided by the French, the former French East Indiaman *Duc de Duras*. She wasn't a purpose-built warship; she wasn't agile; she certainly wasn't fast. But with 42 guns, she was more powerfully armed than most frigates of the time. In addition, she was far more powerful than any ship Jones had commanded up to that point.

Jones named his new command *Bonhomme Richard* in recognition of Benjamin Franklin, known as the author of *Poor Richard's Almanac*. It would not be the last time a U.S. Navy ship would be named for a political leader who was in a position to influence naval policy.

In addition, Jones was provided with a small squadron for his next deployment against the British Isles. His squadron included the 36-gun American frigate *Alliance,* the French 26-gun small frigate *Pallas,* the French 12-gun brig *Vengeance,* and the French 12-gun cutter *Le Cerf.*

The three French ships were commanded by French officers, and *Alliance* was commanded by a former French naval officer, who had been commissioned into the Continental Navy, and who clearly was mentally unstable. The latter officer was an ongoing problem for Jones during the deployment, and when there was serious combat action, he was more of a help to the enemy than to Jones.

Before departing from Lorient in August 1778, the French minister of marine confronted Jones with a document that seriously undercut his command authority. The document stipulated that any of his captains could leave his squadron if they disagreed with Jones' orders. The agreement was a guarantee of difficulties, if not the complete failure of the deployment. Jones signed the document, however, probably in the belief it was the only way he would get his squadron to sea.

This time Jones planned to circumnavigate the British Isles by sailing northeast along the Atlantic coasts of Ireland and Scotland, over the top of Scotland and then southeast along the North Sea coasts of Scotland and England. As with his deployment in *Ranger,* Jones hoped to attack at least one port along the way, but although he came close at one point along the Yorkshire coast, that part of his plan never worked out.

On the other hand, as he sailed along the coasts, Nelson roiled the countryside. Militias were called out and anxious messages were sent to the admiralty for Royal Navy ships to protect threatened ports. There was widespread fear in the coastal communities, where Jones' exploits were becoming legendary. British newspaper accounts of Jones' actions confirm the fear and national resentment he precipitated.

Finally, as Jones sailed southeast and down along England's Yorkshire coast, his moment in history arrived. He was approaching the city of Scarborough when he sighted a 40-ship British convoy. It was a Baltic convoy, loaded with naval stores for the Royal Navy and the British merchant marine. It was a choice target, an answer to an aggressive commodore's prayers.

Bonhomme Richard vs. HMS *Serapis*

The British convoy was escorted by two Royal Navy ships: HMS *Countess of Scarborough,* a small 20-gun converted merchantman that had been taken up into naval service, and HMS *Serapis,* a large, fast, 44-gun frigate, with an experienced Royal Navy captain, Richard Pearson. [58]

As events developed, Jones was not able to get at the convoy before it reached the safety of Scarborough harbor. What then developed was a single-ship battle between *Bonhomme Richard* and *Serapis,* an action that became known as the Battle off Flamborough Head.

Initially it was an uneven match. *Serapis* was faster, more agile, and had a faster rate of fire. Captain Pearson simply maneuvered around Jones and *Bonhomme Richard,* while methodically pounding his enemy. If he had continued those tactics, Pearson would undoubtedly have carried the day. But he did not. Why he did not is an interesting question. Perhaps it was chance. Perhaps Pearson was reacting to a sudden shift in wind or sea conditions. Perhaps it was overconfidence on the part of the British captain. It could even have been a mistake by Serapis' helmsman. But whatever else it was, it also was fatal to the British ship.

At one point the combatants came together for a second time, and this time Jones grappled his ship firmly to *Serapis*. Once the two ships were grappled together, Pearson's advantage of speed and agility was negated. Further, Jones had a relatively large contingent of Marines aboard. Many of the Marines were positioned on *Bonhomme Richard's* fighting tops and in her rigging, and they swept *Serapis'* exposed decks with musket fire. In the meantime, *Serapis'* guns continued to fire into *Bonhomme Richard* from point blank range, with her fire actually passing in one side of the American ship and out the other.

During this phase of the fighting Pearson shouted across to ask if Jones had struck his colors. Jones' reply was a reflection of his character and has become a part of U.S. Navy lore: "I have not yet begun to fight." Over the years commentators have claimed that those were not Jones' actual words. On the other hand and of greater significance, no one has ever claimed that those words do not match the *meaning* of Jones' response.

As the battle raged on, a sailor from *Bonhomme Richard* was dropping hand grenades onto the main deck of *Serapis* from one of *Bonhomme Richard's* yardarms. One of the grenades found its way through a hatch and exploded on *Serapis'* gun deck, where it ignited powder bags being used to serve the ship's guns. The explosions wiped out the major portion of Pearson's main armament and its gun crews.

The tide of battle had turned, and it was Pearson who finally struck his colors. The convoy was safe in Scarborough, and he decided to end the carnage. No one could have faulted him for his decision, and eventually he was recognized with a knighthood for having saved the convoy. An anecdotal story has it that when Jones heard of Pearson's knighthood, he responded: "If we meet again, I'll make him a Lord."

For Jones' part, his victory wasn't a matter of superior tactics. It was a matter of iron-hard determination that carried Jones and his ship past the point when almost any other captain would have surrendered and on to ultimate victory.

It also is important to remember that, when all was said and done, it was the crew of *Bonhomme Richard* that fought through the horrors of combat off Flamborough Head to give Jones and America a victory that was crucial in America's fight for independence. In the Epilogue of *John Paul Jones: America's First Sea Warrior* I wrote of the performance of *Bonhomme Richard's* crew in the action off Scarborough:

> The Battle off Flamborough Head was a vision of hell. With a few notable exceptions, it was fought and won by anonymous men. Those rank-and-file warfighters who endured for more than three hours of horrendous combat—soaked in sweat, choking on gunpowder smoke, and splattered with blood—deserve more than a passing reference in our nation's history. Scores of them died during the fight, and as far as we know, all the dead were buried at sea. Scores more were wounded and would live with the marks of their fight to stay alive on 23 September 1779. By Jones's own account, about half of *Bonhomme Richard's* crew of three hundred plus were either killed or wounded.
>
> *Bonhomme Richard's* crew members endured the unspeakable to preserve the priceless. They were not sophisticated men; many, no doubt, could not even read. But there is no doubt that the sum of their strength was as essential to winning the battle off Flamborough Head as was the leadership of John Paul Jones. Their incredible ability to continue doing their duty—and more—under the most appalling combat conditions was as important as a force multiplier as was the astonishing mental and physical toughness of their captain. [59]

The Aftermath

Although Jones' victory was a tribute to his courage and combat skills, a single-ship victory in the Age of Sail was not usually considered of great strategic importance. But just as his victory over *Drake* had taken on inordinate psychological importance so did his victory over *Serapis*.

The news of the Battle off Flamborough Head was another crucial break in the long series of Continental Navy defeats at sea.

In addition, it accelerated the doubts in London, where both the West Indies and India were considered to be more important colonies than America, about the wisdom of pursuing the war in America. The ongoing war with France was a much more serious affair. Britain could survive the loss of the American Colonies; it could not survive a loss to Napoleonic France.

With his victories over *Drake* and *Serapis,* Jones demonstrated that the Continental Navy could not only win in combat against the greatest naval power of the time, he also showed that the emerging United States of America, notwithstanding its birth struggles, had the will and the naval capability to strike at the very homeland of Great Britain. And when all was said and done, it was the American will, not military superiority, that resulted in The Treaty of Paris in September 1783 and American independence.

A Coffin with no Nameplate

Jones died alone in Paris in 1792, almost ten years after the Treaty of Paris confirmed America's independence. He was buried in a small cemetery at the edge of Paris. As that city grew, the cemetery quickly was overrun, and for a century, Jones' burial place wasn't known. And sadly, no one cared.

It was President Theodore Roosevelt who finally initiated the hunt for Jones' remains, and after a six-year search that came close to failing, his body was located and was returned to the United States with appropriate ceremony. Jones' crypt is located under the golden dome of the impressive U.S. Naval Academy Chapel. His epitaph is carved in marble: "He gave our Navy its earliest traditions of heroism and victory."

Arguably his greatest achievement, however, was to grasp the broad strategic potential of maritime power. It was a remarkable achievement, considering Jones was serving in an improvised, nascent navy that was fighting against a global power with the most powerful navy of the era. He was arguably the American navy's first sea power visionary and an officer who sensed the relationship between the navy and America's coming rise to global preeminence.

In 1778, Jones wrote to a friend who was the captain of an American privateer. The vision he described would have seemed to be totally outlandish at the time:

> When the Enemies land force is once conquered and expelled (from) the Continent, our Marine (navy) will rise as if by enchantment, and become within the memory of Persons now living, the wonder and Envy of the World. [60]

That was a stunning prediction at the time, and although it took a little longer than Jones predicted, it was a prophecy that came true. And the beginning of the transition of the U.S. Navy into a truly global force coincided with the discovery of Jones' burial site in France.

Validation

In *John Paul Jones: America's First Sea Warrior,* I tried to assess Jones' career, not in terms of his celebrity, his love affairs, or his personality. I placed the focus on his character and as a naval officer in extremely unusual and challenging circumstances, one who did important things at sea for all Americans, despite immense obstacles.

Among the book's reviews, there was one that had particular meaning for me. It appeared with the book's Amazon.com listing and it was from a reviewer simply identified as a Lieutenant Colonel in Baghdad. It read in part: "I enjoyed this book. Admiral Callo presented a balanced history that placed the strategic, operational and tactical achievements of John Paul Jones's career in perspective."

The fact that a serving officer in a current combat theater saw the book in that way was, for me, an ultimate validation. It confirmed my effort to move John Paul Jones beyond the superficial contemporary analyses that fail to address the important role he played in securing American independence.

JOSEPH CALLO

The End of a Warfighter

John Paul Jones' death was very different from the heroic end, state funeral, and interment at St. Paul's of Admiral Lord Nelson. Jones died alone in his small second story apartment on a nondescript Paris street. He was found face down on his bed.

If it were not for a Parisian who believed that someday Jones' body would be reclaimed by his country, he would have wound up in an unmarked grave, and his remains would have never been found. In fact, it took a hundred years, an archeological dig, and the particular interest of President Teddy Roosevelt to find Jones' remains and return him to the United States with appropriate honor.

The manner of Jones' death established him, in a literary sense, as a truly tragic figure. He died with the knowledge that no one really understood why he fought America's battles at sea. And he took his knowledge of that into eternity.

Jones had not fought for wealth or for glory. He fought for a cause that he considered to be transcending: liberty. And he provided a clue to the urgency of that commitment in a letter written to Robert Morris, a member of the Continental Congress, in October 1776: "The situation of America is new in the annals of mankind, her affairs cry haste, and speed must answer them." [61]

During Jones' last days, there had been no life companion or life-long friend who really understood why he did what he did, and sadly, he surely realized that. In a significant way, he was like most of those who dedicate themselves to endure the horrors of war to prevent greater horrors. They don't speak their stories, even to those closest to them, because they know that no one could really understand.

Their stories are told only in their eyes, and when death shaded Jones' eyes, there would never again be an opportunity for someone who really cared for him to read his real story.

EPILOGUE

The sea is calm tonight
The tide is full, the moon lies fair
Upon the straits.

Matthew Arnold

On Thursday, July 15, 2009 I held my first great-grandchild in my arms. Dominic had been launched into the world on June 26, 2009, the first child of my granddaughter Emily and her husband Adam.

When I held him closely, he looked up at me without fear. His dark, dark blue eyes were fixed with penetrating curiosity. "Who or what is this?" they asked. His arms and legs were pumping, not frantically, but with the measured pace of a long distance swimmer. I could feel the strength that had been gathering daily in his small body. He showed no apprehension as I held him closely. His eyes were locked on my eyes, asking his question over and over.

I knew he could feel the rhythms of my body as I held him against my chest, something different from the rhythms of his mother, father and the others who had met him before me.

Could he sense the throbbing of USS *Sarasota's* engines that had become part of me more than fifty years ago? Could he feel the slow rise and fall of the deep ocean swells I absorbed as I discovered the honest strength of *Carmali* in the open ocean off the coast of St. Maarten? Was there something of the remnants of the screaming winds of Hurricane Frederick transferring from me to him? Could he feel the gentle lapping of the water on the boat's

341

hull as I sat under a canopy of stars in Marina Cay in the British Virgin Islands?

You bet he could, and they were now part of him, and I wondered how he would respond to those rhythms and how they would influence his life. I wondered to whom he would pass them. There was one thing sure: this book's epilogue is a prologue for Dominic.

APPENDIX A

MY IMMEDIATE FAMILY

My grandparents on my father's side, Joseph and Maria Callo, emigrated from Sicily to New York City. Initially they lived in Harlem, and then they lived for many years in The Bronx. My father had one older brother and two younger brothers.

My mother's parents, Patrick and Ellen Brennan, emigrated from County Tipperary in Ireland to New York City. At some point—perhaps around 1920—they moved to Hastings-on-Hudson, about twenty miles up the Hudson River from New York City. My mother had two older brothers and a younger sister and brother.

Both my sister (three years older) and I were born in and grew up in the Borough of The Bronx in New York City.

In June 1952, I married Susan Jones. In May 1954, Joseph F. Callo III was born in Portsmouth Naval Hospital, Virginia. In May 1954, James D. Callo was born in St. Albans Naval Hospital, New York. In April 1956, Mary Ellen Callo was born in Doctors' Hospital, New York City. On August 25, 1958, Kathleen E. Callo was born in Doctor's Hospital. On January 26, 1962, Patricia A. Callo was born in Phelps Memorial Hospital, New York.

In 1976 Susan and I separated, and in 1978 we divorced.

In March 1979, I married Sally Chin McElwreath, who has a son, Robert J. McElwreath III by a previous marriage.

Grandchildren:

      Emily born in December 1978

      Thomas born in August 1982

      Jacob born in April 1983

      Audra born in June 1985

      Rima born in March 1987

      David born in April 1994

      Henry born in July 1994

      Jordan born in January 1996

      Benedict born in February 1996

      Kelsey born (on my birthday) in December 1996

      Zoe born in August 2000

      Max born in June 2002

Great-grandchildren:

      Dominic born in June 2009

      Alexander born in January 2012

APPENDIX B

WHAT'S IN A NAME?

Names of Sailboats I have Skippered

Over the years, I have skippered many sailboats; most were bareboat charters in the Caribbean. In the case of the bareboat charters, the boats were named by individual owners who had placed their boat in a charter operation. In many cases, the boat names were pretty straightforward. Personal names were common. Some were whimsical, and a few were hard to figure out.

In a number of cases, the names had particularly interesting meanings, and some were rich in symbolism.

Each boat had a personality and each became a part of my learning experiences at sea.

Ree-Raa 1942-46—From the Gaelic: A place or state where exuberance and revelry prevail.

Spindrift 1962-1972 (approximately)—Windblown sea spray and the name I would have painted on the transom of my sailing dinghy, if I'd had the time.

Breezin' Up 1976—Nicely symbolic in the sense that it was the first boat Sally and I sailed in the British Virgin Islands.

Poco Joya 1997—From Spanish: small jewel.

Shore Duck 1998—Some day I may understand this one.

Restless 1978—Clearly symbolic of the frequent feelings of those who enjoy sailing.

Fenson Bligh 1979—Author of a spy novel.

Carmali 1979-82—A name made up with parts of the first names of the children of the original owner of the boat. We decided not to rename the boat when we purchased it from the original owner.

Igel 1983—From German: hedgehog

Vagamundo 1985—A possible corruption of "vagabundo," which is Spanish for "vagabond"

M-37-2 1986—The only boat I sailed that was identified by a number. It made me sound like a secret agent on the VHF radio.

Uprohr 1987—Presumable derived from the owner's name.

Jazz 1988—At least it's easy as a VHF call sign.

Free Spirit 1988—More obvious symbolism.

Antigone 1990—The name of two different women in Greek mythology—also can mean "in place of a mother."

Kokopelli 1991—A fertility deity for several Southwest American Indian tribes, including the Hopi and Zuni—also represents an Indian spirit of music—in recent years a Kokopelli icon has been used to symbolize the American Southwest.

Espadone 1992/93—From Spanish: sword.

Vera 1993—Probably the owner's girlfriend or wife.

Sam 1994—Another easy VHF call sign.

Wild Turkey 1995—A species of large turkey native to North America—also the brand name for a well-known brand of bourbon whisky. I wonder which the owner had in mind.

Legacy 1996—Perhaps the source of the boat's purchase price.

Scipionne 1997—This is a really tough one to figure.

Haleakala 1998—The huge volcano that makes up most of the Hawaiian Island of Maui.

Lonestar IV 1999—A single star was part of the Long Expedition (1819), Austin Colony (1821) and several flags of the early Republic of Texas. Some say that the star represented the wish of many Texans to achieve statehood in the United States. Others say it originally represented Texas as the lone state of Mexico, which was attempting to uphold its rights under the Mexican Constitution of 1824. A flag with a single star was raised at the Alamo (1836) according to a journal entry by David Crockett. The "David G. Burnet" flag, with a blue background and with a large golden star central was adopted by the Congress of the Republic of Texas in December of 1836. It continued in use as a battle flag after being superseded in January of 1839. The 1839 design has been used to symbolize the Republic and the "Lone Star State" ever since. (From SHG Resources)

Bonac Witch 2000—The small Bonac community at the eastern tip of Long Island traces its linage to sixteenth century English colonists from Kent and Dorset, England. Since arriving in America, they earned their living by fishing the local waters. In addition, they have preserved the special dialect of English they brought with them three-plus centuries ago.

Panta Rhei 2002—An ancient Greek phrase meaning "everything is in a state of flux."

La Murielle 2002—Another wife or girlfriend?

Marcella D 2004 (twice)—Probably yet another wife or girlfriend.

Baraka 2005—A French slang word for good luck, also in Islamic and Arab-influenced languages the word means a blessing from God.

Calypso Rose 2006—Calypso music in the Caribbean originated in Trinidad and Tobago in the early 1900s and has African roots. It is believed to stem from a phrase meaning "keep going" or "continue on." Calypso also was a spoken language used to transmit news among the Caribbean Islands. In a different context: in Homer's *Odyssey*, Calypso was a daughter of Atlas and a sea nymph inhabiting the island of Ogygia. She loved Odysseus who was shipwrecked on the island and detained him there for seven years. We are left to wonder about who Rose was.

Glascarnoch 2007—Loch Glascarnoch, a reservoir 7km long, is about halfway between Ullapool and Inverness. When the glen was flooded, stands of trees were covered and now a lot of driftwood (with many shapely, ornamental pieces for house or garden) has been blown eastwards to accumulate in the small bays. A good family walk, with no special footwear needed, unless you leave the path to gather driftwood. (From *Walking Scotland*.)

Wandering Eye 2007—I believe the owner was an ophthalmologist.

NOTES

1. *The Influence of Sea Power Upon History,1660-1783,* Captain A.T. Mahan (Boston, Little, Brown and Company, 1894)

2. *The Quotable Sailor,* edited by Christopher Caswell (The Lyons Press, Guilford, Connecticut, 2001), 1

3. There were two parts of the NROTC program: Regular (US Navy) and Contract (US Navy Reserve). Regular (USN) students were on all-paid scholarships, and they had four years of obligated active duty upon commissioning. Contract students (USNR) were not on scholarship, and we had two years of obligated active duty upon commissioning.

4. *Naval History* magazine, October 2008, article by Paul Stillwell, "Looking Back," 2

5. *H.M.S. Surprise* by Patrick O'Brian (New York, London W.W. Norton & Company, 1973) 260

6. *Watch Officers's Guide* ed. by Lee, Brown, Morabito, Colenda (Annapolis, Naval Institute Press, 1987) 3

7. *HMS Surprise,* Patrick O'Brian (New York and London, W.W. Norton & Company, 1994) 260

8. *The Dispatches and Letters of Vice Admiral Lord Viscount Nelson,* Vol. I ed. by Sir Nicholas Harris Nicolas (London, Henry Colburn, 1844), 424

9. "Round File": in the Navy administrative process, the wastebasket.

10. There was one pay billet in the unit: the administrative officer. In addition, members of the unit were able to earn points toward eventual retirement from the U.S. Navy Reserve.

11. Then-Captain Stroh went on to become a vice admiral and was involved as a carrier battle group commander in the naval quarantine of Cuba during the Cuban Missile Crisis.

12. The historic New York Naval Shipyard—often referred to as The Brooklyn Navy Yard—was established in 1801. Robert Fulton's steam launch was built there in 1815. Hundreds of ships, many famous and many not, were built and repaired there before the yard was closed in 1966. It is now an industrial development site.

13. *Maritime Supremacy and the Opening of the Western Mind,* Peter Padfield (Woodstock and New York, Overlook Press, 2000) 1

14. Dyer is a well known manufacturer of sailing dinghies and larger boats in Warren, Rhode Island.

15. The airport has since been enlarged and it's presently served with a regular schedule of twin-engine, propeller-driven commuter planes of American Eagle Airline. It still has a single runway that ends all too abruptly at the water's edge, and it still does not accommodate wide-body jet aircraft.

16. Simon and Nancy Scott went on to establish Cruising Guide Publications in Dunedin, Florida.

17. *The Cruising Guide to the Virgin Islands,* 13th Edition, written and edited by Nancy and Simon Scott (Dunedin, FL, Cruising Guide Publications, Inc. , 2007-2008) 175

18. *Mariner's Mirror,* Vol. 13 380

19. Just use Seven-Up for the batter instead of milk

20. *The Life and Character of John Paul Jones,* John Henry Sherburne (Adriance, Sherman & Co., New York, 1851) 230

21. *The Life of Nelson* by A.T. Mahan (London, Sampson Low, Marston & Company, 1897) 397, 398

22. The udjat eye symbol was used in ancient Egypt to represent Horus the sun god.

23. *The Life of Nelson,* Robert Southey (John Murray, London, 1813), 230-31

24. *The Dispatches and Letters of Vice Admiral Lord Viscount Nelson,* Vol. VII ed. by Sir Nicholas Harris Nicolas (London, Henry Colburn, 1845), 35 footnote

25. Ibid. 244

26. Ibid. 252

27. The items in the Lily Lambert McCarthy Collection at the Royal Naval Museum are described in the 228-page book *Remembering Nelson* (published privately by Lily Lambert McCarthy and the Royal Naval Museum, 1995)

28. *The Quotable Sailor,* ed. by Christopher Caswell (Guilford, Connecticut: The Lyons Press 2001) 135

29. There are more than 40 state-owned Pousadas in Portugal. They include former castles, manor houses, monasteries and convents that have been converted into inns and hotels. The architecture and settings reflect the regions in which these unique facilities are located.

30.*Sagres—Past and Present,* Owen C. Watkins (The Peacock Press of Holt, 1994) 3

31.*The Dispatches and Letters of Vice Admiral Lord Viscount Nelson,* Vol. II ed. by Sir Nicholas Harris Nicolas (London, Henry Colburn, 1844) 341

32.Ibid. 379

33.Ibid. 421

34.Ibid. 434

35.Ibid. 435

36.Australia II has since been moved to the Western Australian Maritime Museum in Fremantle.

37.In 2002 a new-purpose-built and architecturally dramatic Western Australian Maritime Museum was opened at Victoria Quay along the Fremantle Waterfront. The historic Commissariat Building at the Museum's former site on Cliff Street now houses the Museum's shipwreck exhibits.

38.The prize system of the Age of Sail was a procedure whereby captured ships were sold and the proceeds divided among the captain, officers and crew of the capturing ship or ships. The admirals who were in command of the capturing ship, even if they were not at the scene of the action, also shared in the prize money.

39.*Nelson,* Carola Oman (London: The Reprint Society), 1947) 9

40.*Nelson in the Caribbean—The Hero Emerges, 1784-1785,* Joseph F. Callo (Annapolis: Naval Institute Press, 2003)

41.*Horatio Nelson,* Tom Pocock (London: The Bodley Head, 1987), 132

42.*The Dispatches and Letters of Vice Admiral Lord Viscount Nelson,* Vol. VII ed. by Sir Nicholas Harris Nicolas (London: Henry Colburn, 1845),. 80

43.*Nelson and his World,* Tom Pocock (London: Book Club Associates, 1974), 126

44.*Nelson—The New Letters,* Colin White (Woodbridge, Suffolk and Rochester, New York: The Boydell Press, 2005)

45.Ibid, xii

46.*The Dispatches and Letters of Vice Admiral Lord Viscount Nelson,* Vol. I ed. by Sir Nicholas Harris Nicolas (London: Henry Colburn, 1845), 187

47.*The Life of Nelson by A.T. Mahan,* Vol. II, (London: Sampson Low, Marston & Company, Limited 1897) 397, 398

48.*Who's Who in Naval History,* written and edited by Alistair Wilson and Joseph Callo (London: Routledge, 2004)

49. *John Paul Jones: America's First Sea Warrior.* Joseph Callo (Annapolis: Naval Institute Press, 2006)

50. *The Dispatches and Letters of Vice Admiral Lord Viscount Nelson,* Vol. IV ed. by Sir Nicholas Harris Nicolas (London: Henry Colburn, 1845), 277

51. The John Paul Jones Cottage Museum is located on the grounds of the Arbigland Estate, near Kirkbean, Southwest of Dumfries, Scotland

52. *How the Scots Invented the Modern World,* Arthur Herman (New York: Crown Publishers, 2001), vii

53. *John Paul Jones: America's First Sea Warrior,* Joseph Callo (Annapolis: Naval Institute Press, 2006), 3

54. *Common Sense,* Thomas Paine (Rockville Manor, Maryland, Arc Manor, 2008) 8

55. The first ships commissioned by the Continental Congress were eight former merchant vessels: *Alfred,* 24-guns, *Columbus,* 20 guns, *Andrew Doria,* 14 guns, *Cabot,* 14 guns, *Providence,* 12 guns, *Hornet,* 10 guns, *Wasp,* 8 guns, *Fly,* 8 guns.

56. *The Life and Correspondence of John Paul Jones,* Robert C. Sands (New York: A. Chandler, 1830), 304-309

57. *Military History,* July/August 2008 Issue, 26-33

58. Although HMS *Serapis* was "rated" at 44 guns, it is believed that she actually had 46 or more guns when she encountered the Continental Ship *Bonhomme Richard.* It was not unusual for a warship of the time to actually have more guns than it was "rated" for at commissioning.

59. *John Paul Jones: America's First Sea Warrior,* Joseph Callo (Annapolis: Naval Institute Press, 2006), 188

60. *U.S. Naval History Division, Naval Documents of the American Revolution* (Washington, DC: Government Printing Office, 1964}, 6: 1303; John Paul Jones Papers, reel 3, document 459

61. Ibid., reel I, document 53).

Joe Callo's previous book, *John Paul Jones: America's First Sea Warrior* earned the Naval Order's Samuel Eliot Morison Award. He has also written three books about Admiral Lord Nelson, was U.S. editor for *Who's Who in Naval* History, and he writes frequently on naval subjects for magazines and newspapers. Joe is a Yale University NROTC graduate. He earned a Surface Warfare designation during two years of sea duty in the US Navy's Atlantic Amphibious Force and retired from the U.S. Navy Reserve as a rear admiral. Joe was a senior advertising agency executive and a producer for NBC-TV and PBS programs. He earned a Peabody Award as line producer for the NBC-TV prime time program, "Tut: The Boy King" and a Telly Award for his script "The Second Life of 20 West Ninth," which aired on the History Channel and PBS. He is also a *Naval History* magazine Author of the Year. As a sailor, Joe has skippered boats up to 50 feet in length, and he crewed in the recreation of Captain Cook's around-the-world square rigger *Endeavour*.

BOOKS BY REAR ADMIRAL JOE CALLO

Legacy of Leadership is a penetrating view of the leadership of Great Britain's Admiral Lord Nelson at his history-shaping Battles of Cape Saint Vincent, Santa Cruz, the Nile, Copenhagen, and Trafalgar.

After two centuries of biographies and historical analyses by countless authors, Britain's greatest admiral speaks for himself in *Nelson Speaks—Admiral Lord Nelson in his own Words.*

Nelson in the Caribbean—The Hero Emerges, 1784-1787 is an unusual view of critical elements of leadership at a formative early phase of Admiral Lord Nelson's astonishing career.

In *Who's Who in Naval History—from 1550 to the Present,* Joe Callo provides 300-plus concise biographies of noteworthy American naval personnel, from the American Revolution forward.

John Paul Jones: America's First Sea Warrior avoids both hero worship and cynicism while illuminating critical and often neglected characteristics of America's leading naval hero in the War of Independence.

"OLD IRONSIDES" AND HMS JAVA
A STORY OF 1812

HMS *Java* and the USS *Constitution* (the famous "Old Ironsides") face off in the War of 1812's most spectacular blue-water frigate action. Their separate stories begin in August 1812—one in England and the other in New England. Then, the tension and suspense rise, week-by-week, as the ships cruise the Atlantic, slowly and inevitably coming together for the final life-and-death climax.

The Perfect Wreck is not only the first full-length book ever written about the battle between the USS *Constitution* and HMS *Java*, it is a gem of Creative Nonfiction. It has the exhaustive research of a scholarly history book; but it is beautifully presented in the form of a novel.

A highly recommended must-read for every naval enthusiast—indeed, for every American!

Stephen Coonts
NY Times best-selling author

WWW.FIRESHIPPRESS.COM
Interesting • Informative • Authoritative

The Riddle of the Sands
by Erskine Childers

Two sail-boaters cruising off the coast of Germany on a vacation. To their amazement they discover a German military exercise—a trial-run for the invasion of England.

From that starting point we are whisked through a series of mysteries, bluffs, counter-bluffs, and wild nautical maneuvers as our sail-boaters try to learn more and get their information back to England. Through it all, Childers brilliantly captures the style and attitudes of the day. His use of military terms and concepts is creditable, and his depiction of small boat sailing is impeccable.

What is astonishing is that the book was written *before* WW-I and correctly anticipates the coming military aggressiveness of Germany. It created a sensation when it was first released, and remains a classic, perhaps THE classic, spy-action-adventure novel to this day.

CLEAR LOWER DECK
BY ROGER PAINE

Do you know where the expression 'grog' comes from? Or why a gun-toting generalissimo in the Philippines distributed medals from a shoebox? Have you heard about Scar, the cat who sunk with the *Bismarck* in World War II and survived to sink twice more in the ships which rescued him?

The answers to these questions, and other true salty stories, can be found in this book by former Royal Navy officer, Roger Paine, as he charts the ups and downs of life, both ashore and afloat. This delightfully irreverent, and occasionally indiscreet, collection of 'yarns' is here to be savoured and treasured.

CPSIA information can be obtained at www.ICGtesting.com
Printed in the USA
LVOW121553260612

287753LV00026B/207/P